BROUGHT TO YOU BY:

SUPERKID ACADEMY
A SIMPLE GUIDE FOR HOME USE

THE SUPERKID CREED II

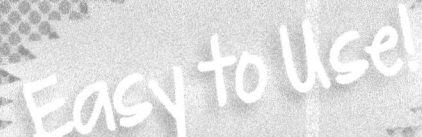

BIBLE STUDY FOR KIDS!

Ordinary kids doing extraordinary things through the power of God's Word!

Unless otherwise noted, all scripture is from the *Holy Bible, New Living Translation* © 1996, 2004, 2007 by Tyndale House Foundation. Used by permission of Tyndale House Publishers Inc., Carol Stream, IL 60188. All rights reserved.

Scriptures marked MSG are from *The Message* © 1993, 1994, 1995, 1996, 2000, 2001, 2002. Used by permission of NavPress Publishing Group.

Scriptures marked NIV are from *The Holy Bible, New International Version* © 1973, 1978, 1984, 2011 by Biblica Inc.™ Used by permission. All rights reserved worldwide.

Scriptures marked AMPC are from *The Amplified® Bible, Classic Edition* © 1954, 1958, 1962, 1964, 1965, 1987 by The Lockman Foundation. Used by permission.

Scriptures marked NKJV are from the *New King James Version* © 1982 by Thomas Nelson Inc.

Scriptures marked KJV are from the *King James Version* of the Bible. Public Domain.

ISBN 978-1-60463-360-3   30-1071

Superkid Academy Home Bible Study for Kids—The Superkid Creed II

© 2013, 2017 Eagle Mountain International Church Inc. aka Kenneth Copeland Ministries

Kenneth Copeland Publications
Fort Worth, TX 76192-0001

For more information about Superkid Academy, call 1-800-606-4190 or visit SuperkidAcademy.com.

For more information about Kenneth Copeland Ministries, call 1-800-600-7395 (U.S. only) or +1-817-852-6000 or visit kcm.org.

TABLE OF CONTENTS

WELCOME! v

THE SUPERKID CREED vi

A SIMPLE GUIDE vii

HEALTH & SAFETY DISCLAIMER x

WEEK 1: I LAY HANDS ON THE SICK AND THEY RECOVER 11

WEEK 2: I WIN PEOPLE TO JESUS 27

WEEK 3: I DO NOT LIE—I AM ALWAYS QUICK TO TELL THE TRUTH .. 41

WEEK 4: I DO NOT STEAL 61

WEEK 5: I AM A TITHER AND A GIVER, NOT A TAKER 75

WEEK 6: MY FATHER MAKES ME WEALTHY 89

WEEK 7: I DO NOT COMPLAIN 105

WEEK 8: I WORK HARD TO HELP MY FAMILY 123

WEEK 9: I HONOR AND OBEY MY PARENTS
AND PEOPLE IN AUTHORITY OVER ME 137

WEEK 10: I WALK IN LOVE 155

WEEK 11: I DO NOT GOSSIP, I AM NOT RUDE
AND I AM NEVER MEAN 173

WEEK 12: THE PIRATES IN PROVERBS, PART 1 187

WEEK 13: THE PIRATES IN PROVERBS, PART 2 207

WELCOME!

Dear Parent/Teacher,

I believe you will experience great and exciting things as you begin the faith adventure of *Superkid Academy Home Bible Study for Kids—The Superkid Creed II*.

As you launch into this faith-building time with your family or small group, take the opportunity to seek the Lord's direction about how to minister these lessons for maximum impact. God's Word does not return to Him void, and He will see to it that your children are BLESSED and grow strong in faith as you step out in His Anointing to teach them about Him.

Please keep in mind that we are praying for you. We believe and release our faith for a powerful anointing on you as you teach and impart His wisdom, and that your Superkids are strong in the Lord and mighty for Him.

Remember, we here at Academy Headquarters want to be a resource for you. Make sure you are in our contact base so we can keep in touch. And, let us know how we can better serve you and your Superkids.

We love you and look forward to hearing from you!

Love,

Commander Kellie

Commander Kellie

THE SUPERKID CREED

I am a Superkid—Servant and child of the Most High God.
Jesus is my Savior and my Lord.
I am filled with His Holy Spirit.
I obey His written Word.
I hear every word that He speaks to me, and I obey quickly without arguing.
I live and walk by faith, not by what I see.
I walk in the power of my strong spirit.
I am full of wisdom and understanding.
I lay hands on the sick and they recover.
I win people to Jesus.
I do not lie—I am always quick to tell the truth.
I do not steal—I am a tither and a giver, not a taker. My Father makes me wealthy.
I do not complain.
I work hard to help my family.
I honor and obey my parents and people in authority over me.
I walk in love—I do not gossip, I am not rude and I am never mean.
I put others first and I am not selfish.
I treat other people with respect.
I am always grateful for everything good in my life.
I am fiercely loyal.
I am full of courage and I refuse fear of any kind.
I am merciful and kind.
I am generous and fair-minded.
I do not get offended, and I am quick to forgive.
I always do what is right and I do it right.
I do all things with excellence.
I am diligent and I am not a quitter.
I only allow my eyes and ears and mouth to let in good things.
I keep my heart pure.
I live my life in honor and humility.
I allow nothing to come before God.

LEADING YOUR SUPERKID ACADEMY: A SIMPLE GUIDE FOR HOME USE

We are excited that you have brought Superkid Academy into your living room with the Home Bible Study for Kids! This powerful, Bible-based curriculum will guide your children into building a strong, personal relationship with the Lord and inspire them to live an extraordinary, faith-filled life.

Each of the 13 weeks included in this study provide five days of lessons, including a:

- **Lesson Introduction From Commander Kellie:** As the creator of Superkid Academy with more than 20 years' experience ministering to children, Kellie Copeland has a unique anointing and perspective for reaching children with the uncompromised Word of God. She passes on her wisdom through these timeless segments.
- **Lesson Outline:** Each lesson contains three main points, subpoints and supporting scriptures to empower you to clearly communicate the truth to your children.
- **Memory Verse:** Throughout the week, your kids will have the opportunity to memorize and understand a scripture. More than that, they'll learn how to apply it directly to their lives.
- **Bible Lesson:** Each Bible Lesson reinforces the memory verse and the principle behind it. Discussion questions will help you lead your children through not only comprehending the passage of scripture, but also giving it meaning in their lives.
- **Giving Lesson:** Each week, you will have the opportunity to teach your children about the importance of tithing and giving so they can be "blessed to be a blessing" in the Body of Christ.
- **Game Time:** Reinforces the message and gives families an occasion to celebrate what they've learned in a fun way.
- **Activity Page:** Reinforces the lesson through acrostics, word searches, mazes and other activities.
- **Supplements:** Support the memory verse and lesson—two will be provided each week, including:
    - **Object Lesson:** Illustrates the focus of the lesson and provides visual and hands-on elements to the teaching.
    - **Real Deal:** Highlights a historical person, place or event that illustrates the current lesson's theme.
    - **Storybook Theaters, You-Solve-It Mysteries and Read-Aloud Stories:** Reinforces the message with creative, read-aloud stories.
    - **Food Fun:** Takes you and your children into the kitchen where you will discuss, illustrate and experience God's truth, using everyday items.
    - **Academy Lab:** Brings the lesson and science together.

And, don't forget the enclosed Praise and Worship CD! These original, upbeat, kid-friendly songs put the Word in your children's minds and hearts. The CD can be listened to around the house or in the car, and the karaoke, sing-along tracks allow your kids to sing their favorite songs.

Making the Curriculum Work for Your Family

Superkid Academy's Home Bible Study for Kids gives you the flexibility to teach your children in a way that works for you. Each week's lesson is divided into five days of teaching. However, we understand that no two families—or their schedules—are the same, so feel free to adjust the lessons to meet your needs. Use all five days of lessons or select only a few to cover each week. Whether you're using the curriculum as part of your home school, as a boost to your family devotions or in a weekly small group, you have the flexibility to make it work for you.

A Homeschool Bible Curriculum

Superkid Academy's Home Bible Study for Kids is easy to use, flexible and interactive—no dry Bible lessons here! It is ideal for a variety of learning styles. Each of the 13 weeks contains five days of lessons—one Bible Lesson, one Giving Lesson, one Game Time and two other lessons or stories to support the week's message. You may choose to use all five days of lessons or pick and choose the ones that work best for your educational structure. Optional variations for several of the lessons have been included to meet a variety of needs.

Each week's Snapshot provides the major points of the lesson and a list of supplies needed for that week, allowing you to easily prepare and customize each week's lessons. Here are just a few additional ideas for customizing for your home school:

- Re-read the Bible passage each day throughout the week to give your children—and you—time to meditate on the highlighted scripture
- Use one or more of the discussion questions as a journaling exercise
- Begin a weekly family Game Night
- Use the Storybook Theaters, Read-Aloud stories or You-Solve-It Mysteries in your nighttime read-aloud routine.

Family Devotions

Superkid Academy's Home Bible Study for Kids empowers you to disciple your children and teach them the Word of God in an easy, fun way. You may choose to use all five days' worth of lessons, or select only a few. Each lesson takes less than 15 minutes, so the curriculum fits easily into your busy life.

Lessons are numbered 1-5, giving you the flexibility to include whichever lesson fits your daily schedule for that week. This allows you freedom to plan around work schedules, church commitments and extracurricular activities. Here are two sample schedules:

5-Day Schedule

Sunday—Church (no lesson)

Monday—Bible Lesson

Tuesday—Object Lesson

Wednesday—Midweek services (no lesson)

Thursday—Giving Lesson

Friday—Storybook Theater

Saturday—Game Time

3-Day Schedule

Sunday—Church (no lesson)

Monday— Bible Lesson

Tuesday—Soccer practice (no lesson)

Wednesday—Giving Lesson

Thursday—Soccer practice (no lesson)

Friday—Object Lesson

Saturday—Family time (no lesson)

A Weekly Small Group

Superkid Academy's Home Bible Study for Kids is designed for use over several days, but a week's worth of lessons can easily be consolidated for a small group. Simply choose the lessons that work best for your location and schedule and allow additional time for discussion and prayer.

Sample Small Group Schedule:

6 p.m.	Bible Lesson with discussion time
6:30 p.m.	Giving Lesson
6:45 p.m.	Object Lesson and prayer time
7:15 p.m.	Game Time
7:45 p.m.	Refreshments
8 p.m.	Closing

Thank you again for implementing Superkid Academy's Home Bible Study for Kids. We stand with you in faith as you disciple your children in the things that matter to Him. Proverbs 22:6 (KJV) says, "Train up a child in the way he should go: and when he is old, he will not depart from it." At Superkid Academy, we are confident that God will bless your efforts, and that you and your children will see the reality of THE BLESSING in all you do (Numbers 6:24-26).

Love,

Commander Kellie

Commander Kellie

HEALTH & SAFETY DISCLAIMER FOR "SUPERKID ACADEMY CURRICULUM"

Superkid Academy is a ministry of Eagle Mountain International Church, aka Kenneth Copeland Ministries (hereafter "EMIC"). The "Superkid Academy Curriculum" (hereafter "SKA Curriculum") provides age-appropriate teaching material to be used in the religious instruction of children. The SKA Curriculum includes physical activities in which children and leaders may participate. Before engaging in any of the physical activities, participants should be in good physical condition as determined by their health care provider. EMIC is not responsible for injuries resulting from the implementation of activities suggested within the SKA Curriculum. Prior to implementing the SKA Curriculum, carefully review your organization's safety and health policies, and determine whether the SKA Curriculum is appropriate for your organization's intended use.

By purchasing the SKA Curriculum, I, individually and/or as authorized representative for my organization, hereby agree to release, defend, hold harmless, and covenant not to sue EMIC, its officers, deacons, ministers, directors, employees, volunteers, contractors, staff, affiliates, agents and attorneys (collectively, the "EMIC Parties"), and the property of EMIC for any claim, including claims for negligence and gross negligence of any one or more of the EMIC Parties, arising out of my use or organization's use of and participation in the SKA Curriculum, participation in the suggested activities contained within the SKA Curriculum, or resulting from first-aid treatment or services rendered as a result of or in connection with the activities or participation in the activities.

WEEK 1: I LAY HANDS ON THE SICK AND THEY RECOVER

 **DAY 1: BIBLE LESSON—
DON'T GIVE UP ON YOUR SICK FRIENDS!** ▶ 14

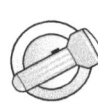 **DAY 2: OBJECT LESSON—
TWO TO TANGO—PARTNERING WITH GOD** ▶ 16

 **DAY 3: GIVING LESSON—
FULLY SUPPLIED** ▶ 18

 DAY 4: REAL DEAL—JOHN G. LAKE ▶ 19

 **DAY 5: GAME TIME—
SIGNED, SEALED, DELIVERED** ▶ 24

 **BONUS: ACTIVITY PAGE—
HEALING—RAISE THE ROOF** ▶ 26

 **Memory Verse:** Heal the sick, raise the dead, cure those with leprosy, and cast out demons. Give as freely as you have received! —Matthew 10:8

Home Bible Study for Kids • Week 1: I Lay Hands on the Sick and They Recover

WEEK 1: SNAPSHOT — I LAY HANDS ON THE SICK AND THEY RECOVER

DAY	TYPE OF LESSON	LESSON TITLE	SUPPLIES
Day 1	Bible Lesson	Don't Give Up on Your Sick Friends!	None
Day 2	Object Lesson	Two to Tango—Partnering With God	A video of two people doing the tango (one that will awe your children)
Day 3	Giving Lesson	Fully Supplied	An empty wallet
Day 4	Real Deal	John G. Lake	Photos (pictures from the internet), Map to show the places where John G. Lake traveled Optional Costume: Early 20th century man's suit or a nice suit
Day 5	Game Time	Signed, Sealed, Delivered	Stopwatch, Heavy oversized jacket, Baseball cap, Oversized shoes (large boots or flippers), Scarf, 8 Pieces of paper, 8 24-Inch strings, 4 Safety pins, Tape, Marker
Bonus	Activity Page	Healing—Raise the Roof	1 Copy for each child, Crayons or colored pencils

Lesson Introduction:

What stops Christians from laying hands on the sick? Fear of being rejected or laughed at, perhaps. I think the biggest fear would be that nothing will happen, and the person won't get healed. If Christians are afraid of this, they aren't BELIEVING Mark 16:15-17, but DOUBTING it!

Today, as you take your Superkids through God's Word about laying hands on the sick, FAITH WILL COME (Romans 10:17). You can then lead them to an on-purpose choice to believe!

Driving out fear will enable and excite your kids to freely give to others what has been given to them. Help your Superkids know that while Jesus did ask us to lay hands on the sick and to believe, *He didn't ask us to heal anyone.* That's His part. And He is *always* faithful to do His part!

No fear! Let's go!

Love,

Commander Kellie

Commander Kellie

Series: The Superkid Creed II

Home Bible Study for Kids • Week 1: I Lay Hands on the Sick and They Recover

Lesson Outline:

This week your children will learn that they can lay hands on the sick and see them recover, just as Jesus did! God has called your Superkids to be the hands that heal the sick. They just need to be bold enough to step out in the Name of Jesus, and trust that He will do all the healing when they step out in faith!

I. JESUS TOOK ALL OUR SICKNESSES AND DISEASES
Matthew 8:16-17

   a. The touch of His hand healed everyone. Luke 4:40

   b. People were healed when they touched Him. Luke 6:17-19

   c. Friends made an opening in the roof to bring their sick friend to Him! Mark 2:1-4 NIV

   d. Jesus didn't care about the roof! He healed the man! Mark 2:5-12

   e. Jesus was always willing to heal. Matthew 8:1-3

II. JESUS GAVE HIS DISCIPLES THE AUTHORITY TO HEAL THE SICK
Matthew 10:1, 7-8

   a. He said to give healing freely. Matthew 10:7-8

   b. Peter and John knew the crippled man didn't need money. Acts 3:1-5

   c. They obeyed Jesus and freely gave the man what he needed—healing! Acts 3:6-11

III. JESUS SAID MIRACULOUS SIGNS WOULD FOLLOW THOSE WHO BELIEVE Mark 16:15-17

   a. They can place their hands on the sick, and they will be healed. Mark 16:18

   b. Superkids understand that the same power that raised Jesus from the dead lives in us! Ephesians 1:19-20

   c. It makes our bodies alive. Romans 8:11

   d. Like the friends brought the man to Jesus, you bring Jesus to the people you lay hands on.

   e. Since Jesus gave you healing so freely, you freely give it to others!

Be BOLD! Be a believer.

Superkid, when you lay your hands on the sick, they *will* recover!

Home Bible Study for Kids • Week 1: I Lay Hands on the Sick and They Recover

DAY 1: BIBLE LESSON — DON'T GIVE UP ON YOUR SICK FRIENDS!

Memory Verse: Heal the sick, raise the dead, cure those with leprosy, and cast out demons. Give as freely as you have received! —Matthew 10:8

It's so important that your children begin hearing from God and responding in faith, especially when it comes to healing. At the end of the discussion, there is an opportunity for all to pray together for someone they know who is sick, listen to the Holy Spirit, and do what He says to do for that person. Or, maybe they believe the Lord is telling them to go and "lay hands on that person," or He gives them a craft idea to make for the person that has several healing scriptures written on it. He may simply direct them to pray the prayer of faith over the person and believe. (These things are all biblical choices.) Don't forget that Jesus obeyed His Father when He spit in the dirt and made mud to put onto the blind man's eyes. So BE BOLD! Step out in faith where the Holy Spirit leads—He will ALWAYS back you up!

Read Mark 2:1-12 NIV:
Putting Your Faith to Work!

A few days later, when Jesus again entered Capernaum, the people heard that he had come home. They gathered in such large numbers that there was no room left, not even outside the door, and he preached the word to them. Some men came, bringing to him a paralyzed man carried by four of them. Since they could not get him to Jesus because of the crowd, they made an opening in the roof above Jesus by digging through it and then lowered the mat the man was lying on. When Jesus saw their faith, he said to the paralyzed man, "Son, your sins are forgiven."

Now some teachers of the law were sitting there, thinking to themselves, "Why does this fellow talk like that? He's blaspheming! Who can forgive sins but God alone?"

Immediately Jesus knew in his spirit that this was what they were thinking in their hearts, and he said to them, "Why are you thinking these things? Which is easier: to say to this paralyzed man, 'Your sins are forgiven,' or to say, 'Get up, take your mat and walk'? But I want you to know that the Son of Man has authority on earth to forgive sins." So he said to the man, "I tell you, get up, take your mat and go home." He got up, took his mat and walked out in full view of them all. This amazed everyone and they praised God, saying, "We have never seen anything like this!"

Discussion Questions:

1. **How did the four men get the paralyzed man to Jesus?**

    They dug a hole in the roof and lowered him down into the room in front of Jesus.

Home Bible Study for Kids • Week 1: I Lay Hands on the Sick and They Recover

2. **What did you notice about the four men who carried the paralyzed man? What made them succeed?**

   They didn't give up! They kept on trying to get the man to Jesus until they succeeded.

3. **Whose faith did Jesus notice—the paralyzed man's or the four men's faith who carried him?**

   The four men's faith. Jesus noticed their faith by their actions!

4. **What would have happened if the four men had given up on getting to Jesus?**

   The paralyzed man would have remained sick.

5. **Mark 16:17-18 NKJV says, "These signs will follow those who believe…they will lay hands on the sick, and they will recover." Do you know anyone you can carry to the Healer as the four men did?**

   Answers will vary. Let your Superkids come up with the names of people they want to pray for.

6. **As believers, we are called to carry the gospel to the world—this includes Jesus' healing power. Take a few minutes today to pray for the sick friends you know, and then ask the Holy Spirit how you can "carry" Jesus' healing power to them. Remember, when you pray, BELIEVE that He will answer you, and then DO what He says!**

   Let the children pray together, and then wait to hear what they believe the Holy Spirit is telling them to do about a particular sick person. Allow the time for them to hear from the Lord on their own. Don't give up praying and believing God for the person's healing.

Notes:

Series: The Superkid Creed II

Home Bible Study for Kids • Week 1: I Lay Hands on the Sick and They Recover

DAY 2: OBJECT LESSON — TWO TO TANGO—PARTNERING WITH GOD

Suggested Time: 10 minutes

Key Scripture: *These miraculous signs will accompany those who believe: They will cast out demons in my name, and they will speak in new languages. They will be able to handle snakes with safety, and if they drink anything poisonous, it won't hurt them. They will be able to place their hands on the sick, and they will be healed.* —Mark 16:17-18

Teacher Tip: There's no fear when it comes to being silly with your kids, nor when it is time to lay hands on someone and see them healed! Have fun, and don't be afraid to go all out with this object lesson.

Supplies: ☐ A video of two people doing the tango (one that will awe your children)

Prior to Lesson:

Play the video of people doing the tango. It's best to use videos of kids or professionals doing the tango. Make sure you watch the video fully to make sure it's age-appropriate.

Learn a basic tango spin and lead your children in a few dance moves. (They don't have to be perfect, the important thing is that they follow your lead as you all dance.)

Lesson Instructions:

Superkids, today we're going to talk about dancing. That's right! Dancing. Have you ever heard the common phrase, "It takes two to tango"? Well, that is certainly a true statement. Watch this… *(Begin pretending to tango by yourself. Feel free to make your own music by humming or singing.)*

Does this look like a tango to you? *(Continue trying to dance the tango by yourself. Feel free to be silly!)* OK, I'm sure I look ridiculous because it really does take TWO to tango. Let's look at how it's really done. *(Take time to show the video of two people doing the tango correctly.)*

The tango is an amazing dance when it is done correctly. But you always need two people. A two-person dance is called a "partner dance," and you can see why—because you need a partner to do it correctly. In partner dancing, one of the partners is the "lead" and the other is the "follow." Let's try it. *(Choose one of the children to help you.)* I'll lead and you follow. *(Do a few moves with your helper. Perhaps imitate a few moves you saw in the tango video or do a few steps to the left and then to the right, with a spin at the end. Take the time to practice leading and following with each child, or if you have a large group, allow children to take turns with each other leading and then following.)*

When you were the partner who followed, were you stressed out about coming up with dance moves? No, because I was telling you where to go and what to do. When I lifted my arm to spin you, all you had to do was spin. It's easy as long as you know how to follow and you have a good leader partner.

Series: The Superkid Creed II

Home Bible Study for Kids • Week 1: I Lay Hands on the Sick and They Recover

Superkids, isn't it amazing that God wants to partner with us? He clearly tells us in Mark 16:17-18: "These miraculous signs will accompany those who believe: They will cast out demons in my name, and they will speak in new languages. They will be able to handle snakes with safety, and if they drink anything poisonous, it won't hurt them. They will be able to place their hands on the sick, and they will be healed."

God wants to partner with us and use OUR hands to heal the sick! When we go, we don't have to be worried or afraid we might not know what to say or that we are the one responsible to get someone healed. When we learn to FOLLOW God's lead, He is the One who does the healing. We just use our hands and follow what He said to do in His Word by commanding them to be healed in Jesus' Name! Just like in the dance, we have to trust our Partner, Jesus, who will never lead us in the wrong way.

Begin to trust God as your Partner today! Let Him lead your hands, your voice and your faith! Speak and believe that if He says you will lay hands on the sick and see them recover, that's *exactly* what will happen!

Notes: _____

Home Bible Study for Kids • Week 1: I Lay Hands on the Sick and They Recover

DAY 3: GIVING LESSON — FULLY SUPPLIED

Suggested Time: 10 minutes

Offering Scripture: Peter and John went to the Temple one afternoon to take part in the three o'clock prayer service. As they approached the Temple, a man lame from birth was being carried in. Each day he was put beside the Temple gate, the one called the Beautiful Gate, so he could beg from the people going into the Temple. When he saw Peter and John about to enter, he asked them for some money. Peter and John looked at him intently, and Peter said, "Look at us!" The lame man looked at them eagerly, expecting some money. But Peter said, "I don't have any silver or gold for you. But I'll give you what I have. In the name of Jesus Christ the Nazarene, get up and walk!" Then Peter took the lame man by the right hand and helped him up. And as he did, the man's feet and ankles were instantly healed and strengthened. He jumped up, stood on his feet, and began to walk! Then, walking, leaping, and praising God, he went into the Temple with them. —Acts 3:1-8

Teacher Tip: Take the time to listen to your children's stories as you ask the questions.

Supplies: ☐ An empty wallet

Lesson Instructions:

(Start by frantically looking through the empty wallet several times.)

Superkids, I really wanted to give an offering to God today, but it seems that I don't have any money. *(Open wallet toward your kids to show it is empty.)* Have you ever wanted to give God an offering but thought you didn't have anything to give? Today, we're going to look at how Peter and John gave, even though they had no money at the time (read Acts 3:1-8).

In Bible times, people who couldn't support themselves financially would have family members or friends place them outside the Temple gates. As people passed by, they would ask for money from the people coming in and going out of the Temple. When the crippled man asked Peter and John for money, they didn't have any money to give him at that time. But, instead of walking away, they did what they had often seen Jesus do and gave the crippled man what he really needed—healing!

Peter and John were not the only ones who were given the power to heal in the Name of Jesus! When you asked Jesus into your heart, you were given the same power. You are BLESSED because of Jesus. You have MANY spiritual gifts and many ways you can give.

So, Superkids, what are some things we can give that don't cost money? Have you ever felt in your heart Jesus talking to you about giving something you have to someone else? *(Allow time for the children to answer your questions.)* Now, let's ask God this week to show us ways we can give offerings to Him from the gifts He has already given us. Remember, with Jesus, we are never without something to give!

DAY 4: REAL DEAL — JOHN G. LAKE

Suggested Time: 15 minutes

Memory Verse: Heal the sick, raise the dead, cure those with leprosy, and cast out demons. Give as freely as you have received! —Matthew 10:8

Concept: Highlighting an interesting historical place, figure or event that illustrates the theme of the day. The theme of the day is: I lay hands on the sick, and they recover.

Teacher Tip: This segment has many possible variations. Choose the best that fits your family/group, and have fun! We suggest getting as familiar as possible with the script prior to instructing this lesson. Printed photos will help to keep your kids engaged. You can even write notes for yourself on the back of them to read as you teach this lesson!

Supplies: ☐ Photos (pictures from the internet), ☐ Map to show the places where John G. Lake traveled
Optional Costume: ☐ Early 20th century-looking man's suit or a nice suit

Intro:

John G. Lake's ministry revealed that God's power to heal reached beyond the time Jesus was here on earth. He taught that Christianity is a "strong man's gospel," and God wants EVERYONE to experience His health and wholeness.

John G. Lake also trained others how to heal people and cast out devils by the power of God. He evangelized North America, South Africa and other nations.

Lesson:
Overcoming Sickness:

John G. Lake was born in Ontario, Canada, March 18, 1870, into a very sick family. One of 16 children, he grew up in Canada and then Michigan in a house full of disease, doctor visits and death. In fact, 8 of his brothers had passed away before he became an adult. He was also sick with a digestive disease that nearly killed him.[1]

But when John was 16, he received Jesus into his heart at a Salvation Army meeting. After years of uncomfortable treatments, John was on the brink of death and prayed, "Lord, I am finished with the world and the flesh, with the doctor and the devil. From today, I lean on the arm of God." And he was healed!

Then, John got rheumatism in his legs, but he knew it was NOT God's will for him to be sick. He heard of John Alexander Dowie's Divine Healing Home in Chicago and went to a meeting where his legs were straightened by the power of God. He saw many others get healed, too. He knew then that God's miracles were for today and didn't end with stories from the New Testament Church.

Home Bible Study for Kids • Week 1: I Lay Hands on the Sick and They Recover

Healing for His Family:

In 1891, John married Jennie Stevens. Five years later, she was diagnosed with tuberculosis and an incurable heart disease. She soon became an invalid. At the same time, John's other brothers and sisters were lying on their deathbeds. John was determined to help them all receive healing.

So, John took his brother, who'd been an invalid with bleeding kidneys for years, to Dowie's healing home, first. He was healed! Next, he took his sister, who was dying of five cancers, and she was healed! Even after such healings, another of his sisters whom he was especially close to lay dying of an issue of blood. He received a telephone call telling him if he wanted to see her alive, he should come see her one last time. When he arrived, she appeared to be dead, but Lake was determined. He sent a telegram to John Alexander Dowie in Chicago, asking him to pray. Lake received an answer back: "Hold on to God. I am praying. She will live." John continued to pray, and an hour later, she woke up and was well within a few days!

At the same time, John's wife, Jennie, was getting worse. Her heart was giving out as she struggled with tuberculosis. Sometimes, she was paralyzed. The doctors gave her a short time to live, and even their family ministers told John to be reconciled to the will of God and let her die. John was so discouraged by the minister. He thought about their children and how much he loved his wife. *How could her death be God's will?* He began to pray, and when he opened his Bible, it fell open to Acts 10:38, KJV: "God anointed Jesus of Nazareth with the Holy Ghost and with power: who went about doing good, and healing all that were *OPPRESSED OF THE DEVIL;* for God was with him." As he read, Lake said, "Like a flash from the blue, these words pierced my heart. 'Oppressed of *the devil!'* Then *God* was not the author of sickness, and the people whom Jesus healed had not been made sick by God! He decided to make an appointment with the Healer instead of death for his wife. John called and telegraphed friends and family asking them to pray because at 9:30 a.m. a few days later, he was going to lay hands on his wife, and she would be healed.

On April 28, 1898, at 9:30 a.m., John laid his hands on his wife and prayed for her, and she was healed! This began John and Jennie's healing ministry. The sick began flocking to their home to be prayed for when they heard of Jennie's miracle in the news. As time went by, even though John became a very wealthy businessman, the call of God was constantly tugging at his heart.

Called to South Africa:

In 1907, John Lake was baptized in the Holy Spirit. The same year, he received a four-hour vision from the Lord in which God told him he would be going to Africa! He was determined to trust in God only, so he and Jennie gave away all they owned and looked to God for their supply.

In February 1908, John left with a group of missionaries and his family to go to South Africa. He had just enough money to buy the tickets for their voyage. He had $1.25 left in his pocket for himself, his wife and seven children, but he knew God had spoken and that He would provide. And God did provide—every step of the way! By the time the Lakes got off the ship, someone had given them $200 and they had been offered a fully furnished house in Johannesburg.

Shortly after, John was asked to preach in a church for a few weeks while the pastor took a leave of absence. As John preached, a mighty outpouring of the power of God came into that church and spilled into the community. News of the signs, wonders and miracles happening in the church services brought hundreds of people pouring into the area, opening the door for five years of powerful ministry throughout all of South Africa.

Home Bible Study for Kids • Week 1: I Lay Hands on the Sick and They Recover

In fact, John G. Lake's ministry in South Africa became noted for signs, wonders and miracles! In one area, people were dying of a plague, but everyone was too afraid to touch the dead to bury them. John began burying the dead because he was not afraid. The doctors and scientists told him the disease was highly contagious, and he would die if he didn't stop helping people who had the plague and burying those who had died from it. John G. Lake said, "No…when disease touches my hand, it dies." He challenged the doctors, saying he could prove it. So, the doctors placed a sample of plague-infested saliva from a dead man's mouth onto John's hand and watched through a microscope with great surprise as the germs died on contact with his hand!

John also challenged Buddhists, Yogis, Confucianists and hypnotists that his God was the true God. He told them that Jesus would heal a lady with a locked hip. So, John let them try to heal the lady themselves for months until finally, he told them to step aside. He laid his hands on her and prayed in the Name of Jesus. She was instantly healed!

On one occasion, John had to leave a healing meeting early, so he laid his hands on a rock and prayed, transferring the healing anointing on him to the rock. He told the congregation to touch the rock and they would receive healing. Lepers, and many others who touched it, were healed and restored!

Another time, a plague had overtaken a city, but John and another man prayed until the Lord showed him a vision of demons hovering over the city. In the vision, John saw them all leave as he and his friend prayed. The next day, the city was miraculously delivered from the plague. It disappeared just as he had seen in the vision!

One Sunday, while pastoring a church in South Africa, John and his congregation were praying at their service. A member got up and requested prayer for a cousin in Wales, U.K., who was violently insane and in a mental institution. As they prayed, John sensed a powerful anointing come on him from the Holy Spirit. He suddenly found himself in the spirit, approaching the mental institution in Wales, 7,000 miles away! He noticed the big doors and then found himself standing next to the insane woman who was strapped to a cot, wagging her head back and forth and muttering incoherently. John knelt down, put his hand on her forehead and prayed for her, strongly, in the Name of Jesus Christ, the Son of God, for the demons to come out of her, and commanded her to be healed by the power of God. She snapped out of her madness, opened her eyes and smiled up at him. He knew she was healed and in the next moment, John became aware, once again, that he was kneeling in prayer back in his church in South Africa! After three weeks, his church member received a letter from a relative saying that the cousin who had been in the mental institution for seven years had suddenly become well. The mental institution had no explanation, but the woman had been restored and discharged from the facility! God had transported John miraculously in the spirit to Wales and back to South Africa just as He did with Philip in Acts 8:39-40.

Sadly, John's wife, Jennie, died in December 1908 while he was away at a meeting a long distance from their home. She had worked too hard to care for the sick who were camping in the Lakes' front yard, waiting for John to come back and pray for them to be healed.

John was heartbroken, but continued his work in South Africa. In 1909, about a year after Jennie's death, he decided to move his family back to the United States to raise more money and recruit more missionaries for the work in South Africa. While they were gone, the ministry continued in South Africa through a national named Elias Letawba who built Patmos Bible School, which graduated thousands of trained workers who carried the gospel throughout all Africa!

Two years later, John returned to South Africa with $3,000 and eight more missionaries. For the next three years he worked very hard, and by 1913 his ministry included 1250 preachers, 625 churches, and 100,000 people who had been born again, as well as countless miracles, signs and wonders.

Home Bible Study for Kids • Week 1: I Lay Hands on the Sick and They Recover

After John and his children returned to America the second time, in 1913, they traveled around the country, going from city to city, visiting old friends and resting. During that year, John met and married Florence Switzer. They moved to Spokane, Washington, and eventually had five children together.

Lake's Divine Healing Rooms:

While in Spokane, in 1915, John opened "Lake's Divine Healing Rooms"[2] where he trained his students to be "healing technicians." He taught them how to help people receive their healing by the power of God. His healing technicians were taught the Word of God in classrooms and then sent out to sick people's homes to get them healed. They were not allowed to return until the person was healed. Sometimes, it was instant, and sometimes it took weeks. But, everyone always came back with the report that God's healing power worked!

Many people didn't believe God was really healing people in John's meetings and in the healing rooms, so he invited a team composed of people from the Better Business Bureau, doctors, lawyers, educators and businessmen to confirm that people were truly being healed by the power of God. After the committee had interviewed some of the people they had heard about who were healed, John G. Lake said, "Two members of the committee saw us privately and said that the committee was astounded. They said, 'We soon found out, upon investigation, you did not tell half of it.'" They were overwhelmed by the great and miraculous healings by the power of God.

In just five years, over 100,000 documented cases of sickness were healed in John G. Lake's healing rooms in Spokane, including:

- A pastor who had violent fits
- A man with a tumor three times larger than his head sticking out of his shoulder
- Malnourished babies
- Broken bones
- A woman who was left to die from a fibroid tumor, gallstones and missing organs removed through surgery, was healed and her organs regrew!
- An invalid woman suffering from digestive issues, tuberculosis, rheumatism, one of her legs 3 inches shorter than the other and a foot an inch longer than the other was completely healed. Her shorter leg grew an inch each day until she was normal!
- A woman with a 30-pound fibroid tumor in her abdomen
- A boy born with a closed head who was paralyzed and couldn't speak, made totally normal
- Blindness
- Many, many more!

In 1920, John started healing rooms in Portland, Oregon, where there were over 100,000 documented healings, as well. In 1925, John began traveling to create more healing rooms and started churches throughout the United States and Canada.

Making History:

In only five years of ministry in Africa, John G. Lake had started 625 churches, trained 1250 preachers and caused over 100,000 people to come to know Jesus as their Savior and Lord!

Just five years after he began his healing rooms in Spokane, Washington, a government report was released that Spokane was the healthiest city in America. The report stated, "Rev. Lake, through divine healing, has made Spokane the healthiest city in the world, according to United States' statistics." Look how just one man changed his city, his nation and the world because he believed that God is our Healer, even when others didn't!

Outro:

John G. Lake passed away in 1953 at age 65, having lived a full life of ministry, and left a strong heritage of faith. He passed down the knowledge of God's healing power to others, and because of his ministry, there are now over 1,000 healing rooms in 45 different countries.

John G. Lake stated, "It is not TRY but trust. That is the secret of Christ's healing; that is the secret of Christ's salvation. It is trusting Him for it, and believing Him when He says He will do it, and the mind relaxes and the soul comes to rest." His ministry proved that Jesus Christ still heals today, and it is ALWAYS God's will to heal. We just have to LEARN to receive it and LEARN how to minister it to other people!

Variation No. 1:

Entering in costume is an attention grabber for your Superkids. Feel free to present the information as if you were John G. Lake himself!

Variation No. 2:

If you are in a co-op and have other teens or adults involved, consider having another person play John G. Lake, and you can be the interviewer.

---

1 Unless otherwise noted, information in this Real Deal is from *John G. Lake—His Life, His Sermons, His Boldness of Faith,* Kenneth Copeland Publications, 1994.

2 "The Healer: John Graham Lake," http://www.enterhisrest.org/charismata/lake_biography.pdf, from Let Light Shine Out: The Story of The Assemblies of God in the Pacific Northwest by Ward M. Tannenburg, Ph.D (7/16/12).

3 *The Spokesman Review,* Sunday, March 17, 1918, p. 12.

Notes: _____

Home Bible Study for Kids • Week 1: I Lay Hands on the Sick and They Recover

DAY 5: GAME TIME — SIGNED, SEALED, DELIVERED

 **Suggested Time:** 10 minutes

 Memory Verse: Heal the sick, raise the dead, cure those with leprosy, and cast out demons. Give as freely as you have received! —Matthew 10:8

 Teacher Tip: This game can be played in teams with an overall score (add each of their times together) or one by one. (Superkids compete against the clock, each receiving their own time.)

 Supplies: ☐ Stopwatch, ☐ Heavy oversized jacket, ☐ Baseball cap, ☐ Oversized shoes (large boots or flippers), ☐ Scarf, ☐ 8 Pieces of paper, ☐ 8 24-Inch strings (to attach to paper), ☐ 4 Safety pins, ☐ Tape, ☐ Marker (to label papers)

Prior to Game:

First, on each of 4 pieces of paper, write 1 of the following words: SIN, CURSED, SICK, POOR. Attach 1 piece of paper to each article of the costume clothing with a safety pin.

On each of the 4 pieces of paper left over, write 1 word or phrase: SET FREE, BLESSED, HEALED, PROSPEROUS. Attach 1 string to each piece of paper in such a way that it can be worn as a sign around a cadet's neck. Place this second set of 4 pieces of paper around the room to create 4 different "stages."

Decide whether you'd like to have your Superkids play on teams or compete with individual scores.

Game Instructions:

- Ready your cadet(s) to start the relay.
- After starting the stopwatch, have 1 cadet dress quickly in the heavy jacket, baseball cap, scarf and shoes.
- Once the cadet has fully dressed, he or she will go to each "stage," drop 1 piece of costume clothing, and place 1 of the corresponding signs around his/her neck.
- When the cadet arrives back at the start line, stop the clock.
- If there are many children, add players to each team to extend the game if necessary. Combine total time for team scores.

Series: The Superkid Creed II

Home Bible Study for Kids • Week 1: I Lay Hands on the Sick and They Recover

Game Goal:

Replace your old sin "clothes" with the BLESSING of the Word of God, and beat the clock! The Superkid/team who finishes the fastest, wins!

Final Word:

Superkids, Jesus came to your rescue! Your future is signed, sealed and delivered forever. You are healed, set free, BLESSED and prosperous. If you see someone wearing the wrong "clothes" tagged with sin and the curse, ask God to show you what He wants you to do so they can receive their new signs promised in His Word!

Notes: _____

Home Bible Study for Kids • Week 1: I Lay Hands on the Sick and They Recover

ACTIVITY PAGE — HEALING—RAISE THE ROOF

Memory Verse: Heal the sick, raise the dead, cure those with leprosy, and cast out demons. Give as freely as you have received! —Matthew 10:8

Color the page below. Remember that Jesus loves it when we bring our friends to Him for healing!

WEEK 2: I WIN PEOPLE TO JESUS

- **DAY 1: BIBLE LESSON—SHAKE IT OFF** ▸ 30
- **DAY 2: OBJECT LESSON— FILLED TO THE BRIM** ▸ 32
- **DAY 3: GIVING LESSON— MONEY ON A MISSION** ▸ 33
- **DAY 4: ACADEMY LAB— THE GREAT INDICATOR** ▸ 34
- **DAY 5: GAME TIME—SHOW AND TELL** ▸ 36
- **BONUS: ACTIVITY PAGE— SPEAKING UP FOR JESUS** ▸ 38

 **Memory Verse:** So we are Christ's ambassadors; God is making his appeal through us. We speak for Christ when we plead, "Come back to God!" —2 Corinthians 5:20

Home Bible Study for Kids • Week 2: I Win People to Jesus

WEEK 2: SNAPSHOT — I WIN PEOPLE TO JESUS

DAY	TYPE OF LESSON	LESSON TITLE	SUPPLIES
Day 1	Bible Lesson	Shake It Off	None
Day 2	Object Lesson	Filled to the Brim	Baking soda, Vase (a tall, skinny one would be best), ½ Cup vinegar, Food coloring, Glitter (preferably silver), ½ Cup measure, 1 Tablespoon measure, Flat pan
Day 3	Giving Lesson	Money on a Mission	Bible
Day 4	Academy Lab	The Great Indicator	6 Red roses, 2 Sheets of white paper, Scissors, Cotton swabs, Vinegar, Lemon juice, Baking soda, Water, Detergent, 4 Small bowls or cups
Day 5	Game Time	Show and Tell	Strips of paper, Pens, Bowl, Timer (stopwatch) for bigger groups
Bonus	Activity Page	Speaking Up for Jesus	1 Copy for each child, Pencil or pen

Lesson Introduction:

There is a misperception that winning people to Jesus is difficult, or that people say no to the good news about Jesus most of the time. This is simply not true. Let me suggest a mission for you! Take your kids out witnessing (sharing the good news of Jesus with others). But remember, we are fishing for people, and the love of Jesus is the bait! So, go to people in love, not condemnation.

The only sin that keeps people out of heaven is not asking Jesus to come into their hearts. Say, "Is there any reason you can't ask Jesus to come into your heart?" If you haven't done much soul winning, you'll be surprised at how easy it is! Then you can show your Superkids that they can do it, too! Start practicing by asking that question everywhere you go (work, grocery store, parties) and of anyone you meet (friends, neighbors, strangers). Jesus came and looked for the lost (Luke 19:10). We need to go look for them, too! Let's go fishing!

Love,

Commander Kellie

Commander Kellie

Lesson Outline:

This week your children will learn about leading others to Jesus! Jesus is the only way to salvation. So often, we hear from kids and adults: "What about the person in India—or in the remotest village who never hears about Jesus?" We have to understand that God did His part and gave His Son, and Jesus died on the cross so that we can be saved, blessed and healed. God says it is OUR responsibility to GO and TELL the world about what He has done. When you scale it down, we have the easy part!

I. GOD WANTS EVERYONE TO BE SAVED 2 Peter 3:9

    a. God so loved the world that He gave Jesus. John 3:16

    b. Jesus came to seek (look for) and save the lost. Luke 19:10

    c. He died for us while we were still sinners—no one is too bad for Jesus to save. Romans 5:6-8

II. WHEN PETER WAS FILLED WITH THE HOLY SPIRIT, EVERYTHING CHANGED FOR HIM Acts 2:1-3

    a. Jesus called Peter to be a fisher of people. Luke 5:10

    b. He began to preach boldly about Jesus. Acts 2:14-18, 22-24, 32-33, 36

    c. Peter's words pierced the hearts of his listeners, and 3,000 people were saved that day. Acts 2:37-41

    d. God has called you, too. Let's go fishing!

III. GOD GAVE US THE JOB OF BRINGING OTHERS TO HIM 2 Corinthians 5:18

    a. God attracts people through us when we tell them about Jesus. 2 Corinthians 5:19-21

    b. We are God's partners! Jesus did His part on the cross. We do our part when we tell others about Him. 2 Corinthians 6:1-2

    c. Don't be afraid! If people you talk to are not interested in the good news, they are rejecting Jesus, not you! Luke 10:16

    d. Many more people will say yes to the good news, and because of you they will find peace in Jesus.

Notes:

Home Bible Study for Kids • Week 2: I Win People to Jesus

DAY 1: BIBLE LESSON — SHAKE IT OFF

Memory Verse: *So we are Christ's ambassadors; God is making his appeal through us. We speak for Christ when we plead, "Come back to God!"* —2 Corinthians 5:20

In the following passage Jesus gave His disciples the first lesson in soul winning. Some important points are: prayer, healing the sick and preparing for some people to not like what you have to say. Don't take a bad experience with you from person to person. Always share the gospel as a fresh new experience, unoffended by people's rejections. Remember: They aren't rejecting you; they are rejecting God.

Read Luke 10:1-12, 16:
Young Jesus Studies the Word

The Lord now chose seventy-two other disciples and sent them ahead in pairs to all the towns and places he planned to visit. These were his instructions to them: "The harvest is great, but the workers are few. So pray to the Lord who is in charge of the harvest; ask him to send more workers into his fields. Now go, and remember that I am sending you out as lambs among wolves. Don't take any money with you, nor a traveler's bag, nor an extra pair of sandals. And don't stop to greet anyone on the road.

"Whenever you enter someone's home, first say, 'May God's peace be on this house.' If those who live there are peaceful, the blessing will stand; if they are not, the blessing will return to you. Don't move around from home to home. Stay in one place, eating and drinking what they provide. Don't hesitate to accept hospitality, because those who work deserve their pay. If you enter a town and it welcomes you, eat whatever is set before you. Heal the sick, and tell them, 'The Kingdom of God is near you now.' But if a town refuses to welcome you, go out into its streets and say, 'We wipe even the dust of your town from our feet to show that we have abandoned you to your fate. And know this—the Kingdom of God is near!' I assure you, even wicked Sodom will be better off than such a town on judgment day." Then he said to the disciples, "Anyone who accepts your message is also accepting me. And anyone who rejects you is rejecting me. And anyone who rejects me is rejecting God, who sent me."

Discussion Questions:

1. **What did Jesus mean when He said to pray that more workers be sent into the fields for harvest? What kinds of "fields" did He mean?**

    Jesus is talking about believers praying for more workers to be sent to harvest the fields of unsaved souls (people) to tell them about Him. The "fields" are the places where unsaved people are.

2. **Is prayer important when you are about to go soul winning, or what Jesus called being a harvester in the field?**

Series: The Superkid Creed II

It's very important! Not only does prayer equip you to share the gospel, prayer prepares the hearts of the people you will be talking to so they will be ready to receive Jesus as their Savior and Lord. And, as we talked about, it's also important to pray that more workers will be sent out. There are so many souls to be harvested and not enough workers in the field. Even far away, you can make a difference in those remote places or small villages in India where they haven't heard the gospel by praying for them as Jesus said for us to do!

3. **Jesus said He was sending us as _____ among wolves. What did He mean by that?**

   sheep

   In the early church, the gospel was not always a popular message. Then, and even today, many disciples and people of God have been put to death or sent to prison for sharing God's good news of Jesus. Jesus was warning His disciples and us that some people wouldn't like the message, but that shouldn't stop us from telling others about Him. Jesus told His disciples they were like sheep. Remember, a good shepherd takes care of his sheep, protecting them from the wolves. Jesus is the Good Shepherd.

4. **What did Jesus tell the disciples to say as soon as they were received into someone's home? Choose the correct answer.**

   a. You're a sinner, and you're going to hell.

   b. May God's peace be on this house.

   c. You need to get saved!

   Answer: b. Jesus first told His disciples to be a blessing wherever they went. He didn't send them to bring condemnation, but peace, and to pronounce a blessing over their hosts' household!

5. **What were the disciples to do and say if a town rejected them?**

   "We wipe even the dust of your town from our feet to show that we have abandoned you to your fate. And know this—the Kingdom of God is near!" (Luke 10:11)

6. **What does "shaking the dust off your feet" mean, when it comes to people who don't want to hear the gospel? Are they rejecting you or Jesus?**

   If you are "shaking (or wiping) the dust off your feet" before you go to the next place, it's because someone rejected Jesus, not you! Jesus wanted His disciples to not allow one ounce of dust from that town to go with them as they went on to the next town. In essence, He was saying that if you've given it all you've got in sharing the good news and people still reject you, then move on. Don't take that bad experience with you to the next town.

Notes: _____
_____
_____
_____
_____

Home Bible Study for Kids • Week 2: I Win People to Jesus

DAY 2: OBJECT LESSON — FILLED TO THE BRIM

Suggested Time: 7-10 minutes

Memory Verse: So we are Christ's ambassadors; God is making his appeal through us. We speak for Christ when we plead, "Come back to God!" —2 Corinthians 5:20

Teacher Tip: Feel free to do a practice run-through before presenting the lesson if you'd like to see how it looks.

Supplies: ☐ Baking soda, ☐ Vase (a tall, skinny one would be best), ☐ ½ Cup vinegar, ☐ Food coloring (choose any color you'd like), ☐ Glitter (preferably silver because it will show with any food coloring you use; but any color will do), ☐ ½ Cup measure, ☐ 1 Tablespoon measure, ☐ Flat pan

Prior to Lesson:

Set up an empty vase on a table with a pan underneath to demonstrate. Ready your supplies in various bowls to give yourself less to have to think about during the lesson.

Lesson Instructions:

Today, we're talking about sharing Jesus with everyone we know. God gave us the easiest tool to effectively tell people about Jesus! Does anyone know what it is? *(Give time for your kids to answer.)* That's right—the Holy Spirit!

I want to show you how the Holy Spirit is the very best tool we could ever have on our tool belts when it comes to telling people about Jesus. *(Hold the empty vase up so everyone can see it.)*

This vase was like you, Superkids. Before you asked Jesus to come into your hearts, you were empty, and there was no life in you.

(Begin pouring 3 tbsp. baking soda into the vase as you talk.) When you asked Jesus to come into your heart, He filled you with Himself. You became full. *(Put the vase back into the pan.)*

Life with Jesus is fun, colorful and exciting! *(Add about 8 drops of food coloring into the vase.)* Jesus gives our lives meaning.

He makes us sparkle and shine brightly, glowing with His love for people. *(Add the glitter.)*

But God didn't just send us Jesus. He also sent the Holy Spirit as a free gift to all who invite Him to come into their hearts. Superkids, when you accept the Holy Spirit into your life, He changes everything! *(Pour 1/2 cup of vinegar into the vase.)* He makes the gift of Jesus something you can't keep to yourself.

When you have the Holy Spirit inside you, He makes you sparkle and shine! When you let the Holy Spirit become part of you, He gives you the confidence and boldness to share Jesus with your friends and family. Let's make it our mission to let the Holy Spirit guide and direct us on how to share Jesus with others so more people can come to know Him and make Him Lord of their lives, too!

Series: The Superkid Creed II

Home Bible Study for Kids • Week 2: I Win People to Jesus

DAY 3: GIVING LESSON — MONEY ON A MISSION

 Suggested Time: 10 minutes

 Offering Scripture: For this is how God loved the world: He gave his one and only Son, so that everyone who believes in him will not perish but have eternal life. —John 3:16

Supplies: Bible

Lesson Instructions:

Superkids, have you ever wondered where your tithes and offerings go? *(Wait for response.)* Of course, we know we are giving our tithes and offerings to God (Hebrews 7:8), but even your pastor doesn't physically take them to heaven!

Our church (name of church) uses the offerings to pay for things like:

- Pastor and staff
- Bills: phones, water, electricity that keeps us comfortable by running things like the air conditioning when it's hot, or the heat when it's cold outside
- Supporting missionaries
- Toilet paper, soap and paper towels in the church bathrooms
- Summer camp
- Maybe even candy, Bibles or presents to give to people who are visiting church for the first time

Think about it: When you give your offerings, you are giving so more people can come to know Jesus! *(Have your children open their Bibles to John 3:16. If they can, let them read it out loud.)* "For this is how God loved the world: He **gave** his one and only Son, so that everyone who believes in him will not perish but have eternal life."

Wow! God gave the very best He had—Jesus. His love for us was working from the very beginning. We give our offerings because we love God, and we want more people to come to know Him. When you give to God, your money is on a mission, making the way to win more people to Jesus!

What are some other things that our church does to win people to Jesus? *(Discuss outreaches, ministries or other things your kids may not realize their church does to bring more souls into God's kingdom.)*

Notes: _____
_____
_____
_____

Series: The Superkid Creed II

Home Bible Study for Kids • Week 2: I Win People to Jesus

DAY 4: ACADEMY LAB — THE GREAT INDICATOR

 Suggested Time: 10-15 minutes

 Memory Verse: So we are Christ's ambassadors; God is making his appeal through us. We speak for Christ when we plead, "Come back to God!" —2 Corinthians 5:20

 **Teacher Tip:** Do a trial experiment before presenting the lesson for your Superkids to become familiar with mixing the chemicals and the amounts needed. Feel free to let your Superkids help with specific assignments.

Supplies: ☐ 6 Red roses, ☐ 2 Sheets of white paper, ☐ Scissors, ☐ Cotton swabs, ☐ Vinegar, ☐ Lemon juice, ☐ Baking soda, ☐ Water, ☐ Detergent, ☐ 4 Small bowls or cups

Prior to Lesson:

Creating the litmus paper takes some time. So it's a great idea to make some ahead of time. Use approximately half the roses and half a sheet of paper to start. Pull the petals off the roses and rub onto the white paper. The paper will turn purple. Continue until the paper is fully covered with purple. Cut the paper into 4 X 1-inch strips.

It's also helpful to prepare the four small bowls or cups for your test substances: vinegar, lemon juice, baking soda and detergent. You will be adding a tiny bit of water to the baking soda and detergent to make a liquid.

Lesson Instructions:

Today, we are working with what scientists call an *indicator*. In chemistry, an indicator can be many different things that show, or indicate, what type of substance you are dealing with. Some indicators will change color to show if something is an acid or a base.

Scientists use the "potential hydrogen" or "pH" scale in a range from 0-14 to determine what is an acid or a base and measure how acid or alkaline a solution is. Zero is the most acidic and 14 is the most basic. Seven is neutral. Extremely acidic (like battery acid) and extremely basic (like drain cleaner) can be dangerous to handle and should never be ingested! The more acidic the substance, the lower the pH (usually 0-5). Neutral substances have a pH balance of between 6-8, but perfect neutrality is a 7. Most bases are between 9-14 on the pH scale.

Let's test some items to see what happens!

Do you know what test uses color to determine whether something is an acid or a base (alkaline)? It is a "litmus test." To do this test, you have to have what is called "litmus paper." And today, we are going to make our own litmus paper! The important thing about litmus paper is that it has a fairly neutral pH balance. So, we will use roses as our indicator to dye this white paper purple. Begin by taking the rose petals and rubbing the rose onto the white paper. *(Let your kids try this out, so they can see how you made the litmus paper. If you have time and extra roses and paper, they can make their own.)*

Series: The Superkid Creed II

Home Bible Study for Kids • Week 2: I Win People to Jesus

Now, I've already made some of my own litmus strips that we can use to test our items. *(Bring out the prepared strips.)* We are going to test out some of these household items. Remember, since purple is our neutral color, the bases will turn the purple more blue, and the acids will turn it more red.

Let's start with lemon juice. *(Dip your cotton swab into the lemon juice and rub onto the litmus paper—watch as it turns the purple to a more pink color.)* Wow! This must be an acid because it's turning red.

Now let's try the detergent. *(Add a little bit of water and mix well. Then use the cotton swab to rub detergent onto the paper.)* It's blue! So it must be what? You're right—a base!

(Follow the same steps with the vinegar.) It's turning red, so vinegar must be acidic.

(Follow the same steps with the baking soda, mixing with a little water.) Look, it's turning bluish, so baking soda must be a what? Yes! It's a base.

We haven't tested anything neutral yet. What do you think might have a neutral pH balance? Hint: More than half your body is made up of this. Does anyone know? Answer: Water! *(Test with your cotton swab and paper strip.)*

As I was creating this litmus paper I was reminded of the indicator we have living inside us—the Holy Spirit. Jesus made the way for us to receive Him into our hearts after He went to the cross and shed His blood for us—kind of the same way we smeared these roses over this paper. *(Re-demonstrate with the roses and paper, so your kids have a visual.)* We were like this blank sheet of paper not knowing right from wrong, acid from base, but then Jesus' blood made us perfectly balanced in Him and gave us the indicator we needed to live our lives. That same indicator—the Holy Spirit—will also indicate to you who else needs Jesus. He is indicating (speaking) to us all the time, and we know from our memory verse that it is our job to tell others about Jesus to bring their lives into balance, too!

So let's bow our heads today and pray this prayer. *(Allow time for your Superkids to repeat after you.)* "Thank You, Jesus, for giving me Your Holy Spirit. I receive Him as my Indicator. Like our experiment today, I will let my heart indicate who You want me to tell about You. In Jesus' Name. Amen."

Now, get ready for the Holy Spirit to indicate to you, and start bringing people to Jesus!

Notes: _____

DAY 5: GAME TIME — SHOW AND TELL

Suggested Time: 10-15 minutes

Memory Verse: So we are Christ's ambassadors; God is making his appeal through us. We speak for Christ when we plead, "Come back to God!" —2 Corinthians 5:20

Teacher Tip: This game can be played many times over if you only have a few children. If you have many children, it works well to split into 2 teams and have to guess what your teammates are doing. It's a great game for a family night!

Supplies: ☐ Strips of paper, ☐ Pens, ☐ Bowl, ☐ Timer (stopwatch) for bigger groups

Prior to Game:

Cut up strips of paper.

Game Instructions:

There are 3 levels to this game:

1. TELL: You can use words only; no gestures.
2. SHOW: This level is done in charades' style with no words; you must mime/show with gestures only.
3. ONE WORD: You can only use 1 word to enable guessing.

First, each player must write the name of a person, place or a thing on a strip of paper. Make sure everyone understands the words that are written. Check to see words are easily understood and familiar. Fold the paper strips in half and put them into the bowl.

Next, each person must take a strip of paper from the bowl and "TELL" it (Level 1). The person can talk, sing, etc., to help others guess what he or she is attempting to communicate without using the word on their paper. After everyone has drawn a strip of paper and used their words, the papers go back into the bowl.

Level 2: SHOW. Everyone must pick another strip of paper from the bowl, but this time contestants must use gestures to SHOW or act out, charades' style, the word written on the strip of paper. No words or sounds allowed! Continue the game until the bowl is empty again, and put the strips of paper back into the bowl.

Level 3: ONE WORD. Now that everyone has heard many times the various things on the strips of paper, choose 1 word that will let them know which word you're talking about. Each person has a turn until the papers run out.

Game Goal:

To communicate an idea by showing and telling. Eventually people will know exactly what you mean with just 1 word because they've heard about it so many times.

Final Word:

Today, we're talking about winning people to Jesus. Wasn't it fun to tell each other about things and act them out? It's amazing that after each player was showing and telling, it only took one word to understand what someone was talking about! It's time to take that same boldness (and fun) into sharing the gospel. Sometimes, people need to hear the gospel more than once to receive the Lord. They need to hear it, and see it until that wonderful day when that one word from God changes their lives forever! The cool thing is that all of us believers are on the same team to tell people the good news about Jesus!

When we are led by the Holy Spirit, He tells us when to show and when to tell and when to just say one word. It's exciting when we get to be a part of communicating the gospel to people. One Superkid can tell, and then another could show the person the love of God until one day another Superkid comes along with a word from heaven, and BOOM—they get saved on the spot. Most people need to hear about His goodness more than once, so keep being BOLD and expecting God to show you what your mission is every day to win more and more people to Jesus!

Variation:

For a longer version, have each person write on 3 separate slips of paper the name of a person, a place, and a thing. (Example: George Washington—person, Texas—place, *Superkid Academy: The Mission* DVD—thing)

Split into 2 teams and give each person (alternating teams each get a turn) a minute-long turn to go through as many strips of paper as they can until you run out of strips. When the strips have all been used, count the total number each team guessed correctly. Those are that team's points for that level. Then, move on to the next level. Each person is allowed 1 pass (1 opportunity to exchange their slip of paper for another from the bowl) per turn.

Notes:

Home Bible Study for Kids • Week 2: I Win People to Jesus

ACTIVITY PAGE: SPEAKING UP FOR JESUS

Memory Verse: So we are Christ's ambassadors; God is making his appeal through us. We speak for Christ when we plead, "Come back to God!" —2 Corinthians 5:20

Supplies: 1 Copy for each child

Knowing the right words to say can be half the battle when we are "speaking for Christ," telling others about Jesus. Thank God for the help of the HOLY SPIRIT and the WORD of GOD to help us find the best words!

Answer Key:

```
U N I T Y V U F W C V H D I J Y H C
Z F W O N E W A Y O G J S N J P C H
K B U C T V Q V B M U E E H C Q T R
N I K X T F X V T E O S B S O Q H I
F P N B L R L Y E B F T B O U W E S
A E O D S I U C L A F R F M L S A T
T A G S N Q B T L C Y E V F O P L R
H C I V K E Q E H K Q N A D V O I K
E E F X Q D S Z R M X G T J E W N A
R E T A T N R S J T B T F R E E G C
H O L Y S P I R I T Y H S Y U R L V
A O K Q J K Q I B E L I E V E K W R
```

Series: The Superkid Creed II

Home Bible Study for Kids • Week 2: I Win People to Jesus

ACTIVITY PAGE — SPEAKING UP FOR JESUS

Memory Verse: *So we are Christ's ambassadors; God is making his appeal through us. We speak for Christ when we plead, "Come back to God!"* —2 Corinthians 5:20

Name: _____

```
U N I T V U F W C V H D I J Y H C
Z F W O E W A Y O G J S N J P C H
K B U C V Q V B M U E E H C Q T R
N I K X F X V T E O S B S O Q H I
F P N B R L Y E B F T B O U W E S
A E O D I U C L A F R F M L S A T
T A G S Q B T L C Y E V F O P L R
H C I V E Q E H K Q N A D V O I K
E E F X D S Z R M X G T J E W N A
R E T A N R S J T B T F R E E G C
H O L Y P I R I T Y H S Y U R L V
A O K Q K Q I B E L I E V E K W R
```

Find the following words in the puzzle.
Words are hidden ➔ ↓ and ↘

BELIEVE	HOLY SPIRIT	POWER
CHRIST	JESUS	SHOW
COMEBACK	KINDNESS	STRENGTH
FATHER	LIBERTY	TELL
FREE	LOVE	TRUTH
GIFT	ONEWAY	UNITY
HEALING	PEACE	

Notes:

WEEK 3: I DO NOT LIE—
I AM ALWAYS QUICK TO TELL THE TRUTH

DAY 1: BIBLE LESSON— WHO'S YOUR FATHER? ▶ 44

DAY 2: STORYBOOK THEATER— LET'S MAKE A COMPROMISE ▶ 46

DAY 3: GIVING LESSON— "EXTRA"-ORDINARY OFFERING ▶ 53

DAY 4: FOOD FUN— CHOCOLATE SURPRISE ▶ 54

DAY 5: GAME TIME—TRUTH OR LIE ▶ 57

BONUS: ACTIVITY PAGE— TRUTH UNSCRAMBLER ▶ 59

 **Memory Verse:** So stop telling lies. Let us tell our neighbors the truth, for we are all parts of the same body.
—Ephesians 4:25

Home Bible Study for Kids • Week 3: I Do Not Lie—I Am Always Quick to Tell the Truth

WEEK 3: SNAPSHOT — I DO NOT LIE—I AM ALWAYS QUICK TO TELL THE TRUTH

DAY	TYPE OF LESSON	LESSON TITLE	SUPPLIES
Day 1	Bible Lesson	Who's Your Father?	None
Day 2	Storybook Theater	Let's Make a Compromise	Optional Costumes, Props, Art supplies
Day 3	Giving Lesson	"EXTRA"-Ordinary Offering	None
Day 4	Food Fun	Chocolate Surprise	Small jar of pearl or cocktail onions, Small jar of maraschino cherries, 16 Ounces bitter baking chocolate, 16 Ounces sweetened chocolate (color should match the bitter chocolate), 1 Glass drinking water per child, 1 Box of toothpicks, Double boiler, Candy thermometer (optional), Cheese grater, Stirring spoon, Decorative serving plate, Parchment paper for baking, Napkins
Day 5	Game Time	Truth or Lie	None
Bonus	Activity Page	Truth Unscrambler	1 Copy for each child, Pencils

Lesson Introduction:

Today's focus is really as much about making a firm decision to rely on God as it is about not lying. If this is presented as just a "don't do this anymore" lesson it will be difficult for your kids to implement, or even understand, the importance of it. However, if you show them that by telling the truth they're actually allowing God to fix things for them, they'll be motivated to always tell the truth!

It's so simple! God is your Helper, and He said don't lie. If you still choose to lie to get out of trouble, then He can't help you. If you lie to benefit yourself, then God can't bless (or benefit) you.

It's easy to lead the Superkids to a decision for life: no more lies—ever! Amen and amen!

One lie will lead you into another. In Genesis 3, everyone lied: The serpent lied, Eve lied, and Adam lied to God. And we are still dealing with the evil effects of those lies today!

Love,

Commander Kellie

Commander Kellie

Home Bible Study for Kids • Week 3: I Do Not Lie—I Am Always Quick to Tell the Truth

Lesson Outline:

This week your children will learn about making decisions to not lie and be quick to tell the truth. When you make a habit of trusting God to get you out of trouble, lying loses its power. But when you lie, you choose Satan's way. He is the Father of all lies.

I. GOD HATES LYING! Proverbs 6:16-19, 12:22

    a. Satan is a liar and the father of all liars. John 8:44

    b. You don't belong to Satan, so DON'T EVER LIE! Colossians 3:9

    c. Lies are always exposed. Proverbs 12:19

II. PEOPLE LIE FOR DIFFERENT REASONS

    a. Ananias and Sapphira lied to the Lord to impress people. Acts 5:1-2

    b. The Holy Spirit exposed them! Acts 5:3-10

    c. Often kids will lie to get out of trouble.

    d. But lying gets you into more trouble. Proverbs 17:20

III. HONESTY GUIDES GOOD PEOPLE Proverbs 11:3, 5

    a. Lying hurts others. Proverbs 25:18, 26:18-19

    b. Stop telling lies! Let your words be good and helpful. Ephesians 4:25, 29

    c. Be quick to tell the truth, and watch God get you out of trouble! Proverbs 29:25, 11:6

    (Note: Please read scriptures in this order.)

Notes: _____

Home Bible Study for Kids • Week 3: I Do Not Lie—I Am Always Quick to Tell the Truth

DAY 1: BIBLE LESSON — WHO'S YOUR FATHER?

Memory Verse: So stop telling lies. Let us tell our neighbors the truth, for we are all parts of the same body. —Ephesians 4:25

Jesus is the truth. Satan is a liar and the father of all lies. If you receive the truth (Jesus), then your Father is God!

Read John 8:31-38, 42-47:
The Truth or a Lie

Jesus said to the people who believed in him, "You are truly my disciples if you remain faithful to my teachings. And you will know the truth, and the truth will set you free." "But we are descendants of Abraham," they said. "We have never been slaves to anyone. What do you mean, 'You will be set free'?" Jesus replied, "I tell you the truth, everyone who sins is a slave of sin. A slave is not a permanent member of the family, but a son is part of the family forever. So if the Son sets you free, you are truly free. Yes, I realize that you are descendants of Abraham. And yet some of you are trying to kill me because there's no room in your hearts for my message. I am telling you what I saw when I was with my Father. But you are following the advice of your father."

Jesus told them, "If God were your Father, you would love me, because I have come to you from God. I am not here on my own, but he sent me. Why can't you understand what I am saying? It's because you can't even hear me! For you are the children of your father the devil, and you love to do the evil things he does. He was a murderer from the beginning. He has always hated the truth, because there is no truth in him. When he lies, it is consistent with his character; for he is a liar and the father of lies. So when I tell the truth, you just naturally don't believe me! Which of you can truthfully accuse me of sin? And since I am telling you the truth, why don't you believe me? Anyone who belongs to God listens gladly to the words of God. But you don't listen because you don't belong to God."

Discussion Questions:

1. **What did Jesus say would set them free?**

   The truth/knowing the truth

2. **Jesus said that when we sin, we become a slave to sin. What are some sins that are hard to break free from?**

   Answers will vary.

3. **Have you ever experienced being a slave to lying? Do you know what I'm talking about? When you lie once and then keep having to make up more and more and more lies, it feels like you can't get away from them!**

   If your children don't have any experience with this, prepare a story from your own life they can learn from. It helps them to hear your experiences so they are more comfortable sharing their experiences with you.

Series: The Superkid Creed II

4. **Can you tell the difference between God's advice (the truth) and the devil's advice (lies)? Discuss the difference.**

   Continue discussion from question 3 if applicable. The weight and guilt we feel from lying is not from God, but the devil—who is the father of all lies. Our spirits and emotions are affected when we are chained by sin to the devil and his plan for us—which is to steal, kill and destroy. But telling the truth breaks that evil chain and Satan's plan of destruction for us. When we finally tell the truth after lying, it feels like a weight lifted from our shoulders. Most of the time, we wish we had just told the truth from the beginning.

5. **What does the advice of the devil sound like when he is tempting you to lie?**

   Answers will vary. Make sure they hit some main points: "Lying is not a big deal"; "It's just a little lie"; "Everyone does it"; "Well, you didn't exactly lie, you just didn't tell the truth when you could have"; "Just do it this once. It'll get you out of trouble."

6. **Fill in the blank: Jesus said that Satan was a _____ from the beginning. Why do you think the devil wants you to take his advice?**

   murderer

   He wants you to take his advice because he wants to steal from you, kill you and destroy you.

7. **Fill in the blank: Jesus said God wants you to hear the truth, so it will make you _____.**

   free

   Notes: _____

Home Bible Study for Kids • Week 3: I Do Not Lie—I Am Always Quick to Tell the Truth

DAY 2: STORYBOOK THEATER — LET'S MAKE A COMPROMISE

Suggested Time: 15 minutes

Memory Verse: So stop telling lies. Let us tell our neighbors the truth, for we are all parts of the same body. —Ephesians 4:25

Teacher Tip:
- There are many variations, so think outside the box to make this story work best for YOU.
- The Scorekeeper and Sign Holder characters can be combined into one character if you are putting on a show.
- Game show theme music at the beginning of the segment can help set high energy for the show.

List of Characters & Optional Costumes:
- Host/Danny Deceiver/Devil: Upbeat host with a bad agenda; black suit or clothes, sunglasses; wears tag "Danny Deceiver"
- Scorekeeper/Diana: Hollywood game show hostess type/pretty on the outside; pretty dress
- Sign Holder: Holds up audience cue signs; polo shirt and khakis or all black
- Tate: Upstanding Superkid
- Pinster: Not too bright, nose-picker; geeky attire
- Mickie: Trickster and master manipulator; cool outfit
- Sister: Sassy, models a cow outfit

Supplies:
(Variation 1) ☐ Index Cards
(Variation 2) ☐ Copies of the skit
(Variation 3) ☐ 3 contestant booths (easily made with tall boxes and draping material or parchment paper), ☐ Scoreboard, ☐ Felt-tip markers/chalk to write with, ☐ Eraser, ☐ 5 Large poster-sized audience cue signs that read: "APPLAUSE"; "EWWWW!"; "DRUMROLL"; "1-2-3 COMPROMISE!"; "LAUGH"; ☐ Index-sized host cue cards that contain the question and answer options for the show (see script), ☐ 3 Sets of contestant answer signs reading: A, B, C, D (can easily be made by gluing paint sticks or pencils to 5" x 7" cardstock). You should have 12 signs altogether—4 per contestant (Optional) ☐ Game show banner for your set that reads "Let's Make a Compromise!"
(Variation 4) ☐ Whiteboard, ☐ Chalkboard or easel with paper, ☐ Dry-erase markers if using whiteboard, ☐ Colored chalks if using chalkboard, or pencil (art pencils work best) and eraser, ☐ Black marker and rags (to blend chalks) if using paper, ☐ Art smock (to keep your artist's clothes clean)

Variation No. 1:

Read the story as part of your read-aloud time. Remember, familiarizing yourself with the story by reading the story beforehand and giving different voices to each character will help bring life to the story. It's fun to let your children play the audience and use index cards as their cue cards to react in the various ways. Cues in the story should be in ALL CAPITAL LETTERS. They are: APPLAUSE, EWWWW!, DRUMROLL, 1-2-3 COMPROMISE!, LAUGH.

Home Bible Study for Kids • Week 3: I Do Not Lie—I Am Always Quick to Tell the Truth

Variation No. 2:

Read the story as an old-time radio skit, choosing different kids to act out each part. If you are limited on participants, then assign more than one part per person, and change the voice. Make copies of the skit, and have each actor highlight his/her lines.*Great for a large family, Bible study group, or co-op.

Variation No. 3:

Act out the story as a fun skit. Perhaps your children can practice during the day (even creating costumes from everyday items) and then perform it in the evening before the whole family. Before beginning your skit, remember to introduce your cast! *Great for a large family, Bible study group or co-op.

Variation No. 4:

Create a storybook theater where one or more family members sketch the story on a whiteboard, chalkboard or artist's easel as another member reads the story. Initially, there will be a few supplies to purchase, but don't let this be a deterrent from using the illustrated story option! Once the supplies have been purchased, they'll be long-lasting and reusable.

To make your presentation easier, lightly sketch the drawing with a pencil prior to presentation. Time may not allow the picture to be completely drawn and colored at the time of the lesson. Erase pencil lines, so light lines are visible to the artist but not visible to the children. Review the story ahead of time to determine the amount of time needed to complete the illustration while telling the story. When the story begins, use black markers to "draw" the picture, following the sketched pencil lines. Next, apply color using the pastel chalk. Then, blend the color with the rags. Finally, cut the illustration from the board, roll it up, secure it with rubber bands, and share it with one of your children!

STORY:

Some compromises are good like when a brother and sister decide to share a toy. But one thing that should never be compromised is the truth! But that's exactly what the game-show host of the hit TV show *Let's Make a Compromise* always aimed for. But this night was different because this night, they acted like a bunch of ants under a boot.

Much like any other night, the Host appeared on stage in his snazzy black suit and dark sunglasses. He welcomed his lovely assistant, Diana, and she catwalked across the stage in her glorious dress to keep score for all the contestants.

The crowd went wild as the Host said… "Let's Make A Compromise!" He paused for effect, soaking in the audience's praise. "Welcome," he smiled. "I'm your host, Danny." The Sign Holder held up the "APPLAUSE" cue card, though the audience needed no cue. Danny turned to Diana, "This is my lovely Scorekeeper, Diana." The audience cheered again.

"Let's take a look at our contestants!" Danny continued. "Tate, Pinster and Mickie!" From the audience, the 3 contestants walked up and stood behind their contestant booths. Tate was a Superkid. Pinster seemed smart, but very preoccupied with his boogers. Mickie was the coolest contestant by far.

Home Bible Study for Kids • Week 3: I Do Not Lie—I Am Always Quick to Tell the Truth

Danny watched as Pinster ate another booger, and then stuck one behind his ear to save for later. "EW-WWW!" Danny said and the audience followed suit as the "EWWWW!" sign was held up. "I'm gonna call you 'Sinister Pinster.'"

"Cool," replied Pinster.

"Contestants…" Danny said, "raise your hand if you're ready to compromise!" Danny noticed that for some reason, Tate had not raised his hand but continued: "Round 1: What…can you live without?" After some APPLAUSE from the audience, he asked, "There is a new video game in town. It's the latest and the greatest. And you want it really bad…." Mickie nodded mischievously. Danny smiled. "You've already told your parents you want it, but it's a shocking…$100! What's your compromise? Do you:

    A: Try your hand at stealing?

    B: Throw a fit and scream until they buy it for you?

    C: Live without it?

    Or D: Tell your parents there's a school trip that requires $100 to be paid in cash and use the money to buy your new game?"

The contestants weighed their options. "Think carefully," reminded Danny. "Hold up your answer on the count of…help me out, audience!" The Sign Holder held up "1-2-3, COMPROMISE!" and the audience cheered with Danny: "1-2-3, COMPROMISE!"

Danny turned toward the contestants. "Let's see those answers!" Mickie held up the "D" sign, Pinster raised the "A" sign and Tate chose the "C" sign.

"What's the best compromise? Drumroll, please…." The Sign Holder used his "DRUMROLL" cue.

"And the $100 game goes to…" Danny says with excitement, "Mickie with answer 'D: Lie to your parents!' Mickie wins a video game and 50 points for round 1. Coming in second is Pinster, who chose 'A: Steal it,' and has been awarded a free trip worth 30 points!" Pinster threw his fist in the air in victory, "Woohoo!" while Mickie just gave a cool nod. "And Tate…" Danny added, "you're awarded…zilch-o." The Scorekeeper wrote "0" on the board next to Tate's name, "50" next to Mickie's, and "30" next to Pinster's.

Tate was confused. "What? That's not right!" he said. He'd always been taught that lying is <u>never</u> the correct answer.

"You said you could live without it, kid," replied Danny, "No compromise, no points!" The Host quickly moves on: "Round 2! Who…is your BFF?" The Host reads off his cue cards: "Question 2: Your best friend has just been voted the biggest loser of the year and received a major wedgie in the lunchroom. School bullies approach you next and say, 'Looks like losers run in pairs.' What's your compromise? Do you…

    A: Deny that you know your old pal and move tables?

    B: Try to comfort your friend who's in a lot of pain?

    C: Try to give the bullies a wedgie back?

    Or D: Run away like a sissy?

"Ready your answers on the count of *compromise!*" Danny spoke to the contestants. The Sign Holder's cue card lifted, and the people shouted: "1-2-3, COMPROMISE!" Mickie held up "A." Tate chose "B" and Pinster held up "C."

Series: The Superkid Creed II

Home Bible Study for Kids • Week 3: I Do Not Lie—I Am Always Quick to Tell the Truth

"Let's see whose Compromise works best...." The Host walked toward the contestants. "Looks like it's Mickie again with denying that you know your best friend. Mickie, you get 80 points! Pinster, you've been awarded 0 points, another trip and a wedgie." Pinster didn't realize this was a bad thing and raised his fist again. "Yeah!"

"And Tate you get...0 points...again," the Host said as Diana changed the scores.

Tate was astonished, "What kind of game is this?" he asked.

Danny replied, "My game, my rules, kid."

"I don't get anything for being honest and loyal...?"

"Ughhhh... OK, you get to keep your loser friend," the Host replied and the Sign Holder cued the audience to "LAUGH."

"But, that's not fair!" Tate said, though the audience continued to laugh at him.

"That's right!" replied Danny. "It's a...compromise!" The audience roared with LAUGHter until Danny silenced them. "And...round 3! How do you tell them? For this question, imagine your sister is looking for something to wear. She comes out in a new outfit and says..." Danny gestured for the girl playing the Sister to walk out on stage.

Like Diana, the "Sister" entered with a catwalk…but unlike Diana, she was wearing…a cow costume! She said to the contestants: "Hey, brother, does this make me look like a cow?"

"EWWWWW," said the Host. Then, he turned to the contestants: "All right, what's your Compromise? Do you say to her...

    A: You look more like a pig to me.

    B: Of course not! You look beautiful!

    C: Honestly? Yes.

    Or D: I have been momentarily blinded by a UFO and am unable to see your stunning outfit, but you always look great!"

The audience LAUGHed and cheered again. "Ready those answers!" shouted Danny. The contestants thought about it as the Host gave the recap. "Remember, that's 'A: You look like a pig, B: You look beautiful! C: Honestly, yes, D: Blinded by a UFO....' On the count of...1-2-3, COMPROMISE!"

Mickie chose "B." Tate rolled his eyes but held up "C." Pinster wavered and alternated, holding up both the "A" and "D" signs until the Sister walked over to him, took the "A" sign, and smacked him with it, leaving him with only the "D" sign.

"Final answers? This is the second-to-last round."

The contestants nodded as the Sister left. "Congratulations, Mickie! You've got it right, again!" The Audience APPLAUSE was loud as the Host said, "You're awarded 100 points and a new outfit!" The Scorekeeper, Diana, changed the score.

Danny noticed the high score. "Mickie, you're ahead by a landslide. What's your secret?"

Mickie replied, "Well, if I told you the truth, I might not win." Mickie and Danny shared a LAUGH as the audience chimed in, too.

Home Bible Study for Kids • Week 3: I Do Not Lie—I Am Always Quick to Tell the Truth

But Pinster was getting restless. "What about me?"

"Awww, yes, Sinister Pinster," replied the Host. "You're coming in second for that round, with 50 points awarded!"

"All right!" Pinster cheered.

Very smug, Danny added, "And…Tate…your answer receives another zero…. You should try learning from Mickie here."

"Yeah, what's your secret…of losing?" Mickie asked haughtily.

Tate replied, "I'm not going to lie—but, I guess that's not much of a secret."

"But Tate…you're going to go home empty-handed, when you could be winning so much…!" Danny warned.

"Hey, I get to keep my friend, remember?" Tate said with a smile.

"Yeah, but who wants a loser friend," Danny started…

Tate continued, "And I'll probably get to keep my sister from strangling me later on too, right?"

Danny laughed nervously. "Maybe…. Is it hot in here to anyone?"

Tate smiled. "I'm not going to lie no matter what prize you say I can get."

Danny added slyly, "But, it's not a lie. It's a…Compromise!"

Tate knew the answer to this one: "It's a lie if you are compromising the truth!" he said.

Now, Danny felt even more nervous. "Nobody else is hot in here?" As the Host removed his suit jacket, his nametag read: "Danny Deceiver."

"Let's get back on track, shall we?" he continued.

The Sign Holder raised the "APPLAUSE" sign. But now, even the audience was unsure as Danny hurried on. "Round 4…the final round! Here's the last question: You watched a really bad movie with your friends last week, and your parents just found out about it! They have decided to ground you from seeing any of your friends again—even your loser friends, Tate—for the next…drumroll please…." The Sign Holder held up the "DRUMROLL" sign. "For the next 10 years of your life!" Danny continued, "What's your compromise? Do you,

    A: Tell them the truth and lose all your friends.

    B: Tell them whoever said that was a liar because you've never even heard of that movie.

    C: Say that you started watching the movie, but you went to another room because it was bad, and you fell asleep.

    Or D: Tell them that your friends tied you down and forced you to watch it?"

Danny dabbed his sweaty forehead, "Get your answers ready… Ready, audience? 1-2-3, COMPROMISE!"

"Let's see those answers for the final round." Mickie held up "B," for the other people lied. Tate held onto the truth with the answer "A."

And Pinster…Pinster held up the biggest booger he had ever seen! "I've got it!" he yelled excitedly.

Home Bible Study for Kids • Week 3: I Do Not Lie—I Am Always Quick to Tell the Truth

"Hold it up then," Danny said.

Pinster lifted his booger for all to see!

"EWWWW!" The audience and the Host roared. "I meant hold up your answer," Danny said.

Pinster took his booger hand and grabbed the answer "D."

Disgusted, the host turned to find Mickie. He smiled. "Mickie, you were close, but the best possible compromise was actually 'C.' However, you will still be awarded 50 points." Mickie flashed a smile to the audience as Diana began adding up the points.

The Host turned to Pinster. "Pinster, your answer was next, and you are awarded 30 points...."

But Pinster wasn't paying attention—he was too busy smearing boogers on his signs.

"And…" Danny added, "you get to keep your signs!"

Pinster raises the signs in the air with a "Woohoo!"

"Tate, you have once again been awarded the big goose egg—zero, nada, ZIP-a-dee-doo-dah...."

But Tate had heard enough. He knew who Danny really was. "You can keep your prizes, Devil!" In fact, let's take a look at what 'prizes' everyone won, because you only came to steal, kill and destroy!"

Danny just smiled. "OK, well…Pinster wins second-place with 110 points, two free trips and a wedgie. Scorekeeper, what do we have for him, today?"

Diana replied, "Pinster's compromise gets him 110 buckets of slime on his face, a wedgie, a free trip to jail and a trip to…the principal's office!" In unison, Diana and Danny throw their heads back and laugh evilly.

"NO!" Pinster screamed as Security grabbed him and took him backstage.

"Don't forget your signs," said Danny. Danny grabbed the signs and threw them at Pinster.

Hearing Pinster's offstage screams, Mickie grew nervous. "First place prize is better, though…right?" he asked the host.

The Host smiled and rubbed his hands together, replying: "Much better. Tell Mickie what the prize is, Diana."

"For your 280 points, that's how many people will no longer believe you because you lie ALL the time. AND, you get to keep the nightmares from your brand-new video game as well as a beautiful new outfit." Diana gestured as the Sister walked back out bringing with her the cow outfit.

Danny laughed again. "Enjoy the nightmares, little liar.… Ha, ha, ha!"

Tate felt bad for Mickie and Pinster. They had been tricked, but he suddenly remembered what he'd learned at Superkid Academy and spoke loud enough for all the audience to hear: "I resist you, in the Name of Jesus!"

(Address your children:) Now because you're Superkids, you know the scripture that says, "Resist the devil, and he will flee from you" (James 4:7). So what do you think Danny Deceiver, also known as the devil, and his assistant Diana did? *(Allow time for the children to answer.)* That's right, they fled. They ran away!

When Danny and Diana heard the Name of Jesus, they ran out screaming like little girls, because they were totally powerless against that Name. Even their "Security" fled with them. Pinster came back out onto the stage, yelling, "I'm never going to lie again!"

Series: The Superkid Creed II

"I'm gonna work on that too," Mickie said to Tate. They all hugged, and the audience gave a big LAUGH and their best APPLAUSE—but without any need for cue cards. Finally, they too felt free to give an honest response.

THE END

Notes: _____

DAY 3: GIVING LESSON — "EXTRA"-ORDINARY OFFERING

Suggested Time: 10 minutes

Offering Scripture: Then the Lord said to Elijah, "Go and live in the village of Zarephath, near the city of Sidon. I have instructed a widow there to feed you." So he went to Zarephath. As he arrived at the gates of the village, he saw a widow gathering sticks, and he asked her, "Would you please bring me a little water in a cup?" As she was going to get it, he called to her, "Bring me a bite of bread, too." But she said, "I swear by the Lord your God that I don't have a single piece of bread in the house. And I have only a handful of flour left in the jar and a little cooking oil in the bottom of the jug. I was just gathering a few sticks to cook this last meal, and then my son and I will die." But Elijah said to her, "Don't be afraid! Go ahead and do just what you've said, but make a little bread for me first. Then use what's left to prepare a meal for yourself and your son. For this is what the Lord, the God of Israel, says: There will always be flour and olive oil left in your containers until the time when the Lord sends rain and the crops grow again!" So she did as Elijah said, and she and Elijah and her family continued to eat for many days. There was always enough flour and olive oil left in the containers, just as the Lord had promised through Elijah.
—1 Kings 17:8-16

Lesson Instructions:

Superkids, are you ready to see some "EXTRA"-ordinary things show up in your life?

Have you ever seen God perform a miracle? *(Wait for responses.)*

Today, we're going to read about a time when God did something completely "EXTRA"-ordinary. Read 1 Kings 17:8-16.

Think about it: All the widow had left was a small amount of oil and flour, and a very small amount of wood to cook it over. This was even less than normal! She and her son would starve on what they had left. But Elijah had heard from God, and he knew God would bless this widow if she obeyed his instructions.

But the widow had to place her whole trust in God, and because of her obedience, she received an "EXTRA"-ordinary blessing! Elijah was right. The Lord multiplied the small amount of food the widow had and, as a result, Elijah, the widow and her son ate from that food for many days and ended up with lots of EXTRA food!

It works exactly the same way today. When we put our trust in our heavenly Father, He *always* provides the "EXTRA" stuff in our lives. The Word tells us, "God is not a man, that he should lie" (Numbers 23:19, KJV). You can fully place your trust and hope in the Lord. Everything HE says IS true.

Remember, when it's time to give—there's nothing ordinary about it. When you give to God with a joyful and obedient heart, you will see what "EXTRA"-ordinary things He does in return!

Home Bible Study for Kids • Week 3: I Do Not Lie—I Am Always Quick to Tell the Truth

DAY 4: FOOD FUN — CHOCOLATE SURPRISE

 **Suggested Time:** 10 minutes

 Memory Verse: So stop telling lies. Let us tell our neighbors the truth, for we are all parts of the same body. —Ephesians 4:25

 **Teacher Tip:** Keeping a straight face is vital to pulling this off. You can't let your children suspect something is amiss. Do your best to make sure the chocolate-covered onions look like the chocolate-covered cherries. (For small groups, make enough for all. For larger groups, make a few and choose volunteers.)

Overview: In this lesson, you will make some chocolate-covered onions and pass them off as chocolate-covered cherries. You will then relate it to the lesson on lying. When someone is expecting sweet chocolate and cherries and bites into an onion surrounded by bitter chocolate instead, the expression on his/her face makes the point of how bitter it is when we lie.

Ingredients: ☐ Small jar of pearl or cocktail onions, ☐ Small jar of maraschino cherries, ☐ 16 Ounces of bitter baking chocolate, ☐ 16 Ounces of sweet chocolate (color should match the bitter chocolate)

Supplies: ☐ 1 Glass of drinking water per child, ☐ Box of toothpicks, ☐ Double boiler, ☐ Candy thermometer (optional), ☐ Cheese grater, ☐ Stirring spoon, ☐ Decorative serving plate, ☐ Parchment paper for baking, ☐ Napkins

Prior to Lesson:

Before the lesson, prepare the chocolate-covered pearl onions using bitter chocolate, and make chocolate-covered cherries with sweet chocolate by following the recipe below.

On a party plate, make a beautiful display of your chocolate treats. Put the chocolate-covered onions on one side of the platter, and the chocolate-covered cherries on the other. Make sure you know which is which! You can garnish or decorate the serving plate in such a way that allows only you to know which are cherries and which are onions.

Keep your creations chilled until you are about to start the lesson.

Recipe:

- First, drain and place the cocktail onions and maraschino cherries in the refrigerator to cool. Keep them separate. Remove and discard any stems.
- Grate ¾ of the sweet chocolate into the double boiler. (If you don't have a double boiler, you can create one using water in a saucepan or soup pot with a glass or metal bowl stacked on top.)

Series: The Superkid Creed II

- Set the top part (or bowl) of the double boiler pan over lightly simmering water (in the pot) and stir the chocolate as it melts.
- Do not allow the water to come to a rolling boil because the chocolate will burn. When the chocolate reaches 100° F (if you have a candy thermometer), remove it from the heat.
- Stir in small chunks of the remaining sweet chocolate. As the chunks melt and you stir, it will "temper" the chocolate so it will harden and become shiny as it cools.
- When the temperature cools to around 90° F, it is ready for dipping. Stick toothpicks into the cherries, dip them into the chocolate, and set them on parchment paper to cool. Leave the toothpick in each chocolate-covered cherry to use for serving.
- Repeat the process with the bitter baking chocolate and pearl onions.

Lesson Instructions:

Today, I have a very special dessert for you. Do you like chocolate-covered cherries? *(If you have a large group, choose volunteers who like chocolate-covered cherries.)*

Yum! I do. *(Eat a chocolate-covered cherry, and if there's another adult present, allow him or her to try one and get their reaction.)* So tasty!

These are special because I made them just for you, so I'm going to hand them out, and we'll all eat them on the count of three. *(Place each one on a napkin, and hand them out to whomever is eating. Get one for yourself also, and if you feel brave, try the onion this time!)* Ready: 1-2-3. (Everybody eats.) YUCK!

Superkids, that's what deceit and lies taste like!

(Ask the children to describe what it tasted like.)

I apologize, but I made half our treats from sweet chocolate and cherries, and the other half from bitter chocolate and pearl onions.

How did it make you feel to get a chocolate-covered onion when you were expecting a chocolate-covered cherry? *(You can coax them along with, "Did you feel disappointed?" etc.)*

I can understand how you feel. They both look really good, but there was a big difference, wasn't there? Proverbs12:19 says, "Truthful words stand the test of time, but lies are soon exposed."

Could anyone eat a chocolate-covered onion and believe it was a cherry? No! As soon as someone takes a bite, they will know and not be happy!

That's the way it is with lying. It puts a bad taste in the mouth of the person being lied to. If someone in a store sold you a box of chocolate-covered cherries and they turned out to be onions, don't you think that person would be in big trouble? You would be back down there asking for your money back because they deceived you!

Some people lie because they are trying to get out of trouble. But lying always makes everything worse. Proverbs 25:18 tells us that lying hurts people just as if we hit them. God loves people and doesn't hurt them. So as children of God, we speak the truth in love and encourage others.

When we are told a lie, it can leave a bad taste in our mouths, too. So would you like to try one of the REAL cherries now? *(Give each taster a glass of water to rinse the bad taste from their mouths.)*

Home Bible Study for Kids • Week 3: I Do Not Lie—I Am Always Quick to Tell the Truth

As children of God, we get rid of that bad taste by forgiving others. When we find out they have deceived us, we pray the Lord will bless them, not hurt them. When we act in love, it takes the bad taste out of our mouths! *(Hand out the chocolate-covered cherries for everyone to enjoy.)*

Repeat after me:

> I speak the truth in love.
>
> I do not lie because lying hurts me and others.
>
> I forgive those who have lied to me.
>
> I pray that God will bless them.

(Feel free to make a show of eating a chocolate-covered onion at the end of the lesson, so the children will see you shared in their discomfort!)

Notes: _____

Series: The Superkid Creed II

Home Bible Study for Kids • Week 3: I Do Not Lie—I Am Always Quick to Tell the Truth

DAY 5: GAME TIME — TRUTH OR LIE

Suggested Time: 10 minutes

Memory Verse: *So stop telling lies. Let us tell our neighbors the truth, for we are all parts of the same body.* —Ephesians 4:25

Prior to Game:

Make sure you are ready with the questions. If you want to find other interesting "truths/facts" that would be of more interest to your children, feel free to use those instead. If you'd like to keep score, prepare paper and pen or a scoreboard.

Game Instructions:

We're going to play a game. YOU must determine or figure out what's the truth, and what's a lie. I'm going to read 3 interesting facts, but only 2 will be true and 1 will be false. So you have to be quick to tell the truth. The instant you hear me say something untrue, raise your hand and put up the number of the lie on your fingers. For example, if you think No. 2 is false, raise your hand and put up two fingers. But you can only raise your hand 1 time while I read. At the very end of my statement, I'll say "Which one is *not* true?" And if you haven't put your hand up yet, pick No. 1, No. 2 or No. 3 as quickly as you can. The first person to raise his or her hand with the correct answer wins the round.

Question No. 1: Sloths

1. Some sloths can turn their head almost 360 degrees.
2. All sloths have 3 toes.
3. Sloths can stick their tongues 10-12 inches out of their mouths.

Which one is not true?

Answer: No. 2. Sloths have either 2 or 3 toes. It's the 3-toed sloths that can turn their heads almost 360 degrees.

Question No. 2: Food

1. Chewing gum burns about 60 calories per hour.
2. Strawberries have more vitamin C than oranges.
3. The world's heaviest onion weighed more than a man's head.

Series: The Superkid Creed II

Home Bible Study for Kids • Week 3: I Do Not Lie—I Am Always Quick to Tell the Truth

Which one is not true?

Answer: No. 1. Chewing gum burns about 11 calories per hour.

Question No. 3: Animal anatomy

1. A shrimp's heart is located in its head.
2. An ostrich's eyes are the same size as its brain.
3. Cat urine glows under a black light.

Which one is not true?

Answer: No. 2. An ostrich's eyes are larger than its brain.

Question No. 4: Weather

1. A bolt of lightning is about 5 times hotter than the surface of the sun.
2. Raindrops are shaped more like hamburger buns than actual drops.
3. Africa is the driest continent on the earth.

Which one is not true?

Answer: No. 2. Antarctica is the driest continent on the earth.

Question No. 5: Humans

1. Most of the dust in your home is actually dead skin particles.
2. While in outer space, humans become a little shorter because there is no gravity to pull them down.
3. It is impossible to sneeze with your eyes open.

Which one is not true?

Answer No. 3. Humans get a little taller in space because there is no gravity to pull them down.

Game Goal:

To be able to quickly figure out what's true and what is a lie.

Final Word:

Some of those questions were really tricky! Some of the true statements sounded ridiculous and yet they were true! Who knew that raindrops looked like hamburger buns, not the shape we consider to be actual drops?

It's important to make a habit of telling the truth. No matter how crazy the truth sounds, people will still believe us if we are known for always telling the truth, not lies. Just think how much easier it will be for unbelievers to hear about the truth of Jesus when they know you are one of those people who never tells a lie.

Home Bible Study for Kids • Week 3: I Do Not Lie—I Am Always Quick to Tell the Truth

ACTIVITY PAGE — TRUTH UNSCRAMBLER

Memory Verse: So stop telling lies. Let us tell our neighbors the truth, for we are all parts of the same body. —Ephesians 4:25

Supplies: ☐ 1 Copy for each child, ☐ Bible

Answer Key:

Unscramble the bolded words to find the TRUTH from the Word of God—your Bible!

1. John 8:32: You will know the **HURTT** ___truth___, and the **HURTT** ___truth___ will set you free.

2. Ephesians 4:25, 29: Stop Telling Lies! —Let your words be **DOGO** ___good___ and **PHELLUF** ___helpful___.

3. Proverbs 17:20: Lying gets you into more **BLUETOR** ___trouble___.

4. Proverbs 29:25: **RIFEANG** ___fearing___ people is dangerous, but trusting **DOG** ___God___ is safe!

5. Proverbs 11:5: The Godly are **TIDRECED** ___directed___ by **YENOSHT** ___honesty___.

Series: The Superkid Creed II

Home Bible Study for Kids • Week 3: I Do Not Lie—I Am Always Quick to Tell the Truth

ACTIVITY PAGE — TRUTH UNSCRAMBLER

Memory Verse: So stop telling lies. Let us tell our neighbors the truth, for we are all parts of the same body. —Ephesians 4:25

Name: _____

TRUTH UNSCRAMBLER
. –Ephesians 4:25

Unscramble the bolded words to find the TRUTH from the Word of God—your Bible!

1. John 8:32: You will know the **HURTT** _____, and the **HURTT** _____ will set you free.

2. Ephesians 4:25, 29: Stop Telling Lies! —Let your words be **DOGO** _____ and **PHELLUF** _____.

3. Proverbs 17:20: Lying gets you into more **BLUETOR** _____.

4. Proverbs 29:25: **RIFEANG** _____ people is dangerous, but trusting **DOG** _____ is safe!

5. Proverbs 11:5: The Godly are **TIDRECED** _____ by **YENOSHT** _____,

WEEK 4: I DO NOT STEAL

- **DAY 1: BIBLE LESSON—LET THE THIEF STEAL NO MORE** ▶ 64
- **DAY 2: YOU-SOLVE-IT MYSTERY—CHERRY PICKIN'** ▶ 66
- **DAY 3: GIVING LESSON—KNOW THE SOURCE** ▶ 68
- **DAY 4: OBJECT LESSON—FOCUS** ▶ 69
- **DAY 5: GAME TIME—TAKE AWAY** ▶ 71
- **BONUS: ACTIVITY PAGE—WHO'S A THIEF?** ▶ 72

Memory Verse: If you are a thief, quit stealing. Instead, use your hands for good hard work, and then give generously to others in need. —Ephesians 4:28

Home Bible Study for Kids • Week 4: I Do Not Steal

WEEK 4: SNAPSHOT — I DO NOT STEAL

DAY	TYPE OF LESSON	LESSON TITLE	SUPPLIES
Day 1	Bible Lesson	Let the Thief Steal No More	None
Day 2	You-Solve-It Mystery	Cherry Pickin'	"CLUE!" sign or flashing light Optional Costume: A cute blouse or red shirt if narrating as Superkid Amelia
Day 3	Giving Lesson	Know the Source	Paycheck stub or personal check, Bible
Day 4	Object Lesson	Focus	2 Oranges or baseballs, Bible
Day 5	Game Time	Take Away	Chairs, Music (that you can start and stop)
Bonus	Activity Page	Who's a Thief?	1 Copy for each child, Pencil or pen

Lesson Introduction:

Just like last week's lesson about lying, this week's lesson is all about God's better way! It's so much more fun for God to give you something than for you to take something that belongs to someone else. We know that everything we do comes back to us as a harvest. (Thank God for forgiveness!) So how can God *give* us the desires of our hearts if we *take* other people's stuff? It doesn't work! And beyond that, it is evidence that the thief is not putting his/her faith in God. I remember when I was 3 years old, and I took my mother's wallet. Shocking, right? Kids do foolish things sometimes—after all, what would a 3-year-old do with a wallet? What makes that especially silly is that my parents would buy me whatever I needed! Help the kids to view stealing as silly, unproductive and just plain dumb! They have a Father who loves them! He will give them something even better than anything they could steal—*and* it's so much sweeter, too. Say, "Ahhh, now that's The Sweet Life!"

Love,

Commander Kellie

Commander Kellie

Lesson Outline:

Stealing is another way of saying, "God, I don't trust or need You to meet my need, I am going to take what I want." This week, help your kids to understand that when we steal, it hurts God, others and ourselves.

I. YOU HAVE TO CHOOSE HOW YOU WILL GET THE THINGS YOU WANT

   a. Satan is a thief who wants to tempt you to steal, too. John 10:10

   b. Stealing opens the door for Satan to work (steal, kill and destroy) in your life.

   c. Stolen stuff isn't fun after you get it. Proverbs 20:17

II. ISRAEL HAD TROUBLE BECAUSE ACHAN WAS A THIEF Joshua 7:1

   a. They lost a battle they should have easily won. Verses 2-8

   b. Achan opened the door to destruction and the Lord couldn't help them. Verses 10-13

   c. All the treasure Achan stole wasn't worth the trouble and deaths he caused. Verses 14-24

   d. The place where Achan died is called the Valley of Trouble. Verses 25-26

III. GOD WANTS TO GIVE YOU THE DESIRES OF YOUR HEART
Psalm 37:3-5

   a. Don't steal to get what you want. Psalm 62:10

   b. Asking God for what you want is much better than scheming (stealing) and killing. James 4:1-2

   c. Stop stealing—believe God, and get to work! Ephesians 4:28

   d. Things you earn or receive from God are more satisfying and more fun! Proverbs 12:12

Notes:

Home Bible Study for Kids • Week 4: I Do Not Steal

DAY 1: BIBLE LESSON — LET THE THIEF STEAL NO MORE

Memory Verse: If you are a thief, quit stealing. Instead, use your hands for good hard work, and then give generously to others in need. —Ephesians 4:28

Paul shares with the Ephesians how to let go of past living without God and embrace The Sweet Life that He has planned for us. It comes with some great things—but we have to let go of the evil: sin, lies, revenge, and yes… stealing!

Read Ephesians 4:17-18, 20-28, 30 MSG:
The Sweet Life

And so I insist—and God backs me up on this—that there be no going along with the crowd, the empty-headed, mindless crowd. They've refused for so long to deal with God that they've lost touch not only with God but with reality itself. But that's no life for you. You learned Christ! My assumption is that you have paid careful attention to him, been well instructed in the truth precisely as we have it in Jesus. Since, then, we do not have the excuse of ignorance, everything—and I do mean everything—connected with that old way of life has to go. It's rotten through and through. Get rid of it! And then take on an entirely new way of life—a God-fashioned life, a life renewed from the inside and working itself into your conduct as God accurately reproduces his character in you. What this adds up to, then, is this: no more lies, no more pretense. Tell your neighbor the truth. In Christ's body we're all connected to each other, after all. When you lie to others, you end up lying to yourself. Go ahead and be angry. You do well to be angry—but don't use your anger as fuel for revenge. And don't stay angry. Don't go to bed angry. Don't give the Devil that kind of foothold in your life. Did you use to make ends meet by stealing? Well, no more! Get an honest job so that you can help others who can't work. Don't grieve God. Don't break his heart. His Holy Spirit, moving and breathing in you, is the most intimate part of your life, making you fit for himself. Don't take such a gift for granted.

Discussion Questions:

1. **What are three things these Scripture verses tell us to not do anymore?**

   Lying, stealing, letting our anger make us sin, revenge, going to bed angry; don't do these things that hurt God's heart.

2. **What are some things we *are* supposed to do?**

   Speak the truth, get an honest job, help others, live a God-fashioned life (The Sweet Life)

3. **What are your actions saying to God if you feel you need to steal? Discuss.**

   You are saying that you don't trust that He will take care of you. You think He's an unfit Father.

Series: The Superkid Creed II

4. **In the last verse, what gift should we never take for granted?**

   The Holy Spirit

5. **How does the Holy Spirit help our lives?**

   Answers will vary. Make sure you hit the main points: He makes us able to lead the new God-fashioned life (the life that God has planned for us). He's our Counselor, Advocate and Standby. He leads and guides our lives in God. He leads us to God's Sweet Life that is planned for us.

6. **Satan is the ultimate thief—he wants to steal away the most important thing from you—your life in Christ Jesus and your relationship with God. But he can't do it without your permission. Fill in the blank: When you put your _____ in God, you will always be telling Satan, "No! I don't need to follow your ways of doing things—stealing is not for me!"**

   trust

   Notes:

DAY 2: YOU-SOLVE-IT MYSTERY — CHERRY PICKIN'

Suggested Time: 10 minutes

Memory Verse: If you are a thief, quit stealing. Instead, use your hands for good hard work, and then give generously to others in need. —Ephesians 4:28

Teacher Tip: Punch it up by dressing up as Superkid Amelia, and telling the story in character, changing your voice and having fun with it.

Supplies: ☐ "CLUE!" sign or flashing light
Optional Costume: ☐ A cute blouse or red shirt if narrating as Superkid Amelia

Background:

Today, your children will hear a mystery story they can solve themselves! Before reading this story, ask the children to listen closely for clues and try to figure it out before you get to the end. **Bolded words** are slightly stressed because they help solve the mystery. For younger kids, you could hold up a "CLUE!" sign, or flash a light when a clue is revealed.

Story: Cherry Pickin'

(Superkid Amelia begins to tell the story):

Every year, Superkid Academy does a HUGE fall outreach! This is one of my favorite events because every squad has their own special booth. I'm in the Red Squad, (soon I'll be in the Blue Squad—I'm just a few tests away from being promoted!) and our booth is the cake- and pie-walk! I love pies. And cakes, too, but mostly pies. They remind me of Christmases at my grandparents' house.

My Nana ALWAYS has pies ready for us when we come for a visit. My squad decided that we would make cherry pies to match our squad color. Get it? Cherries are red, and we're the Red Squad! We thought it was creative. Anyway, so the day before the outreach, my two best friends, Rose and Donna (they are the coolest members of the Red Squad and probably the funniest), and I went to the Academy orchard to pick the ripest and best cherries. It was such a pretty day, birds were chirping, **several squirrels were scurrying about** and bunnies were hopping all over the place. I love our orchard. When we finally located the cherry trees, we set our baskets down and began to pick as many cherries as we could. After a while (more like five minutes), Donna, whose favorite fruit is cherries, sat down and began to eat the cherries we were picking!

"DONNA!" Rose chuckled, as she climbed down the ladder, **"You're eating the cherries faster than we can pick them!"**

"I apologize, Rose. I can't help it. These are the best cherries I've ever eaten in my life! I mean, how can you say no to these?"

Donna held out a cherry to Rose, "Come on Rose, try one!"

"Well, if you insist.... WOW, DONNA! These ARE good!" exclaimed Rose.

"I told you so! I bet these were the fruit that caused Eve to sin in the Garden—after all, the Bible never said it was an *apple,* AND the Academy orchards are the closest thing to Eden I've ever seen."

I finally climbed down the ladder so I could see the damage Donna had already done on the cherries we'd been picking. There were hardly any left in the basket! "Donna," I said, "Rose and I both know how much you like cherries, but could you please quit eating them and start helping us pick them? We have to pick A LOT so we can make all the pies before tomorrow." Rose nodded her head in agreement.

Donna replied, "All right, but only on one condition."

"What's that?" Rose asked.

"I get my own pie," Donna said mischievously, as she popped another cherry in her mouth.

"If that means you'll start helping, then we have a deal," I exclaimed. We shook hands on it and began to work again. We formed an assembly line of sorts. I was at the top of the ladder, picking the cherries then handing them to Rose, who then climbed down the rest of the ladder, handed them to Donna, who placed the cherries in the baskets. **We had placed the baskets on a picnic table nearby.**

After a good 45 minutes of working our assembly line, we finally stopped to see how many baskets we had filled. When we got to the table, both Rose and I could not believe what we saw. The basket was barely full. Thankfully, Commander Kellie had talked to us about walking in love during our morning transmission or I might not have responded very kindly.

"Donna, WHERE are ALL the cherries?" I asked. "We gave you at least five cherries every time!"

"Were you EATING three of them each time?" demanded Rose, who was having a harder time walking in love with Donna.

"Guys, **I wasn't eating them!** I promise! We made a deal! I shook on it..." said Donna. We then heard a noise that answered all our questions.

Superkids, have you solved the mystery? Do you know where all the cherries went? Does anyone know what some of the clues were? *(Allow time for some of the kids to take turns guessing. If no one gets the answer, suggest the clues to them again. Finally, reveal the answer by reading the Solution, and remind the kids about the memory verse.)*

Solution:

We immediately assumed Donna was eating all the cherries, but had we taken the time to observe the situation a little more, we would've seen the cherry pits all around the base of another, nearby cherry tree. As we walked over to the tree, we looked up and saw a family of squirrels munching on the cherries we had just picked! After a good laugh, we apologized to Donna for accusing her and began picking more cherries. This time, we placed them closer to the tree to make sure the squirrels couldn't steal from us anymore!

Home Bible Study for Kids • Week 4: I Do Not Steal

DAY 3: GIVING LESSON — KNOW THE SOURCE

Suggested Time: 10 minutes

Offering Scripture: Trust in the Lord and do good. Then you will live safely in the land and prosper. Take delight in the Lord, and he will give you your heart's desires. Commit everything you do to the Lord. Trust him, and he will help you. —Psalm 37:3-5

Teacher Tip: Your kids don't have to see how much the check is worth, but it is good for them to have a visual and know that your trust is in God, not the bank or your job.

Supplies: ☐ Paycheck stub or personal check, Bible

Lesson Instructions:

When you work a job like *(name a job that you or your spouse do)*, you get paid for what you do. *(Show the paycheck or stub.)* This piece of paper represents the amount of money received for the amount of work done. The person who wrote this told us if we did the job, they'd pay us for our work, and… *voilà,* here it is! Now we're able to pay for things like groceries, clothes and a place to live.

But we don't put our whole trust in getting this paycheck. Our jobs or our bank never claimed to love us or want to protect us from harm. They never said that if we would trust them, they would always meet our needs. However, there *is* Someone who did say that, and it's written here in His Word. *(Show Bible.)*

Let's read Psalm 37:3-5: "Trust in the Lord and do good. Then you will live safely in the land and prosper. Take delight in the Lord, and he will give you your heart's desires. Commit everything you do to the Lord. Trust him, and he will help you."

I hope you know that as a family, we put our trust in God, not a job or the bank or even money. His words written on this paper (the Bible) are way more powerful than any other paper. It is God who provides the job and the money. He is our Source for everything!

Can anyone tell me why God is the best Source? *(Allow your children to answer. Answers may vary.)* Because He created *everything,* and He is the Source of all things. Since He created us, He knows our desires. He even knows what we need before we need it. Could a bank or an employer do that? No! But God can. He knows what will make you the happiest because He knows the ins and outs of your heart.

So, when we give, let's keep that in mind. He is always our Source—and He's the best Source, too. When we give to Him, He *always* knows how to out-give us, because He is the One who gave us life. And He wants to give us the desires of our hearts!

Home Bible Study for Kids • Week 4: I Do Not Steal

DAY 4: OBJECT LESSON — FOCUS

 Suggested Time: 5-7 minutes

 Memory Verse: If you are a thief, quit stealing. Instead, use your hands for good hard work, and then give generously to others in need. —Ephesians 4:28

Supplies: ☐ 2 Oranges or baseballs, ☐ Bible

Lesson Instructions:

Today, we're going to talk about focus!

(Pull out the two oranges, and hold them at a normal distance.) What size would you say these oranges are? Would you say they're small compared to a basketball, for example? *(Yes, they're small.)* But they're big compared to a grape, aren't they? But, they certainly aren't giant. I can hold them in my hand or throw them into the air. I couldn't throw an elephant into the air because an elephant is huge! A refrigerator or desk isn't as big as an elephant, but I couldn't play catch with it, could I?

What about a house? That's really big. I definitely couldn't pick that up! So, I guess all in all these are very small, unless…. *(Now place an orange in front of one of the children's eyes at a close distance but still allowing the child to be able to see clearly.)* How big does it look now? *(Give each child a turn if your group is small.)* Now they SEEM huge. But they are still pretty small.

Why does the orange look so huge when it's right in front of your eyes? Yes, that's right. Because it is so close, that's all your eyes can *focus* on! But did the size of the orange change? No, it didn't, but your focus did.

Did you know your mind can focus? If you focus on God and His Word, you'll see what He sees. You may have a need, but if you are focused on God's Word, you will believe what He says, then He will *always* meet your need!

(Now take your Bible and hold it far enough away so your Superkids can't read it.) Will you read this for me, please? *(They should say something like they can't read it because it's too far away.)* Oh, right! That's because I need to bring God's Word closer to you so your eyes can focus on it. Let's read Philippians 4:19. *(Read the verse out loud with the children.)* "And this same God who takes care of me will supply all your needs from his glorious riches, which have been given to us in Christ Jesus."

When you stay focused on God's Word, you will be at peace because you are trusting Him. But, on the other hand, if you are focused on your need instead of God and what He says about it, then your need gets really big in your own eyes—even if that need is as small as this orange. You will begin to worry that your need will never be met.

This is the way people think who steal. Since they don't see God as their Source, they take things into their own hands. So, if they see something they want, they steal it.

What those people don't realize is that the thief has to pay back sevenfold when he is caught. So, instead of getting ahead, they actually get further and further behind.

Series: The Superkid Creed II

Home Bible Study for Kids • Week 4: I Do Not Steal

The more you focus on the need, the more discouraged you will get. So, let's focus on God instead!

When God gave the command, "Thou shalt not steal" (Exodus 20:15 KJV), it wasn't because He didn't want you to have things. He gave the command to protect you. He loves you and wants to meet all your needs. The reason Superkids don't steal is because they know God loves them, and He is their Source. They focus on God and His Word, not on their need.

Everyone say this after me: "My focus is on God and His Word. He loves me, and He is my Source!" Amen, I agree. Now, let's eat these oranges! *(Or play ball if you used baseballs.)*

Notes: _____

Home Bible Study for Kids • Week 4: I Do Not Steal

DAY 5: GAME TIME

TAKE AWAY

Suggested Time: 10 minutes

Memory Verse: If you are a thief, quit stealing. Instead, use your hands for good hard work, and then give generously to others in need. —Ephesians 4:28

Supplies: ☐ Chairs, ☐ Music (that you can start and stop)

Prior to Game:

Count how many kids are present and make sure you have enough chairs for all but 1 of them. Place the chairs facing outward in a circle.

Game Instructions:

Note: Game is played like musical chairs.

- When the music starts, have your children circle around the chairs.
- When the music stops, everyone must find a vacant chair to sit in.
- Whoever is not seated when the music stops, is out.
- Remove 1 chair and begin to play again.
- Repeat this process until there is only 1 chair left and 2 children playing.
- Whoever sits first in the final seat when the music stops, wins.

Game Goal:

To be the final player to sit in the last seat when the music stops and win the game.

Final Word:

In our game today, we saw how someone could want a seat so badly that friends were willing to steal someone else's seat just to win. Aren't you glad this was just a game? God wants to give us the desires of our hearts so we never have to take something that doesn't belong to us. In real life, no one wins when he or she steals! But God will *always* reward us when we do what is right!

Home Bible Study for Kids • Week 4: I Do Not Steal

ACTIVITY PAGE — WHO'S A THIEF?

Memory Verse: If you are a thief, quit stealing. Instead, use your hands for good hard work, and then give generously to others in need. —Ephesians 4:28

Supplies: ☐ One copy for each child

Stealing does not belong in a Superkid's life! In fact, it's as ridiculous as a monkey on a computer! Find 10 ridiculous things that don't belong in the photo below.

Answer Key:

Series: The Superkid Creed II

Home Bible Study for Kids • Week 4: I Do Not Steal

ACTIVITY PAGE

WHO'S A THIEF?

 Memory Verse: If you are a thief, quit stealing. Instead, use your hands for good hard work, and then give generously to others in need. —Ephesians 4:28

Stealing does not belong in a Superkid's life! In fact, it's as ridiculous as a monkey on a computer! Find 10 ridiculous things that don't belong in the photo below.

Home Bible Study for Kids • Week 4: I Do Not Steal

Notes:

WEEK 5: I AM A TITHER AND A GIVER, NOT A TAKER

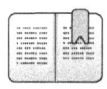 **DAY 1: BIBLE LESSON—MORE BLESSED** ▶ 78

 **DAY 2: ACADEMY LAB— SALT OF THE EARTH** ▶ 80

 **DAY 3: GIVING LESSON— A MORE-THAN-ENOUGH GOD** ▶ 82

 **DAY 4: OBJECT LESSON— GIVE AND LET GIVE** ▶ 83

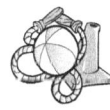 **DAY 5: GAME TIME—WHITE OUT** ▶ 85

 **BONUS: ACTIVITY PAGE—THE BLESSING** ▶ 87

 **Memory Verse:** *Give freely and become more wealthy; be stingy and lose everything.* —Proverbs 11:24

Home Bible Study for Kids • Week 5: I Am a Tither and a Giver, Not a Taker

WEEK 5: SNAPSHOT — I AM A TITHER AND A GIVER, NOT A TAKER

DAY	TYPE OF LESSON	LESSON TITLE	SUPPLIES
Day 1	Bible Lesson	More Blessed	None
Day 2	Academy Lab	Salt of the Earth	Salt shaker full of salt, Periodic table of elements chart
Day 3	Giving Lesson	A More-Than-Enough God	10 $1 bills, Small empty pitcher, Big pitcher filled to the brim with water, Large bowl
Day 4	Object Lesson	Give and Let Give	10 Small toys or trinkets (such as army men)
Day 5	Game Time	White Out	1 Box of chocolate sandwich cookies with white filling (how many you purchase will depend on size of group), Napkins, Table, Chairs, Dropcloth or old tablecloth, Plate, Napkin or cleaning wipe
Bonus	Activity Page	The Blessing	1 Copy for each child, Bibles

Lesson Introduction:

The last several weeks, you have been teaching your Superkids who their Source is. If our Superkids establish God as their Source now, they will have that mindset forever. They will always look to God for direction, for help and promotion. I once heard a preacher say, "I don't need God to make me rich, I can do that on my own." In his attempt to be humble, he left God out of an area of his life that actually Satan would love to take charge over. The love of money is the root of all evil, so it's Satan's root, too.

By giving God our 10 percent, we shut the door on the devil and place ourselves firmly in God's hands. He can do so much more for us with what's left over than we can do with the whole thing! This concept leads you into a great setup for next week's theme: "My Father Makes Me Wealthy." Yes, He does!

Love,

Commander Kellie

Lesson Outline:

As adults, you've often heard about the benefits of giving your tithes and offerings. Some people might say that kids are too young to understand these concepts. But much like teaching basic math, it's best to start now teaching them that the top 10 percent ALWAYS belongs to God. Better yet, when you put that 10 percent in God's hands, He'll protect the other 90! That's some powerful math!

I. TITHING HONORS GOD AND SHOWS THAT HE IS YOUR SOURCE
Proverbs 3:9-10

    a. Tithing is giving 10 percent of your money to God.

    b. When you don't tithe, you've robbed God! Malachi 3:8-9

    c. Tithing opens the door for God to bless you. Malachi 3:10-12

    d. God said, "Put Me to the test"—so try it!

II. WHEN GOD BLESSES YOU, THERE'S NO SORROW—JUST JOY
Proverbs 10:22

    a. Zacchaeus was a taker—he cheated people when he collected their taxes. Luke 19:8-10

    b. Everything changed when he met Jesus!

    c. He gave back to people more than he had taken, and gave to the poor!

    d. Zacchaeus was full of joy and started acting like Jesus! Proverbs 21:26

III. GIVE FREELY, AND BE MORE WEALTHY? SOUNDS CRAZY BUT IT'S NOT! Proverbs 11:24

    a. Trusting in money will bring you down. Proverbs 11:28

    b. Will you do without if you give? Luke 6:38 NKJV

    c. No! God will give you even more, so be a joyful giver! 2 Corinthians 9:6-11

Notes: _____

Home Bible Study for Kids • Week 5: I Am a Tither and a Giver, Not a Taker

DAY 1: BIBLE LESSON — MORE BLESSED

Memory Verse: Give freely and become more wealthy; be stingy and lose everything. —Proverbs 11:24

Many people like to be stingy or hush-hush when it comes to talking about money and gifts. But when you give God's way, there is NOTHING to feel ashamed about. In fact, Jesus said that it is more blessed to give than to receive. Give your kids the gift of opening up and talking to them transparently about giving. And take the time to let them share with you, too. You will be blessed that you did!

Read Isaiah 55:1-2:
God's Best

Is anyone thirsty? Come and drink—even if you have no money! Come, take your choice of wine or milk—it's all free! Why spend your money on food that does not give you strength? Why pay for food that does you no good? Listen to me, and you will eat what is good. You will enjoy the finest food.

Read Malachi 3:8-11 MSG:
Robbing God?

"Begin by being honest. Do honest people rob God? But you rob me day after day. You ask, 'How have we robbed you?' The tithe and the offering—that's how! And now you're under a curse—the whole lot of you—because you're robbing me. Bring your full tithe to the Temple treasury so there will be ample provisions in my Temple. Test me in this and see if I don't open up heaven itself to you and pour out blessings beyond your wildest dreams. For my part, I will defend you against marauders, protect your wheat fields and vegetable gardens against plunderers." The Message of God-of-the-Angel-Armies.

Read 2 Corinthians 9:6-9:
Giving Generously

Remember this—a farmer who plants only a few seeds will get a small crop. But the one who plants generously will get a generous crop. You must each decide in your heart how much to give. And don't give reluctantly or in response to pressure. "For God loves a person who gives cheerfully." And God will generously provide all you need. Then you will always have everything you need and plenty left over to share with others. As the Scriptures say, "They share freely and give generously to the poor. Their good deeds will be remembered forever."

Series: The Superkid Creed II

Home Bible Study for Kids • Week 5: I Am a Tither and a Giver, Not a Taker

Discussion Questions:

1. **What did God say we needed to do to have the best—for free?**

   Come and listen to Him.

2. **How much of our increase (the things we get) belongs to God?**

   Ten percent

3. **What did God say to test Him in when we give Him our 10 percent?**

   That He will pour us out a blessing beyond our wildest dreams!

4. **God loves a _____ giver!**

   cheerful

5. **When you give, you are to give from your heart, but NOT in response to_____.**

   pressure

6. **When we give, it's good to remember that giving under *pressure* is wrong. Can you name an instance when someone begged you or pressured you to give them something? Discuss.**

   (Share a story from your own life with your children if they don't have a story of their own to share. Remember, sharing from your own life helps your kids to open up.)

7. **How did you feel after giving under pressure?**

   Not excited as you should be—as if you'd been stolen from.

8. **When you give God's way, with a cheerful heart, you get the most blessed. Acts 20:35 says, "It is more blessed to give than to receive." What was the best feeling you ever had when you gave something away? Why?**

   (Challenge your kids to open up about the most rewarding gift they've given. Kids are such givers that usually they will remember a time that they gave an extra-special gift. Allow time for them to share.)

Notes:

Home Bible Study for Kids • Week 5: I Am a Tither and a Giver, Not a Taker

DAY 2: ACADEMY LAB — SALT OF THE EARTH

Suggested Time: 7-10 minutes

Memory Verse: *Give freely and become more wealthy; be stingy and lose everything.*
—Proverbs 11:24

Supplies: ☐ Salt shaker full of salt, ☐ Periodic table of elements chart

Prior to Lesson:

It's easy to find a periodic table online and print it out. Make sure it's big enough to read. If printing is difficult, use a computer or tablet to show the children.

Lesson Instructions:

Does anyone know what I have in my hand? That's right, it's salt—common table salt. It's the same stuff you sometimes shake onto your food. Many people think of salt just as a seasoning—something you just have in your kitchen—but it's really a whole lot more!

Salt is a chemical needed to keep us alive. Our bodies can't make salt by themselves, but they need it for our blood, sweat and digestive systems, and to help our nerves work.

Do you know what the Bible says about salt? Jesus said in Matthew 5:13 that as believers in Him, you are the salt of the earth. That means you should bring the life of the One who is in us to the people around us!

I took some time to study salt and found out what it's made of. I think it's pretty interesting. Did you know that salt is made of two different elements? *Elements* are categories, or groupings, of matter in their purest form, according to their atomic weights and numbers.

On this chart *(show the periodic table),* you see all sorts of elements from metals to gases. For example, we can see the letters "Fe," which stands for *iron.* Iron is a metal that's used to make nails for building, skillets for cooking in and stoves for heating.

"O" stands for *oxygen,* which is a gas that's part of the air we breathe. You can't see air, but you can see how it affects things around you, like when the wind blows the leaves on a tree.

Does anyone know which two elements make salt? *(Allow children to try and guess which two elements make salt.)* Those are good guesses! Salt is made of a metal and a gas, but not iron and oxygen. It's made of *sodium* and *chlorine.*

Sodium is a soft metal and is represented by "Na" on this chart. It's very reactive, and if you put it in water, it will explode and catch on fire. Isn't that amazing? Sounds like dangerous stuff, right? Chlorine is represented by "Cl" on the chart, and is dangerous stuff, too. Chlorine gas is poisonous and can kill you. So we have two very dangerous elements, but when we combine them, they become life-giving salt. That's pretty cool!

Series: The Superkid Creed II

Home Bible Study for Kids • Week 5: I Am a Tither and a Giver, Not a Taker

There are a lot of cool things about salt. Sodium and chlorine have to come together to form it. So let's talk about why and how they come together to form salt. The smallest part of an element is called an *atom,* and atoms have tiny electrical parts called *electrons* that fly in orbit around them all the time. When sodium and chlorine come together, they form a bond when the sodium atom gives one of its electrons to the chlorine atom. This action causes them to bond, or lock together, in unity to form what we call *salt. (Show the children the salt again.)*

The reason sodium is so explosive is because it has one too many electrons. It isn't until it gives that extra electron away that it becomes a BLESSING and not a curse. That's a lot like our tithe. The tithe belongs to God. When we keep the tithe for ourselves and don't give it to God, then that opens the door for the devil to attack our goods. It makes things very explosive for us. Things can start breaking or cost more than they should because the devourer begins to steal from us. And that is no good! Even though we are Christians and going to heaven, life won't be very much fun on earth if we keep the tithe for ourselves. But when we bring the tithe to God, it's part of the covenant of BLESSING we have with Him that allows Him to rebuke the devourer for us.

Malachi 3:10-11 says the Lord will stop the devil from taking our stuff, and He opens the windows of heaven to pour out a BLESSING on us. When we are blessed, then we can bless others and truly be the salt of the earth!

Say this after me: "I am a tither. I am in covenant with God. He rebukes the devourer for me. The windows of heaven are open, and BLESSINGS are pouring out on me. I bless others, and I am the salt of the earth! Amen."

Notes:

Home Bible Study for Kids • Week 5: I Am a Tither and a Giver, Not a Taker

DAY 3: GIVING LESSON — A MORE-THAN-ENOUGH GOD

Suggested Time: 10 minutes

Offering Scripture: "Bring all the tithes into the storehouse so there will be enough food in my Temple. If you do," says the Lord of Heaven's Armies, "I will open the windows of heaven for you. I will pour out a blessing so great you won't have enough room to take it in! Try it! Put me to the test!"
—Malachi 3:10

Supplies: ☐ 10 $1 bills, ☐ Small empty pitcher, ☐ Big pitcher filled to the brim with water, ☐ Large bowl to put under the small pitcher

Lesson Instructions:

Today, we're talking more about tithing. Who remembers what tithing is? *(Allow your Superkids to answer.)* Yes, you're right! The tithe is 10 percent (or one out of 10) of whatever we receive. It belongs to God. Let me give you an example:

(Choose one of your kids to help you. Give your helper ten $1 bills.) I just gave _____ $10.

So, if the tithe is 10 percent of the $10, how much would that be? *(Allow time for children to answer.)* That's right—$1!

Now that we all know what the tithe is, let's find out *why* we tithe. God said He will bless us when we tithe—and open up the windows of heaven for us, and pour out more than enough when we give Him first what's His.

Now, let me *show* you what happens when you tithe. *(Hold out your hand to your helper.)* Please hand me 10 percent of the $10 I gave you *(Allow your helper to figure out what he or she needs to do and hand you $1 out of the $10).* Good job! You just gave your tithe, and by doing this, you did what the Lord asked you to do in His Word.

(Pick up the small pitcher and give it to the Superkid, who will hold it over the large bowl.) This represents you. *(Pick up the larger pitcher.)* This larger represents God. *(Begin pouring the water from the larger pitcher into the smaller pitcher.)* God said He would pour out a BLESSING on you. *(Fill the pitcher halfway up.)* Would God only bless us halfway? *(Wait for a response.)* No!

(Now fill the smaller pitcher almost to the top.) Did God say He would bless us *just enough*? *(Wait for a response.)* No!

(Continue to fill the pitcher until it is overflowing all over your Superkid's hands.) We just read in His Word that He pours out THE BLESSING so great it can't help but get all over us. God wants to bless you, and when you give your tithe, He can bless you more than you could ever imagine. As you give your tithes and offerings today, thank God for THE BLESSING that overflows in your life!

Series: The Superkid Creed II

Home Bible Study for Kids • Week 5: I Am a Tither and a Giver, Not a Taker

DAY 4: OBJECT LESSON — GIVE AND LET GIVE

 Suggested Time: 10 minutes

 Memory Verse: Give freely and become more wealthy; be stingy and lose everything. —Proverbs 11:24

 **Teacher Tip:** Choosing one of the older kids who can do the math may be helpful to you.

Supplies: ☐ 10 small toys or trinkets (such as army men)

Lesson Instructions:

(Set up the 10 small toys or trinkets on a nearby table so all the children can see them. Choose one of your children to be a helper.) Say, "_____, I have all these toys, and because I love you, I'm going to give them to you! All I want from you is that you take care of them and enjoy them. Also, I'd like you to give one away. How do you feel about that? *(Let your helper express his or her feelings about the request.)* Remember, you still get to keep all nine of the other toys to do whatever you want with them. *(Thank your helper and ask him or her to sit down.)* I believe you'll find the right person to bless with one of the toys!

Now let's read God's instruction to Adam in Genesis 2 about the fruit He gave to him. (Read aloud Genesis 2:8-9, 15-17, *The Message*.)

> Then God planted a garden in Eden, in the east. He put the Man he had just made in it. God made all kinds of trees grow from the ground, trees beautiful to look at and good to eat. The Tree-of-Life was in the middle of the garden, also the Tree-of-Knowledge-of-Good-and-Evil. God took the Man and set him down in the Garden of Eden to work the ground and keep it in order. God commanded the Man, "You can eat from any tree in the garden, except from the Tree-of-Knowledge-of-Good-and-Evil. Don't eat from it. The moment you eat from that tree, you're dead."

Why would God give something to Adam and Eve, but then ask them to give something back? *(Allow your children time to answer.)*

What would happen if I just kept giving you every toy you wanted—all the toys you could imagine—but I never taught you how to give any of them away? *(Answers will vary. They would probably become selfish and stingy, and the house would become so crammed with toys, there wouldn't be room for anything else.)*

It would be sad if I were your parent and loved you so much that I gave you everything, BUT I never taught you how to give. You'd be blessed, but not blessed to be a blessing to others. You'd be so spoiled! God knows how to give the best gifts, but He also teaches us how to be the best gift givers, just as He tried to do with Adam in the Garden of Eden.

Let's make sure that we are always allowing God to bless us to be a blessing by tithing and giving…not just to get, get, get. Because we know He knows how to give, give, give!

Series: The Superkid Creed II

Home Bible Study for Kids • Week 5: I Am a Tither and a Giver, Not a Taker

(Ask your helper who received the toys:) Now do you know why I want you to give one of those toys away? You'll make the way for God to bless you even more, and you'll be a blessing to someone else!

Notes: _____

Home Bible Study for Kids • Week 5: I Am a Tither and a Giver, Not a Taker

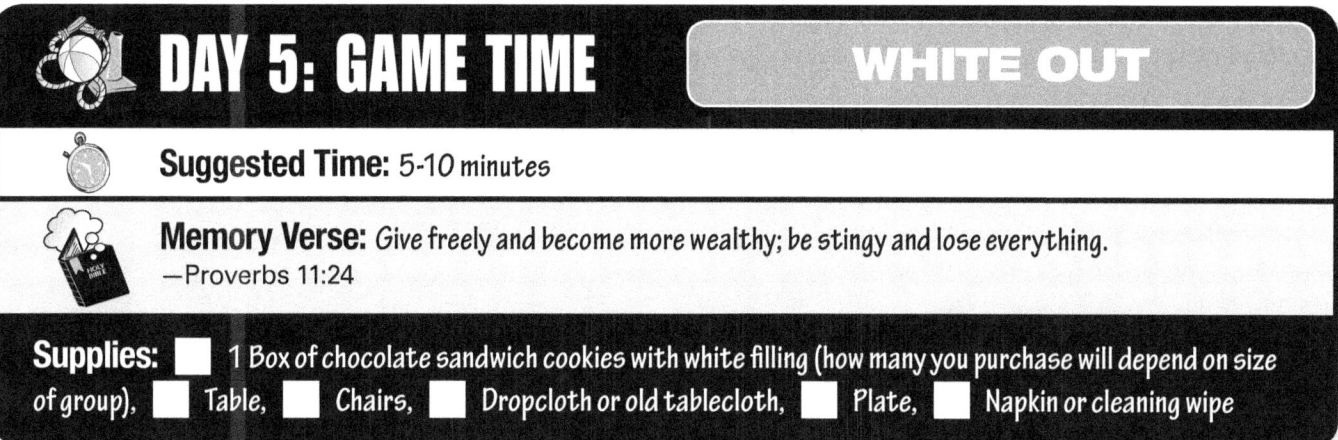

DAY 5: GAME TIME — WHITE OUT

Suggested Time: 5-10 minutes

Memory Verse: Give freely and become more wealthy; be stingy and lose everything. —Proverbs 11:24

Supplies: ☐ 1 Box of chocolate sandwich cookies with white filling (how many you purchase will depend on size of group), ☐ Table, ☐ Chairs, ☐ Dropcloth or old tablecloth, ☐ Plate, ☐ Napkin or cleaning wipe

Prior to Game:

Determine how many kids will play, the number of rounds you'll play, and the number of cookies you'll need. Assemble all your supplies, making sure you will have enough chairs and cookies. Use the dropcloth or old tablecloth underneath the game area because this game is a bit messy.

Game Instructions:

This is a great team game if you have a larger group. You can have your cadet play relay style. If you have a small number of children, cadets will compete against each other, one-on-one.

First, ask the cadets to take their seats and sit on their hands. Place 3 cookies on a table in front of each cadet. Instruct them to use only their mouths (no hands!) to eat just the middle filling—NONE OF THE CHOCOLATE COOKIE! Have each cadet pick up the chocolate cookie with his or her teeth as best they can and put it on the plate. Start the round.

Once a cadet eats all the filling and puts the chocolate cookies on the plate, the next cadet can begin.

Game Goal:

Whoever eats all the white filling out of each of the cookies first, wins, and the round starts again with the next players. Can be played for several rounds or on a team relay.

Final Word:

Did everyone enjoy eating the filling out of the cookies? When you live the SPIRIT-FILLED life, people who meet you will know that you are different because of your generous heart. Imagine what it would be like to get a new bag of cookies, open them up, and find out someone took the yummy filling out! That would be GROSS, SAD and very disappointing. That's how people feel when they encounter people who claim to be Christians, and act like a TAKER and not a GIVER.

Home Bible Study for Kids • Week 5: I Am a Tither and a Giver, Not a Taker

Don't take the Spirit filling out of your giving. And let people enjoy being around you, because they can always count on you to follow the Holy Spirit in being generous!

Notes:

Home Bible Study for Kids • Week 5: I Am a Tither and a Giver, Not a Taker

ACTIVITY PAGE — THE BLESSING

Memory Verse: Give freely and become more wealthy; be stingy and lose everything. —Proverbs 11:24

Teacher Tip: For younger Superkids, feel free to help them find the answers in their Bible by reading the scriptures to them.

Supplies: ☐ 1 Copy for each child, ☐ Bibles

Answer Key:

THE BLESSING

Complete the crossword below using your Bible- Luke 19:1-10

ACROSS
1. Zacchaeus decided to give _____ of his wealth to the poor! (**half**)
4. What helped Zacchaeus to see Jesus? (**sycamore**)
7. Zacchaeus took Jesus to eat at his _____ (**home**)
8. Zacchaeus felt great ____ to host Jesus in his home and be a giver. (**joy**)
9. Whal was Zacchaeus' job? (Luke 19:8-10) (**taxcollector**)
10. Zacchaeus even said that he would pay back _____ times the amount he cheated people. (**four**)

DOWN
2. How did people react to Jesus eating with the tax collector? (**angry**)
3. Jesus saw Zacchaeus and called him down by _____. (**name**)
4. Jesus said _____ has come to Zacchaeus' house today. (**salvation**)
5. Zacchaeus was a _____ man, so he climbed the tree. (**short**)
6. The people didn't understand why Jesus would eat wilh a _____. (**sinner**)
8. Where did Zacchaeus live? (**jericho**)

Series: The Superkid Creed II

Home Bible Study for Kids • Week 5: I Am a Tither and a Giver, Not a Taker

ACTIVITY PAGE — THE BLESSING

Memory Verse: Give freely and become more wealthy; be stingy and lose everything.
—Proverbs 11:24

Name: _____

THE BLESSING

Complete the crossword below using your Bible- Luke 19:1-10

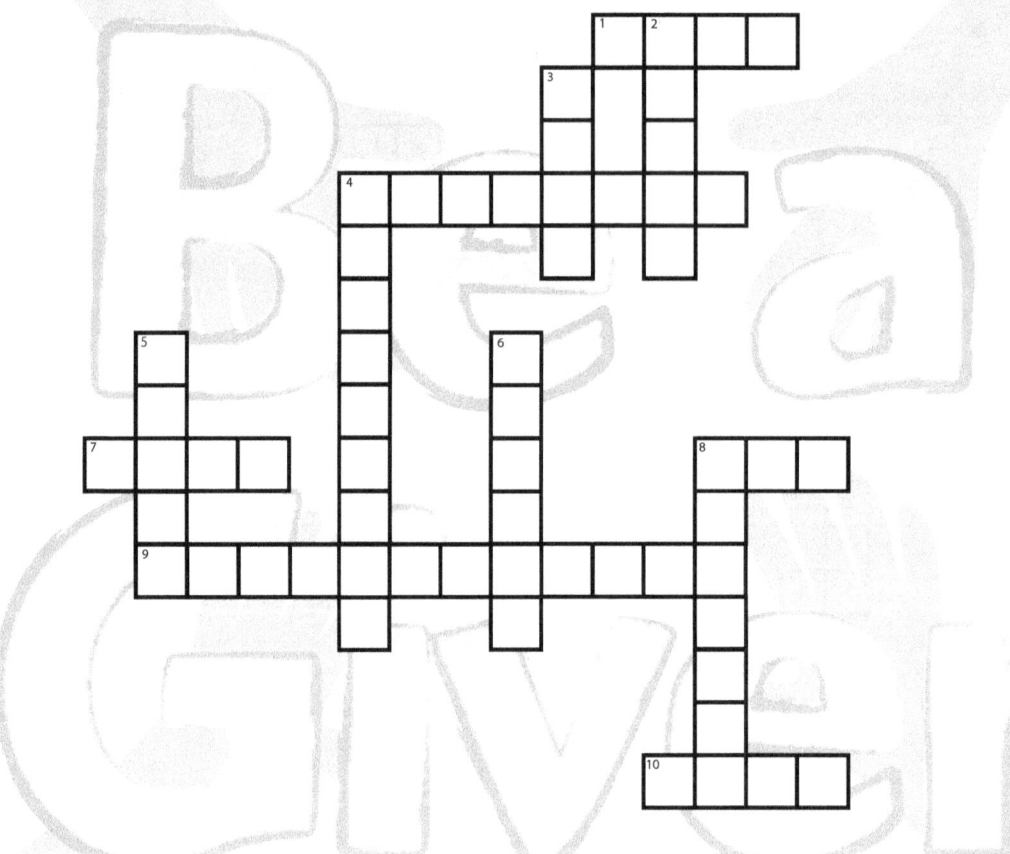

ACROSS

1. Zacchaeus decided to give _____ of his wealth to the poor!
4. What helped Zacchaeus to see Jesus?
7. Zacchaeus took Jesus to eat at his _____.
8. Zacchaeus felt great ____ to host Zaccheus in his home and be a giver.
9. What was Zacchaeus' job? (Luke 19:8-10)
10. Zaccheus even said that he would pay back _____ times the amount he cheated people.

DOWN

2. How did people react to Jesus eating with the tax collector?
3. Jesus saw Zacchaeus and called him down by _____.
4. Jesus said _____ has come to Zacchaeus' house today.
5. Zacchaeus was a _____ man, so he climbed the tree.
6. The people didn't understand why Jesus would eat with a _____.
8. Where did Zacchaeus live?

WEEK 6: MY FATHER MAKES ME WEALTHY

- DAY 1: BIBLE LESSON—TRUE WEALTH ▸ 92
- DAY 2: REAL DEAL—BISHOP DAVID OYEDEPO ▸ 94
- DAY 3: GIVING LESSON—PICTURE-PERFECT BLESSINGS ▸ 98
- DAY 4: FOOD FUN—LIFE AND HEALTH IN GOD'S WEALTH ▸ 99
- DAY 5: GAME TIME—POCKET CHANGE ▸ 102
- BONUS: ACTIVITY PAGE—A PICTURE OF WEALTH ▸ 103

Memory Verse: THE BLESSING of The LORD makes a person rich, and he adds no sorrow with it.
—Proverbs 10:22

Home Bible Study for Kids • Week 6: My Father Makes Me Wealthy

WEEK 6: SNAPSHOT — MY FATHER MAKES ME WEALTHY

DAY	TYPE OF LESSON	LESSON TITLE	SUPPLIES
Day 1	Bible Lesson	True Wealth	None
Day 2	Real Deal	Bishop David Oyedepo	Photos of Bishop Oyedepo and his church (pictures from the internet), Map of Africa, Pictures of Africa Optional Costume: Nice, current suit or traditional Nigerian clothing
Day 3	Giving Lesson	Picture-Perfect Blessings	Pictures of famous pieces of art (Make sure one is a picture of the Mona Lisa.)
Day 4	Food Fun	Life and Health in God's Wealth	Ingredients: (Multiplied by the number of batches you will make—you will need at least double of all ingredients) 1 Cup WARM water (110° F), 1/4 Ounce packet active dry yeast, 2 1/4 Teaspoons vegetable oil or spray, 2 3/4 Cups bread flour, 1 Tablespoon granulated sugar, 1 Teaspoon kosher salt, plus more for sprinkling, 6 Cups hot water, 1/4 Cup baking soda, Butter, Cinnamon, sugar for sprinkling (optional) Supplies: Oven, Clear mixing bowls and measuring cups, A set of measuring spoons, Clean cutting board or work surface, Parchment baking paper, Saucepan or pot, Spatula, Oven glove or potholder, Apron, Clean soft towel, Bread knife, 2 Trays
Day 5	Game Time	Pocket Change	Large bucket filled with washed change (pennies, nickels, dimes and quarters), Straws, 2 Small cups, Table, Stopwatch
Bonus	Activity Page	A Picture of Wealth	1 Copy for each child

Lesson Introduction:

As you bring this word to your Superkids this week, there are a few things to keep in mind. First, as you teach, remember to bring this down to their level and circumstances. Help them recognize ways they can get sidetracked from God being their Source. For instance: Kids want *stuff!* They may want something today and forget about it tomorrow, but today *they gotta have it!* They can become impatient, or worse, a thief! "Stuff" isn't what life is made of. And, waiting on God instead of pressuring parents or coming up with other scheming ideas, helps make certain that the "stuff" you *must* have will last beyond tomorrow!

Another thing to keep in mind is that as TV news gets worse and worse, and the economy appears doomed forever, kids can take on those worries without understanding them. Help them see that, as believers, we don't let worry dominate our thinking (Matthew 6:31-32). God takes care of us!

And lastly, parents—as your Superkids' "Commanders," the devil would like you to shy away from using the word *wealthy*. The world thinks a Christian should be poor, but that's not what God's Word says! Are we going to agree

Series: The Superkid Creed II

with God or buy into the devil's lie? I think I know your answer to that question, so use the word *wealthy* confidently, boldly and often! Our Superkids will be givers and receivers who have more than enough to be generous to others!

Love,

Commander Kellie

Commander Kellie

Lesson Outline:

This week your children will learn that "wealthy" isn't a dirty word. It's a Bible word! God has called your Superkids to be blessed and prosperous enough so that they can ALWAYS be a blessing to other people! When we learn how God likes to bless His kids, we become more like Him—able to BE a blessing, not just receive one.

I. PEOPLE SOMETIMES TRY TO BECOME RICH IN BAD WAYS

a. Waiting on God is better than cheating and stealing. Psalm 62:5-8, 10

b. Trusting in God is better than being greedy and fighting. Proverbs 28:25

c. Asking God is better than scheming and killing. James 4:1-2

d. Don't get busy chasing *stuff* and forget to chase after a relationship with your heavenly Father. Luke 12:13-21

II. YOUR FATHER WANTS TO TAKE CARE OF YOU Luke 12

a. Don't worry about everyday life. Verses 22-27

b. He cares *wonderfully* for you—so have faith! Verse 28

c. He knows everything you need. Verses 29-30

d. Seek the Father above everything else—He wants to give you the Kingdom! Verses 31-32

III. MAKE A DECISION TO RELY ONLY ON THE LORD

a. Abraham promised the Lord he would not let anyone else claim to have made him rich but God. Genesis 14:22-23

b. Abraham was wealthy and his descendants even wealthier. Genesis 26:13

c. This is a great deal! Proverbs 10:22

d. Say yes to the Father's invitation to be BLESSED!

Home Bible Study for Kids • Week 6: My Father Makes Me Wealthy

DAY 1: BIBLE LESSON — TRUE WEALTH

Memory Verse: THE BLESSING of The LORD makes a person rich, and he adds no sorrow with it. —Proverbs 10:22

God is not against you having nice things and being rich. He is against those nice things and riches having you! Our memory verse says, "THE BLESSING of *The LORD* makes a person rich…" so you can see it is His will that we prosper. But the difference between being rich God's way and the world's way is huge! In God's way, there is only BLESSING, joy and peace. In the world's way of greed and stinginess, there is sorrow and death. Let's read what Jesus had to say about wealth God's way!

Read Luke 12:15-34:
Jesus Teaches Us True Wealth!

Then he said, "Beware! Guard against every kind of greed. Life is not measured by how much you own." Then he told them a story: "A rich man had a fertile farm that produced fine crops. He said to himself, 'What should I do? I don't have room for all my crops.' Then he said, 'I know! I'll tear down my barns and build bigger ones. Then I'll have room enough to store all my wheat and other goods. And I'll sit back and say to myself, "My friend, you have enough stored away for years to come. Now take it easy! Eat, drink, and be merry!"'

"But God said to him, 'You fool! You will die this very night. Then who will get everything you worked for?'

"Yes, a person is a fool to store up earthly wealth but not have a rich relationship with God." Then, turning to his disciples, Jesus said, "That is why I tell you not to worry about everyday life—whether you have enough food to eat or enough clothes to wear. For life is more than food, and your body more than clothing. Look at the ravens. They don't plant or harvest or store food in barns, for God feeds them. And you are far more valuable to him than any birds! Can all your worries add a single moment to your life? And if worry can't accomplish a little thing like that, what's the use of worrying over bigger things?

"Look at the lilies and how they grow. They don't work or make their clothing, yet Solomon in all his glory was not dressed as beautifully as they are. And if God cares so wonderfully for flowers that are here today and thrown into the fire tomorrow, he will certainly care for you. Why do you have so little faith?

"And don't be concerned about what to eat and what to drink. Don't worry about such things. These things dominate the thoughts of unbelievers all over the world, but your Father already knows your needs. Seek the Kingdom of God above all else, and he will give you everything you need. So don't be afraid, little flock. For it gives your Father great happiness to give you the Kingdom. Sell your possessions and give to those in need. This will store up treasure for you in heaven! And the purses of heaven never get old or develop holes. Your treasure will be safe; no thief can steal it and no moth can destroy it. Wherever your treasure is, there the desires of your heart will also be."

Series: The Superkid Creed II

Discussion Questions:

Fill in the blanks.

1. **Verse 15: Beware! Guard against every kind of** _____. **Life is not measured by how much you**_____.

   greed/own

2. **Verse 21: A person is a**_____ **to store up earthly wealth, but not have a rich** _____ **with God.**

   fool/relationship

3. **Verse 28: And if God**_____ **so wonderfully for flowers that are here today and thrown into the** _____**tomorrow, he will** _____ **care for you.**

   cares/fire/certainly

4. **Verse 31: Seek the** _____ **of God above all else, and he will give you**_____ **you need.**

   Kingdom/everything

5. **Verse 32: So don't be** _____, **little flock. For it gives your Father great** _____ **to give you the Kingdom.**

   afraid/happiness

6. **Verse 34: Wherever your** _____ **is, there the desires of your** _____ **will also be.**

   treasure/heart

In John 10:10, Jesus said, "My purpose is to give them a rich and satisfying life." How can you have that? One of the ways is to always speak the truth: Make it a habit to say: "JESUS is BLESSING me," especially if you are about to complain about something. This is the best time to get THE BLESSING of God working in your life! Instead of complaining, start praising God and thanking Him for His goodness in your life. You'll forget all about what you were going to complain about, and the joy of the Lord will rise up in your heart instead and bring you the victory!

Notes: _____

Home Bible Study for Kids • Week 6: My Father Makes Me Wealthy

DAY 2: REAL DEAL — BISHOP DAVID OYEDEPO

Suggested Time: 15 minutes

Memory Verse: THE BLESSING of The LORD makes a person rich, and he adds no sorrow with it. — Proverbs 10:22

Concept: Highlighting an interesting historical place, figure or event that illustrates the theme of the day. The theme of the day is: My Father makes me wealthy.

Teacher Tip: Use media such as photos, on screen or printed, videos or props is helpful to keep the Superkids engaged and gives more clarity to your presentation. Bishop Oyedepo is still ministering around the world—so you may want to research more recent facts.

Supplies: ☐ Photos (pictures from the internet), ☐ Map of Africa, ☐ Pictures of Africa
Optional Costume: ☐ Nice, current suit or traditional Nigerian clothing

Intro:

Many wealthy people profess they are "self-made" men. Bishop David Oyedepo (Oy-YE-depo) knows exactly where his wealth came from—the Lord. Bishop David Oyedepo is a pastor, minister and CEO of Living Faith World Outreach Ministries in Nigeria, Africa. Refusing the aid of the Nigerian government and money from other countries, he trusted God to bring Nigeria out of poverty and make it like a Garden of Eden.

Lesson:
Humble Beginnings:

David Oyedepo was born in Nigeria, Africa, on Sept. 27, 1954, into a family of mixed faiths. His father was a Muslim and his mother a Christian. Early on, God was watching over David. His teacher led him to the Lord while he was in high school. From then on, David put his whole trust in the Lord and believed that what He said in His Word—the Bible—He would do.

At age 16, David's brother died of the measles. But David had already learned that Jesus was not just a healer in New Testament times, but He heals *today*. So, he and his mother secretly carried his brother's body outside the city limits. David got down on his knees and cried out in faith, "Jesus! Jesus! Jesus!" His brother immediately came back to life!

David continued to read the Word of God and trust everything he read as he went through college and got his Ph.D. in human development. Even after he received his degrees, he continued to put himself through what he called the "school of the Holy Spirit." He started reading about revivals around the world and books on faith by ministers like Kenneth E. Hagin, T.L. Osborn and Smith Wigglesworth. But as he read the struggles of the Church in the New Testament and saw the poor and broken Christians in Nigeria, he was not satisfied to let the prosperity gospel be only something he read about in the lives of Abraham, Isaac, King David and Solomon. He asked himself, *What revelation did Old Testament saints have that we don't?*

In March 1981, David Oyedepo set aside three days to find the answer to that question. All he did for three days was read the Bible, Gloria Copeland's book *God's Will Is Prosperity* and Kenneth Copeland's book *The Laws of Prosperity*. On the third day, Bishop Oyedepo discovered the key that much of the Church had been missing: *covenant!* The Old Testament prophets and kings understood that prosperity was part of the covenant God had made with Abraham—you can find that covenant written in Genesis 28. When you trust and obey the Lord—you will be blessed. The New Testament states that we have become heirs to that same covenant when we accept Jesus as our Lord and Savior. With that revelation, Oyedepo began praising the Lord and shouting, "That's it! I can never be poor!"

Two months later (May 2, 1981) in an 18-hour vision, God showed him many, many dying and beaten people sobbing, deformed and crying out in pain. The Lord spoke to him in this vision, saying, "The hour has come to liberate the world from all oppressions of the devil, through the preaching of the word of faith, and I am sending you to undertake this task."

Shortly after the vision, he founded Liberation Faith Hour Ministries and began a weekly teaching program called *Faith Liberation Hour.*

In September 1983, David and his wife, Faith, were ordained as ministers by Pastor Enoch Adeboyo. David Oyedepo was 29 years old when he began his first church in Kaduna. He was preaching to only four members, but knew he was called to be a full-time minister. At that time, Nigerian Christians were so poor that no one could afford to be a full-time minister—especially if you refused to stoop to corruption. He was preaching in a makeshift structure, built from woven grass, that was dubbed "The Grass Cathedral." People laughed at his dream of being a full-time minister, but David continued in faith and even confessed that one day he would have a sanctuary that would seat 50,000 people, and his ministry would own airplanes and take the gospel to other parts of the world. Despite people's jeers, his church grew, and he was ordained a bishop in 1988.

In September 1989, the Lord told him to reach out to the city of Lagos, the former capital of Nigeria. He obeyed God's instruction and purchased 530 acres on the outskirts of the city. Again, people said he would fail, but he started a church, Winner's Chapel, that grew so quickly, people began standing in the streets to hear the Word of God preached. It was soon clear they needed a bigger building, which led to the building of Faith Tabernacle. In preparation for the building, Bishop Oyedepo dedicated the 530 acres to become the headquarters of his ministry and called it "Canaanland."

In Ministry:
Winner's Circle/Living Faith Church:

In 1998, Bishop David Oyedepo set out to build Faith Tabernacle, a structure that would seat over 50,000 people. It was built debt-free by Nigerian people—and in just 12 months! Experts said the building would take over three years to complete. But on Sept. 18, 1999, Faith Tabernacle was completed with seating for 50,400 people with an overflow capacity of 250,000!

When Bishop Oyedepo started his first church, Winner's Chapel, in Kaduna in 1983, he had four members, a Volkswagen Beetle and an old building. Now, the church in Kaduna has more than 20,000 members and Winner's Circle in Lagos has more than 100,000 members, with more than 350 buses to help bring people to church!

Oyedepo has established more than 3,000 churches all over Nigeria and in 65 cities in other parts of Africa, Britain and the United States. The church owns multiple airplanes to preach the gospel around the world! All were paid for in cash.

Home Bible Study for Kids • Week 6: My Father Makes Me Wealthy

World Mission Agency:

David Oyedepo has also established 36 mission stations in 28 African nations. These stations include hospitals, maternity wards, schools and other relief programs.

In Education:

In 2002, Covenant University was founded by Winner's Chapel on the Canaanland property. It, too, was built debt-free and began with three colleges including more than 20 departments, and student and teacher housing. The university now offers more than 43 graduate and undergraduate degrees with room for 7500 students.

Faith Academy was built as a full-boarding secondary school for more than 7,000 students, ages 12-17. There are now more than 12 of these schools throughout Nigeria.

Oyedepo also built Kingdom Heritage Schools for elementary-aged children, 6-11, including nursery age. There are now more than 60 nurseries and elementary schools across Nigeria.

In 2008, Bishop Oyedepo founded the National Education Commission with a mission statement: "It is our goal to ensure that our school system produces total personalities who shall be pathfinders and trailblazers in their various endeavors by helping them discover themselves, get them connected to their Creator and be in touch with their divine purposes and covenant dreams."

David Oyedepo also built another college, Landmark University, in Omu Aran, Nigeria, that opened in 2011 and has further plans to build five more colleges in other African nations.

In Business and Housing:

Canaanland is a self-sustaining facility with businesses including Dominion House Publishing, House of Hebron Bottled Water Processing Plant, schools, restaurants and a bank. Housing for thousands of workers, students and families, both members and nonmembers of Oyedepo's church, is available with 24-hour security surveillance. It is one of the safest places in the world in the middle of one of the poorest nations in the world!

Dominion Publishing House (DPH):

Bishop Oyedepo founded the publishing house in 1992. It has published more than 4 million copies of inspirational books, minibooks, magazines and more in multiple languages. At its commissioning, Dr. Oyedepo stated, "Knowledge, which is a product of learning, is a key factor in the liberation of man. The degree of truth you know, determines your degree of freedom...." Bishop Oyedepo has written more than 70 titles DPH publishes.

Testimonies of healings, marriage and business success have been pouring in from people around the world who have read and been blessed by the books Dominion Publishing House has produced. In 1996, DPH won the Economic Community of West African States (ECOWAS) Gold Award, and Dr. David Oyedepo won the Gold Award for author of the year!

In Family:

Bishop David Oyedepo has been happily married to Florence (known as Faith) Akano since 1982. They have four children who are now adults. All are serving the Lord faithfully and help in their parents' mission to spread the gospel.

Series: The Superkid Creed II

Pastor Faith Oyedepo has been a true partner in her husband's ministry and has helped families across Africa learn how to create a strong family unit. Her books and ministry are centered on marriage, family, youth, relationships and the empowerment of women. She has also established the Faith Oyedepo Foundation. The Foundation provides healthcare facilities for orphans, widows, the sick and needy—especially in remote areas of Nigeria. It also provides scholarships for the underprivileged.

Making History:

In 2011, *Forbes* magazine named Bishop Oyedepo the wealthiest minister in Nigeria, with an estimated net worth of $150 million. The magazine also noted that he has homes in Nigeria, London and the United States, and owns four private jets.

In 2005, the *Guinness World Records* recorded the Oyedepos' church, Faith Tabernacle, which seats 50,000 people, as the largest church auditorium in the world. A July 2012 *Nigeria News* article stated: "Faith Tabernacle is presently the largest church building in the world, with a seating capacity of 50,400 people and an outside overflow capacity of over 250,000, with four services every Sunday."[4] Canaanland started as 530 acres and now covers 10,500 acres.[5]

Outro:

Bishop David Oyedepo knows what it means to be blessed by God in every area of life. He has shared THE BLESSING of the Lord with millions of people across the globe through his churches, missions, ministries, schools and universities, relief programs, businesses, family and publishing company. He is a true picture of 2 Corinthians 9:8 (NKJV): "And God is able to make all grace abound toward you, that you, always having all sufficiency in all things, may have an abundance for every good work."

With all he owns and the work he has accomplished, Bishop David Oyedepo makes a point to give the glory to God. He says, "If you want to duplicate my success, you have to love Jesus like I do. If you give tithes and offerings from compulsion or in order to get something back from God, you may as well keep your money. **The secret of my success is that I'm lovesick for Jesus, and love motivates everything I do.**"

Variation No. 1:

Entering in costume is an attention grabber for your Superkids. Feel free to present the information as if you were Bishop David Oyedepo himself!

Variation No. 2:

If you are in a co-op or have other teens or adults involved, consider having another person play Bishop David Oyedepo and you can be the interviewer!

---

[4] "Living Faith World Outreach aka Winners Chapel," *Nigeria News,* July 5, 2012, http://articles.onlinenigeria.com/nigerian-churches/4281-living-faith-worldoutreach-aka-winners-chapel.html (9/20/12).

[5] *Nigeria News,* July 5, 2012.

Home Bible Study for Kids • Week 6: My Father Makes Me Wealthy

DAY 3: GIVING LESSON — PICTURE-PERFECT BLESSINGS

Suggested Time: 10 minutes

Offering Scripture: *God's blessing makes life rich; nothing we do can improve on God.*
—Proverbs 10:22 MSG

Supplies: ☐ Pictures of famous pieces of art (Make sure one is a picture of the Mona Lisa.)

Lesson Instructions:

Superkids, today we're going to look at some beautiful art. Have you ever seen a painting and thought it was the most beautiful thing you'd ever seen?

Let's take a look at some paintings now! *(Show your kids several pictures of the paintings.)* Which is your favorite painting? What is your favorite part of this painting? What do you think the artist might have been thinking when he or she painted it?

For centuries, people have been looking at these works of art. *(Hold up the picture of the Mona Lisa.)* Does anyone know the name of this famous painting? Yes, you're right! It is called the Mona Lisa. It was painted in 1503 by a famous Italian Renaissance artist named Leonardo da Vinci. The Mona Lisa is known as one of the most famous paintings in the world! It is on the wall of one of the most famous art museums in the world called The Louvre in Paris, France. It is protected by some of the best security systems in the world. Thousands of people come to the museum to see it every year.

No artist would ever get the original Mona Lisa and think about repainting it to give her blond hair instead of dark hair. It's a great work of art, so no changes are needed. It would be ruined forever if anyone were to do that.

In our memory verse this week, we learned how God makes us wealthy. Let's read it in *The Message:* "God's blessing makes life rich; nothing we do can improve on God."

As you think about the way you give today, remember, you can always rely on your Father. HE IS PICTURE-PERFECT!

Notes: _____

_____

_____

_____

_____

_____

Series: The Superkid Creed II

Home Bible Study for Kids • Week 6: My Father Makes Me Wealthy

DAY 4: FOOD FUN

LIFE AND HEALTH IN GOD'S WEALTH

Suggested Time: 10 minutes

Memory Verse: THE BLESSING of The LORD makes a person rich, and he adds no sorrow with it. — Proverbs 10:22

Teacher Tip: This lesson requires you to do some things in advance. Start your dough balls at least an hour and a half in advance (they take an hour to rise). Read the instructions carefully, and plan out the time needed to accomplish the prep work. The lesson will take 10 minutes if you cook your pretzels in advance, but add about 35 minutes if you want to make the pretzels with your children.

Ingredients: (Multiplied by the number of batches you will make—you will need at least double of everything)
☐ 1 Cup WARM water (110° F), ☐ 1/4 Ounce packet active dry yeast, ☐ 2 1/4 Teaspoons vegetable oil or spray, ☐ 2 3/4 Cups bread flour, ☐ 1 Tablespoon granulated sugar, ☐ 1 Teaspoon kosher salt, plus more for sprinkling, ☐ 6 Cups hot water, ☐ 1/4 Cup baking soda, ☐ Butter, ☐ Cinnamon, sugar for sprinkling (optional)

Recipe:
1. In a small, clear bowl mix the 1 cup warm water with the 1 tablespoon sugar. Stir until dissolved.
2. Add the 1/4 ounce packet of yeast and stir it in. Let stand for 5-8 minutes until it becomes creamy and has foam on top.
3. While waiting for the yeast to grow, put the 2 3/4 cups bread flour into a mixing bowl, and stir in the 1 teaspoon kosher salt.
4. Make a well in the middle of the flour/salt mixture and pour the yeast/sugar/water into that well. Stir until it begins to form a dough ball and pulls the flour from the wall of the bowl.
5. Place the dough ball on a clean, lightly floured surface and knead it for around 8 minutes until the dough becomes smooth and elastic. If the dough is sticky, you may need to add more flour as you knead.
6. Place the completed dough ball into a greased bowl and roll the dough around until all surfaces have been oiled.
7. Cover with plastic wrap or a damp cloth and set aside in a warm area (70° F or more) to rise (a good trick is to microwave a cup of hot water for 2 minutes, then place your covered dough in the microwave). Let it rise for about an hour or until it has doubled in size. (Stop here if you're cooking the pretzels with your children.)
8. Preheat oven to 475° F.
9. Place risen dough on a clean, floured surface and cut into 12 equal pieces.
10. Roll out each piece until it is about the diameter of a pencil and about 3 feet long.
11. Put 6 cups hot water into a pot and stir in 1/4 cup baking soda.
12. Twist the dough ropes into pretzel shapes and dip them into the hot baking-soda water.
13. When you remove them from the pan, place them on a clean, dry towel to remove the excess water from the

Series: The Superkid Creed II

Home Bible Study for Kids • Week 6: My Father Makes Me Wealthy

bottom of the pretzel, place them on parchment paper lining the baking sheet and sprinkle them with coarse salt. (omit coarse salt at this step if adding cinnamon sugar at step 16)

14. Let the pretzels rise another 15-20 minutes.
15. Place the risen pretzels into your oven preheated to 475° F and bake for 8-10 minutes or until golden brown.
16. Remove from oven and brush with butter. If you did not sprinkle them with coarse salt, you can sprinkle them with cinnamon and sugar at this point.

Supplies: ☐ Oven, ☐ Clear mixing bowls and measuring cups, ☐ Set of measuring spoons, ☐ Clean cutting board or work surface to "work" the dough, ☐ Parchment baking paper, ☐ Saucepan or pot for dipping pretzels into hot soda water, ☐ Spatula for lowering pretzels into the soda water, ☐ Oven glove or potholder, ☐ Apron, ☐ Clean, soft towel, ☐ Bread knife for cutting the pretzels into sample pieces, ☐ 2 Trays

Prior to Lesson:

Unless you plan to make the pretzels with your children *(if so, add about 35 minutes to your lesson)*, make as many batches of pretzels as you need to use as examples and to serve your kids. *(One recipe yields 12 pretzels.)* This is not a meal, so one pretzel can be cut up into a lot of sample pieces if you have a larger group).

- **At least an hour and a half before your lesson** make a dough ball, following the recipe, to the point where the dough is risen by the time you begin your lesson (Steps 1-7).

- Make another dough ball, but **DON'T add yeast** (Steps 1-7).

- **About 5 minutes before your lesson:** Make the yeast/sugar/water mixture in a clear bowl and let it grow for a few minutes before you begin your lesson. It will continue to grow while you're teaching. (Steps 1-2; keep separate)

Before you begin, you should be ready with at least 3 items: risen dough ball with yeast, dough ball without yeast, and the bowl with the yeast/sugar/water mixture.

On one tray or plate, place the ball of dough *without* yeast along with the ball of risen dough containing yeast. Also ready the bowl with the yeast/sugar/water that has been growing for several minutes. On another tray, display some freshly baked pretzels (if prepared beforehand).

Lesson Instructions:

I hope you enjoy our extra special treat today! Most often, it has to be purchased from a specialty restaurant or in a shopping mall or from a vendor on the street. It is so delicious and chewy and tasty. Can you guess what that treat is? Would you like another hint? OK, today we are talking about the Superkid Creed where it says, "My Father makes me wealthy." Some people think that being wealthy only means that you have a lot of money or "dough." Some people call money "dough." So, I made something out of dough just for you! But the dough I'm talking about here is used to make food.

Home Bible Study for Kids • Week 6: My Father Makes Me Wealthy

Today, we'll all be enjoying soft, chewy pretzels! *(Show the children your tray of pretzels if you've prepared them ahead of time.)*

I mentioned that some people think being wealthy just means you have a lot of money, but true godly wealth is a whole lot more than that! God says He will meet all of our needs according to *His* riches in glory in Christ Jesus. Money can only get you things that are bought and sold, but godly wealth meets all of your needs. True joy, for example, can't be bought or sold. It is a fruit of the Spirit of God. Buying things may give you some pleasure and make you temporarily happy, but that happiness will fade, and you will be dissatisfied again. But, the joy of the Lord is always there for you, and God satisfies you.

Can you think of some other things that are blessings from God that can't be bought or sold with money? *(Allow children time to respond. Answers will vary.)* You're right! Things like healing, healthy relationships, wisdom, a loving family and the Holy Spirit, etc., are things that money can't buy.

You may be thinking, *What does that have to do with big, soft, chewy pretzels?* That's a great question. When you make big, soft, chewy pretzels you have to put life into them. One of the ingredients is yeast. Did you know that yeast is alive? When you mix it with warm water and sugar, it actually begins to grow. *(Show the bowl of yeast water.)* I stirred yeast into the warm sugar water before we began, and it has been growing for several minutes. See the foam on top? When yeast grows, it makes bubbles of carbon dioxide. That's the same thing you exhale when you breathe. Those bubbles are what make this foam. It's also what makes your dough rise and makes your pretzels big and soft and chewy!

Yum! It *smells* sweet and yummy, too. Look at these two balls of dough. Can you guess which one has yeast in it? That's right. The big one! It has grown to over twice its original size because there is life in it!

How does this relate to our Memory Verse? Well, when people love money instead of God, there is death in their wealth. The things they spend their money on hurt themselves and others. It can cause fights in their families and with their friends. But, when God makes you wealthy, there's life in it, because He IS life! When you spend the wealth God gives you, it blesses you and those around you. It can bless your relationships with family and friends. God's wealth gives you joy!

So tell me: What is it that adds life to the pretzels and makes them rise and be light and fluffy? *Yeast!* That's right! And what is it that makes you truly wealthy? Our Father God. That's right! You are awesome!

Say this with me: "My Father makes me wealthy, and He adds no sorrow with it!"

Now, are you ready to enjoy some of these pretzels? *(Serve your pretzels, if pre-made. If not, continue with steps 8-16 in your recipe.)*

Notes:

Home Bible Study for Kids • Week 6: My Father Makes Me Wealthy

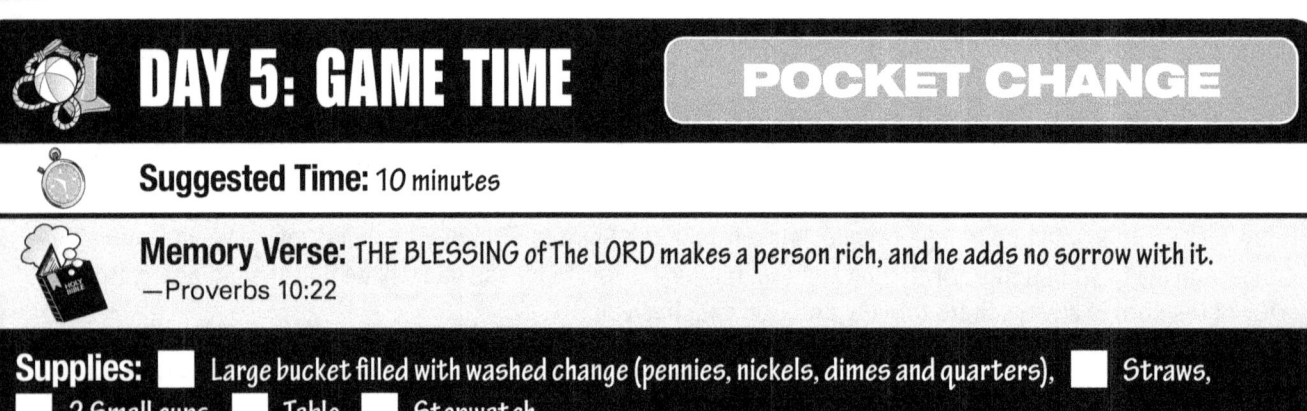

DAY 5: GAME TIME — POCKET CHANGE

Suggested Time: 10 minutes

Memory Verse: THE BLESSING of The LORD makes a person rich, and he adds no sorrow with it. —Proverbs 10:22

Supplies: ☐ Large bucket filled with washed change (pennies, nickels, dimes and quarters), ☐ Straws, ☐ 2 Small cups, ☐ Table, ☐ Stopwatch

Prior to Game:

Wash the change you will be using with soap and water and dry thoroughly.

Game Instructions:

Place the large bucket of change and enough cups in each place on the table for each contestant. Ask the children to put the straws into their mouths and to clasp their hands behind their backs. Cadets must transfer as many coins as possible from the bucket to the small cup by sucking air through the straw to affix coins while transferring from the bucket to their cups.

Start the clock!

Game Goal:

Whoever has the most amount of change in his/her cup at the end of 1 minute, wins.

Final Word:

Today you made yourselves "wealthy." You worked hard, but only ended up with some pocket change to show for it. Our memory verse says that God blesses *without* sorrow. Another way of saying sorrow is painful toil—working yourself to exhaustion. When we don't ask God for His help, we are left to do things all by ourselves. God wants to make us wealthy. All we have to do is follow the Father's way of doing things, and we will be BLESSED His way!

Notes: _____

_____

_____

_____

Series: The Superkid Creed II

Home Bible Study for Kids • Week 6: My Father Makes Me Wealthy

ACTIVITY PAGE — A PICTURE OF WEALTH

 **Memory Verse:** THE BLESSING of The LORD makes a person rich, and he adds no sorrow with it.
—Proverbs 10:22

God wants to paint a picture in your heart. Think and pray about what THE BLESSING means to you. Draw a picture of what the Father shows you.

A PICTURE OF THE BLESSING

Keep the vision in front of you where you can see it. Thank the Lord and say your memory verse every day!

Home Bible Study for Kids • Week 6: My Father Makes Me Wealthy

Notes:

WEEK 7: I DO NOT COMPLAIN

DAY 1: BIBLE LESSON—REJOICING ALWAYS ▸ 108

DAY 2: STORYBOOK THEATER—SHINE LIKE STARS, PART 1 ▸ 110

DAY 3: GIVING LESSON—THANKFUL HEARTS ▸ 118

DAY 4: OBJECT LESSON—WHAT'S IN YOUR GARDEN? ▸ 119

DAY 5: GAME TIME—SHOUT IT OUT! ▸ 121

BONUS: ACTIVITY PAGE—CUT OUT COMPLAINING ▸ 122

Memory Verse: *Do everything without complaining and arguing.* —Philippians 2:14

Home Bible Study for Kids • Week 7: I Do Not Complain

WEEK 7: SNAPSHOT — I DO NOT COMPLAIN

DAY	TYPE OF LESSON	LESSON TITLE	SUPPLIES
Day 1	Bible Lesson	Rejoicing Always	Paper and pens for your children
Day 2	Storybook Theater	Shine Like Stars, Part 1	Pictures of: A nebular cloud in space, comet, particles that have clustered and the cluster becoming a disk, protostar shining in the galaxy, Optional Costumes, Props, Art supplies
Day 3	Giving Lesson	Thankful Hearts	None
Day 4	Object Lesson	What's in Your Garden?	Farmer or gardener outfit, Basket with seed packets and gardening tools or a harvest basket filled with fresh fruit
Day 5	Game Time	Shout It Out!	9 Notecards (more or less depending on size of your group), Marker, Bowl
Bonus	Activity Page	Cut Out Complaining	1 Copy for each child, Safety scissors, Crayons or colored pencils

Lesson Introduction:

I've always told my kids, "If everything has to be perfect or go your way for you to be happy, you'll NEVER be happy!"

Complaining is not just annoying and unappealing to others, it will ultimately rob our Superkids of THE BLESSING of God. It seems like a minor thing in childhood, but as kids grow up and continue to complain, Satan will use it to keep people from walking in God's plan for their lives. It can affect everything. Help them to see that it can be easy to break this habit now and develop a positive, cheerful outlook on life. Not only will the Lord help us if we make a quality decision to stop complaining, but He has filled us with His joy to help us as we go through this change. When there are problems or annoyances big or small, turn to Jesus! He will get you through quickly, and besides, you'll have more fun if you look for the good in any situation.

Remember, you can't complain and walk by faith at the same time.

Love,

Commander Kellie

Commander Kellie

Lesson Outline:

This is truly one of those lessons where a few adjustments make a world of difference, especially with kids. Where can we go these days to get away from complaining? It feels as if it's everywhere—but it doesn't have to be in your home! This week, make your home a complain-free zone, and watch the goodness that can unfold when you do.

I. COMPLAINERS ARE NEVER HAPPY

   a. Israel forgot what God had done for them. Numbers 14:2-11
   b. They were always ungrateful.
   c. They complained even when God BLESSED them. Exodus 14:10-12, 15:24, 16:3, 17:1-3
   d. Do you do this to your mom and dad?

II. WHY NOT COMPLAIN?

   a. They complained so much, God didn't even want to be in their presence. Exodus 33:3
   b. The complainers never received the good things God had for them—are you believing for something?
   c. Complainers have their attention only on themselves. Jude 16
   d. When you complain, others can't see what Jesus has done for you. Philippians 2:14-15

III. WHEN YOU FEEL LIKE COMPLAINING…

   a. Be joyful instead! Don't worry—just tell God your troubles. Philippians 4:4-7
   b. Fix your attention on the good things. Verses 8-9
   c. You can be happy in any situation! Verses 10-12
   d. Remember, you can do all things through Christ! Verse 13

Notes:

Home Bible Study for Kids • Week 7: I Do Not Complain

DAY 1: BIBLE LESSON — REJOICING ALWAYS

 **Memory Verse:** Do everything without complaining and arguing. —Philippians 2:14

Supplies: ☐ Paper and pens for your children

Complaining is a tough habit to break without God's help. But we can do all things through Christ which gives us strength—even rejoice!

Read Philippians 4:4-9, 13:
Rejoice!

Always be full of joy in the Lord. I say it again—rejoice! Let everyone see that you are considerate in all you do. Remember, the Lord is coming soon. Don't worry about anything; instead, pray about everything. Tell God what you need, and thank him for all he has done. Then you will experience God's peace, which exceeds anything we can understand. His peace will guard your hearts and minds as you live in Christ Jesus.

And now, dear brothers and sisters, one final thing. Fix your thoughts on what is true, and honorable, and right, and pure, and lovely, and admirable. Think about things that are excellent and worthy of praise. Keep putting into practice all you learned and received from me—everything you heard from me and saw me doing. Then the God of peace will be with you.

For I can do everything through Christ, who gives me strength.

Discussion Questions:

1. **What should you do when you feel like complaining?**

   Rejoice instead!

2. **What should you think about instead of worrying?**

   Pray about everything.

3. **What will guard our hearts and minds as we live in Christ Jesus?**

   His peace

4. **Can you remember some of the things that we are supposed to fix our minds on?**

   Whatever is true, and honorable, and right, and pure, and lovely, and admirable

Series: The Superkid Creed II

Home Bible Study for Kids • Week 7: I Do Not Complain

5. **In one of the last verses, what does it say we need to do with all that we've learned and heard? (Hint: You do this if you want to get better at something.)**

   Practice!

6. **Complaining can be such a difficult habit to break, but we can do all things through Christ—it just takes some PRACTICE. What are three things you could stop complaining about?**

   (Pass out pens and paper so the children can write their answers. Answers will vary. Tell the children to write down three things they have complained about, and encourage them to share them. Examples: "It's hot," "I'm hungry," "I don't like school.")

7. **Turn your complaints into praise. What are three things you could replace your complaints with and make them into praises?**

   (Have the children write next to each of their own complaints, a praise to God instead. Or use the Activity Page to "cut out complaining." Write your own praises to God to share with the children. Examples: "Thank God for air conditioning!," "I'm so blessed that my parents always feed me!," "Thank You, God, for a place to learn so I don't have to grow up without an education!")

Notes:

Home Bible Study for Kids • Week 7: I Do Not Complain

DAY 2: STORYBOOK THEATER — SHINE LIKE STARS, PART 1

 Suggested Time: 20 minutes

 Key Scripture: Do everything without complaining and arguing (NLT), so that you may become blameless and pure, "children of God without fault in a warped and crooked generation." Then you will shine among them like stars in the sky (NIV). —Philippians 2:14-15

 Concept: "Shine Like Stars" is an illustrated story of how stars are made. Feel free to look up more scientific information about the subject. According to the NIV Bible, believers are able to "shine like stars" when they show themselves blameless and pure by not complaining.

 Teacher Tip: Choose the best variation that works for you. No matter which you choose, having the photos of various stages of becoming a star really helps your kids to have the visual.

List of Characters:
- Narrator: Extremely energetic and dramatic reader!
- Siri: Young and imaginative. Wants to be a star and shine brightly.
- Mariochre *(pronounced: Mary-oker)*: She was part of a cluster that split just before she could become a star. A teacher with a strange accent who shows she's from a different place. Think: old Katharine Hepburn, very dramatic
- Snootie: Bratty sister
- Tootie: Stinky, bratty brother who has a change of heart
- Deena: Pessimist, but very strong
- Cantore: Strongest, but not the smartest
- Mitha: Younger and weak
- Town particles/Complainers/Criers: Naysayers

Optional Props: ☐ Pictures of: A nebular cloud in space, comet, particles that have clustered, the cluster becoming a disk, protostar shining in the galaxy

Supplies:
(Variation 1) ☐ Blank paper, ☐ Crayons or colored pencils
(Variation 2) ☐ Copies of the skit
(Variation 3) ☐ Glitter, Vacuum (to clean up the glitter), Optional: ☐ Create costumes
(Variation 4) ☐ Whiteboard, chalkboard or easel with paper, ☐ Dry-erase markers if using whiteboard, colored chalks if using chalkboard, or pencil (art pencils work best) and eraser, ☐ Black marker and rags (to blend chalks) if using paper, ☐ Art smock (to keep your artist's clothes clean)

Series: The Superkid Creed II

Variation No. 1:

Read the story as part of your read-aloud time. Remember: Reading the story beforehand and giving different voices to each character will help bring life to the story. You may even give your kids a blank sheet of paper (or sketch paper) and crayons or colored pencils to draw what they are seeing in the story or versions of the pictures you've shown them.

Variation No. 2:

Read the story as an old-time radio skit, complete with different actors for each part. If you are limited on participants, then assign more than one part per person, and change the voice. Make copies of the skit and have each actor highlight his/her lines. *Great for a large family, Bible study group or co-op.

Variation No. 3:

Act out the story as a fun skit. Perhaps your children can practice during the day (even creating costumes from everyday items) and then perform it in the evening before the whole family. Before beginning your skit remember to introduce your cast! *Great for a large family, Bible study group or co-op.

Variation No. 4:

Create a storybook theater where one or more family members sketch the story on a whiteboard, chalkboard or artist's easel as another member reads the story. Initially, there will be a few supplies to purchase but don't let this be a deterrent from using the illustrated story option! Once the supplies have been purchased, they'll be long-lasting and reusable.

To make your presentation easier, lightly sketch the drawing with a pencil prior to presentation. Time may not allow the picture to be completely drawn and colored at the time of the lesson. Erase pencil lines, so light lines are visible to the artist but not visible to your children. Review the story ahead of time to determine the amount of time needed to complete the illustration while telling the story. When the story begins, use black markers to "draw" the picture, following the sketched pencil lines. Next, apply color using the pastel chalk. Then, blend the color with the rags. Finally, cut the illustration from the board, roll it up, secure it with rubber bands and share it with one of your children!

STORY:

The Bible says in Philippians 2:14-15, "Do everything without complaining and arguing, so that you may become blameless and pure, 'children of God without fault in a warped and crooked generation.' Then you will shine among them like stars in the sky."

Once upon a time, there were many, many particles floating around in space. *(Show picture of a cloud of dust particles floating in space.)* Growing up together in Nebulae Nursery School, the little pieces of dust floated and floated for eons on end. It took many, many years, but they slowly began to learn how to move and eventually

Home Bible Study for Kids • Week 7: I Do Not Complain

learned how to talk to one another. But always, at the center of their little cores, these little tiny particles of dust wanted to be stars!

Siri was one such little piece of dust. Oh how she desired to be a star! In fact her first word was…"Gravity."

You thought I was going to say *star,* didn't you…. Well the truth is, Siri was always one step ahead of the bunch. But I think I may be getting ahead of myself. Let me rewind a bit.

Long before Siri could speak, a COMET came streaking into her galaxy. *(Show a picture of a comet.)* Siri watched as many of the other particles swiftly moved out of the area when the comet came to town. The old comet's name was Mariochre *(pronounced Mary-oker).* Mariochre was NOT in the prime of her youth when she came through. A failed star, she was running out of steam fast with only her fading tail of light streaking behind her and a dying desire to make her mark on space before her light went completely out. "Who wants to be a star?" Mariochre screamed throughout the gaps and clouds of dust. But, so many were afraid of her vigor as she yelled in her strange and foreign accent. They were scared, too, of the gravity pull that followed her approach. So many particles were not accustomed to change and had never experienced gravity in their lifetimes—they were used to being led on and pushed around by the various elements in the atmosphere. This new force Mariochre brought with her was the biggest change the little particles had ever experienced!

Mariochre approached particle after particle in the nebular cloud. Eventually, she reached the outskirts of Siri's Nebulae Nursery School. Siri had just learned to move and listen. She could understand words, but had still not yet learned to speak.

Mariochre noticed her shining power dwindling to the end as she approached the Nebulae Nursery School. After all, she had never been a true star, and now her taillight was shorter than ever. Even though most of the particles in the nursery were too young to speak, Mariochre screamed most desperately in what could be her last few days: "Who would like to become a star? I can teach you to shine!"

She hollered it over and over. "Who wants to be a star? I can teach you! Please! Anyone?"

Many of the younger particles made fun of her. "Go away, you old bag!" They screamed and laughed at her, "Yeah, we don't need your help, you washed-up comet!"

Mariochre could have cried at their words, but she was too determined—determined that her small amount of light would not go out before she could give somebody, some smart little particle, the secrets to stardom. Again, she yelled in the gaps and space-ways. "Doesn't anyone want to be a star?"

Many refused her in rudeness. Most were too intimidated by the strange pull of her gravity. Others simply failed to believe that they could ever become stars…until she met Siri.

Approaching Siri's cloud, again Mariochre yelled. Her voice was so hoarse from screaming all the way from one part of the galaxy to the next, it was more of a faint cry: "I can teach you to shine! Who wants to be a star?"

Siri saw many of her particle friends begin to disperse. But something inside her wanted what the comet had to offer. She wanted to be a star so much, oh, *so* much! The only problem was, Siri couldn't talk yet. So, she tried to think of a way to get the comet's attention.

Again, Siri heard Mariochre's cry to the particles around her: "Who wants to know the secrets of becoming a star?" Siri wasn't totally sure that the comet knew the secrets she spoke of, but she wanted to shine like a star so badly, she didn't care. In a burst of energy, she pushed against the elements in space and made her way toward Mariochre. And, since most of the particles were moving away from the old comet, Mariochre noticed

Siri instantly.

Mariochre's eyes widened in delight and a smile overtook her face when she saw the young particle approach. In excitement she asked, "Shall I teach you the secret of becoming a star?"

Siri tried to open her mouth to say yes, but she instantly showed her youthfulness with the baby sounds that came out. "Ba-ba-da-da-da."

Siri clamped a hand over her mouth. Would the comet still share her secrets or move on, thinking that Siri was too young to learn? Siri waited in suspense, unsure if Mariochre would hightail it in the other direction. But Mariochre was wise enough to know that teaching a young pupil was often the best way to make a star pupil. If Siri were willing to learn, Mariochre was willing to teach.

Siri never looked back after her first day of learning from Mariochre. Of course, her goal of becoming a star in the vast universe was a lofty one, but she faithfully endured every pressure that came her way.

The first lesson Mariochre taught her was about gravity: "Always follow the leading of gravity. Don't let elements pull you away or distract you." Siri took vigorous notes as she trained. By following in the comet's tail, she quickly learned how to let gravity pull her along. Once she got the hang of it, Mariochre warned her: "It's easy to follow gravity now, while I'm with you and you can see me, but you MUST, absolutely MUST follow, after you can no longer see my light."

When Mariochre spoke this way, Siri would begin to cry. But Mariochre faithfully wiped the tears away from little Siri's face. It was a day like this when Siri spoke her first word. "You must not cry, Siri…" Mariochre said for the hundredth time. Siri let Mariochre wipe away her tears, then closed her eyes and listened to Mariochre's words that always followed, "Though you may no longer see my light, you will still feel my presence in the pull of gravity that I leave behind. You will feel the gravity even stronger than you feel it now."

On this particular day, something clicked in Siri's mind. She realized that Mariochre would never truly leave her! Instantly, Siri opened her eyes and said her first word—the pull that she felt when she was around Mariochre that always led her in the right direction. "G…Gr…Gr…Gravity."

Siri was so pleased with herself! Mariochre was pleased as well, and happy at the rapid growth of her budding pupil. Siri was not only growing older and wiser, but she had been gaining more dust as she followed in Mariochre's tail. As she looked at her dwindling taillight, Mariochre knew what Siri often refused to accept: Her light was almost out.

By the time Mariochre neared the end of her journey, Siri had put on enough dust to be quite substantial. She was growing taller all the time, while Mariochre was slowing down. Siri followed Mariochre faithfully to the last nebular cloud. Particles in the different clouds were always judging Siri for following Mariochre and her strange pull of gravity. But, Siri held close to her mentor.

This last town of a cloud was no different. It was just another cloud full of various types of particles. The difference was that Mariochre began moving so slowly and shining so dimly that Siri knew their time together was short.

Normally, they would have gone on to the next cloud, but Mariochre was too weak. They stayed so long at the cloud that Siri was forced to do something she hadn't done since her young years…get to know other dust particles.

And boy, did she get to know them fast! Mariochre's gravity kicked up a whole lot of dust when she went places. But in the past, she and Siri were able to move on before particles began ganging up against her.

Home Bible Study for Kids • Week 7: I Do Not Complain

One day, a particularly disbelieving particle named Tootie jeered at them both, "Siri, why do you hang around that old comet? She's totally warped!"

As usual, Snootie added, "Yeah, and who does that Mariochre think she is, telling everyone what to do?"

Siri just floated away, hurt by their words. But Mariochre continued to teach her about becoming a star, no matter the opposition. And there was plenty of opposition in that cloud. Particles began grouping up into different clusters. *(Show a picture of dust particles as they cluster.)*

They were all affected by the gravity that Mariochre brought with her. They were concerned too of her warnings about the gravity getting so strong that it would rip their clusters apart. She often warned them: "When I leave you, the gravity will grow so strong, many clusters will be broken apart." After this, she spoke just to her close protégée: "Siri, you must begin to find your own cluster."

Siri was shocked! She always tried to stay away from other particles. Mariochre coughed in her weakness, but continued: "You need to be stronger…*(cough)*…when the different elements come…"

"I don't understand!" Siri interrupted. "I thought you said I was strong enough."

Mariochre just shook her head. "You are strong enough to lead, but when the pressure comes from the helium and hydrogen elements, you'll have to have other particles to stand with so you can withstand the pressure and turn it into heat."

As Mariochre made more and more of a stir, the opposing particles came out of the woodwork. Particles like Snootie and Tootie clustered together against Mariochre. They wanted to get her out of their cloud. They had never liked all the change her gravity brought with her.

Other groups hung around the outskirts to wait and see if what Mariochre predicted would be true. Still other groups formed around the cloud. There were those who didn't even know Mariochre, but were clustered together by the strong gravity that went with her. And, there were particles who had always followed the pressure different elements placed on them to move. The dimmer Mariochre's light became, the more the particles clustered. They were all drawn together by the similar ways they behaved.

Eventually, some, encouraged by Mariochre's teaching, grouped up with Siri, who welcomed them with open arms. They were committed to follow Mariochre's teachings. And, following Mariochre's advice, Siri began to make friends with others like Mitha, Cantore, and Deena. All her friends joined, and Siri soon found that the more particles joined her cluster, the stronger she became. Because her new friends were bringing in other particles, Siri's cluster multiplied at an amazing rate.

Though Mariochre's time was ticking away, she knew that Siri's cluster was strong enough to pull together and overcome pressures from the outside. Still, she continued to warn Siri: "Don't let the pressure of the elements that come pull you away from the gravity and your cluster. Don't let the elements' pressure move you. Just let the gravity continue to draw you together and turn the hydrogen elements into heat."

In one of these teachings, Deena—always one to focus on the downside, asked a very good question—one that even Siri hadn't thought to ask: "What kind of pressure are you talking about?"

Mariochre answered, "Why the pressures of the hydrogen, helium and…"

Deena interrupted the teacher: "No, I mean what will the hydrogen and helium try to do to us? Specifically, what will they use?" Siri had heard of the pressure that the elements put on you often enough. But this demanded a fuller answer than even she had yet to hear.

Series: The Superkid Creed II

Their teacher responded: "They will use anything they can to break you up. There will be unbearable heat. They will try to stir up wars in your cluster to break you apart. But the heat and the pressure are the most unbearable."

Cantore was the largest and physically strongest in the group. He asked the next question: "But how can they actually break us apart if they're not stronger than we are? How is it possible for them to break up our group?"

Mariochre considered all the things she remembered long ago from when she had tried to become a star. Finally, she remembered what broke her group apart. "The No. 1 way they will try to break you up is to get you squabbling. I'm sure they will know that you are strong enough to draw in the elements and turn them into fuel, but they will try their best to make you argue and complain."

Cantore, who had more soot than brains replied: "Huh?"

"Whatever you do, you must not and cannot complain and argue! When you complain, you release the hydrogen fuel before it's ready. And, when you argue with one another, you create weak places in your cluster. If the elements find out they have found a weakness, they will try to drive you apart. You must stay fused together. Even when it gets so unbearably hot before the great FUSION, keep filling up with the fuel that the hydrogen gives you until you burst out and…" Mariochre continued her teaching and unsettled many of the students with her explanation. BUT they all remembered her admonition to not complain or argue—no matter what! It would burn out their fuel or break them up before they fused together to become a star.

Finally, the day arrived. Mariochre's pull had so forced particles into groups that every particle had either formed a cluster or left the nebular cloud altogether. Gravity and the mixture of pressures from the elements had pulled each group together.

Mariochre's taillight blinked in and out in the charged atmosphere. She called Siri to her—right into the center of her gravity. With urgency Mariochre spoke. "Tipping point…" she coughed out: "It will get so hot…the pressure from the outside will try to overcome the energy from the inside. You must overcome *(cough, cough)…*"

Mid-sentence, Mariochre fell into a fit of coughs and her light flickered, making the space around her tremble. Siri, unafraid of the gravity that Mariochre's presence emanated, grabbed Mariochre's hands. A tear rolled down Mariochre's cheek as she continued her plea: "Hold fast to my teaching, and one day you will shine brighter than me. You will shine like a star!"

Mariochre smiled weakly, and Siri sensed the time was near. Her eons of training instantly took over, and she called the particles together. "To the center of gravity! It's time!"

No sooner said, than Mariochre smiled and let out her last bit of sparkle as she watched the great cluster of her stunning pupils group together. The gravity let out from the rest of Mariochre's tail was so powerful that well over half the clusters in the cloud broke away from one another. But Siri and her cluster stayed close in the midst of the storm as the gravity warred against the various elements. They pulled together, despite the warring forces around them, letting the gravity spin them inward to squeeze their little crew of clusters into one flat disk.

Siri's group was yanked on every side as they spun round and round, faster and faster, but they remained close. She watched in compassion as Tootie and Snootie's group were one of the first clusters to be torn in two. She knew the particles would never be able to last on their own.

At one point, the younger and smaller particle, Mitha, had trouble hanging on. She began having doubts as she

tried to take in the elements, but not be moved by the pressure they created. "It's too strong!" She began to cry, and as soon as it left her mouth, the pressure pushed on her section even greater. "I'm losing it. The pressure hurts. We're not…"

Siri was about to leave her central position to help young Mitha, but Deena called out. "Stop! Remember what Mariochre said about complaining. We can do this!"

Everyone agreed, and Siri soon found that their cluster had strengthened. Siri noted that as she and the others encouraged one another, other particles that had been broken away from other clusters were also encouraged and joined their group as well.

One day, Cantore saw Tootie pass by. Considerably smaller since the big pull that gravity had created, Tootie was hardly a particle when Cantore pulled him into the midst of their group.

"Quick, grab my hand!" Cantore called out. With all the strength left in his body, Tootie grabbed Cantore's arm, and Cantore swiftly pulled him in to their cluster. Tootie couldn't have been more thankful, and Siri couldn't have been happier that Tootie decided to join their group.

Still, as the cluster grew larger with more and more dust particles, the gravitational pull grew heavier, and it began pulling more and more helium and hydrogen elements to its center for fuel. And as more elements came into the cluster's core, the cluster grew so very hot! The group was already having a hard time dealing with all the pressures that pushed them.

The added heat put a whole new kind of strain on them. As their numbers grew, their temperature continued to climb, until it was so very, very, unbearably hot. Most of these particles grew up in such cold—it had never been more than 10 kelvins out there. Now, they were up into the high 60 millions! That was 6 million times hotter than they were used to!

Thankfully, Siri knew that it would not be long until they were a protostar, their cluster would fuse and the heat would not bother them. She called out to encourage the others in the painful heat: "Just 10 million more degrees kelvin!" Siri said this to encourage herself even more than to encourage the others. She had never withstood such heat in all her life! She continued to call out: "You can do it! Stick together! Stay strong."

Every day, Siri saw other clusters around theirs lose heart and fade away from pressure or heat. They'd be dashed to particles or become dejected asteroids or failed comets like Mariochre. Some complained in large groups: "Ouch! It's too hot!" Others cried weakly as their clusters disintegrated. "Wahhhhhhh! It's burning me!"

When Tootie heard the cries of other groups, he was tempted to join in their complaints for a while. He had always stayed in the clouds that were cooler. He opened his mouth to complain, but Siri caught him just in time. "Hold tight," she said for the millionth time. "The closer we hold to the center of gravity, the stronger we can become. The stronger we become, the quicker our fuel will fuse so we can be a protostar."

Without thinking, Siri began repeating things she'd heard Mariochre say a thousand times, but never truly grasped their meaning. Now, amidst the heat and pressures from the outside, she understood more than ever what Mariochre had meant by that statement. She was hot too, but once they fused together as a protostar, the heat would not bother them. But they still needed to take in more hydrogen fuel, and they had to get even hotter in order for the fusion to take place.

There was always the temptation, too, that the pressure and problems on the outside might overcome the gravity pull on the inside. But at this stage, Siri was more concerned with an uprising argument or complaint from within that might try to break up their cluster.

Thankfully, the hour came when they finally reached the extremely hot temperature of 70 million kelvins and… BOOM! *(Everyone throws glitter out.)* Their hydrogen fused together to become helium fuel for energy, and their cluster structure fused to be a PROTOSTAR! They were now pushing out their own energy and not just taking in fuel. *(Show a picture of a protostar.)*

Although the heat was no longer an issue because of their structure change, they now faced the challenge of needing to put out more energy. But they were growing stronger every day on their way to becoming a shining, bright star that would last for eons to come!

To Be Continued in Two Weeks…

Notes:

Home Bible Study for Kids • Week 7: I Do Not Complain

DAY 3: GIVING LESSON — THANKFUL HEARTS

Suggested Time: 5-7 minutes

Offering Scripture: Then the Lord said to Moses and Aaron, "How long must I put up with this wicked community and its complaints about me? Yes, I have heard the complaints the Israelites are making against me." —Numbers 14:26-27

Lesson Instructions:

Let me tell you a story about having a thankful heart. God delivered the Israelites out of Egypt and told Moses to lead them into a land flowing with milk and honey. It sounded amazing! Just think, God was promising them a place that would provide more than they could ever even imagine!

All they had to do was trust God and follow His leading. At first, the Israelites followed God's leading, but then they forgot to be thankful for what God was daily providing for them, and they began to complain. They complained about being hungry, and God provided manna to feed them. They complained about only having manna to eat, and God sent birds to them for meat. They complained about needing water, and God gave them water to satisfy their thirst.

When it was time to enter the Promised Land, they sent in spies to check it out. When the report came back that the land was overrun with giants, they complained again! They cried out that God had sent them to die and that they should have stayed in Egypt! (Read Numbers 14:26-27.) "Then the Lord said to Moses and Aaron, 'How long must I put up with this wicked community and its complaints about me? Yes, I have heard the complaints the Israelites are making against me.'"

God gave the Israelites everything they could have ever needed or wanted, but they were never thankful—they only complained.

Since the Israelites never practiced having thankful hearts toward God, they never entered into all He had promised them. They never received the perfect plan He wanted for them.

What are some things WE can thank the Lord for today? *(Allow children to give you several answers.)*

God has given each of us so many BLESSINGS! Today, as we bring our offerings, let's thank the Lord for all He does for us!

Notes: _____

_____

_____

_____

_____

Series: The Superkid Creed II

Home Bible Study for Kids • Week 7: I Do Not Complain

DAY 4: OBJECT LESSON

WHAT'S IN YOUR GARDEN?

 Suggested Time: 5-7 minutes

 Memory Verse: Do everything without complaining and arguing. —Philippians 2:14

 Teacher Tip: Dressing the part of a farmer or gardener increases interest. You can also bring out a basket filled with fresh fruit to let kids sample.

Supplies: ☐ Farmer or gardener outfit, ☐ Basket with seed packets and gardening tools, or a harvest basket filled with fresh fruit

Lesson Instructions:

Have you ever planted something? *(Take the time to allow for answers.)* Farming and gardening can be a lot of hard work, but it's a lot of fun, too! Watching your plants grow and produce fruit is thrilling. It's awesome to see how one little seed can produce so much.

Can anyone tell me why someone would plant a garden? *(Answers will vary.)* Yes, those are all great answers!

Farmers plant seeds because they want a harvest! For example, people plant corn seeds because they want corn. They plant apple seeds because they want apples. If you wanted oranges, would you plant broccoli seeds? Of course not! Can you imagine getting up in the morning with orange juice on your mind, going out into the field and bringing back a bushel of broccoli? Broccoli juice for breakfast is just not the same as orange juice!

It doesn't make sense to plant what you don't want, does it? But people do it every day. They plant things they don't want, all the while hoping to get something out of it that they do want. That's crazy, isn't it?

You see, the words we speak are seeds. God lets US choose what kind of word seeds we plant. There are people complaining about things in their lives and don't realize they're planting seeds for more of the same. You may have heard someone planting the "school is too hard for me" seed when they should be planting the "thank You, Lord, I have the mind of Christ" seed, or the "thank You, Lord, the Holy Spirit is my teacher" seed.

When you speak the Word of God and plant it in faith, it will grow into a crop of what you want. When you complain, God can't bless those words, and your harvest is not going to be something you want!

You may hear someone plant the "I don't have enough" seed instead of the "thank You, Lord, that You meet all my need according to Your riches in glory" seed.

Complaining is the opposite of thankfulness. So, instead of planting that complaining seed, which one of God's promises could we plant? *(Get a few answers.)*

I think the Lord may be reminding *you* of some seeds you have planted that need to be pulled up. We sure don't want to reap a harvest of complaints we have made!

Series: The Superkid Creed II

Home Bible Study for Kids • Week 7: I Do Not Complain

Repeat this after me as we bow our heads and pray: "Lord, I repent. I turn away from complaining, and I choose to be thankful. I pull up those complaining seeds and replace them with thanksgiving seeds. Thank You, Lord, for giving me the Holy Spirit to be my Comforter and Helper. I thank You that I hear and know Your voice, and the voice of a stranger I will not follow. Thank You, Lord, for putting a guard over my mouth and helping me to always give thanks for what You have done for me. Amen!"

I'm so thankful that you are my Superkids!

Notes: _____

Home Bible Study for Kids • Week 7: I Do Not Complain

DAY 5: GAME TIME — SHOUT IT OUT!

 **Suggested Time:** 10 minutes

 Memory Verse: Do everything without complaining and arguing. —Philippians 2:14

 **Supplies:** ☐ 9 Notecards (more or less depending on the size of your group), ☐ Marker, ☐ Bowl in which to put folded notecards

Prior to Game:

Write the following words on 1 notecard each: *dog, fish, cat, bird, elephant, lion, dinosaur, horse, rabbit.*

When notecards are completed, fold and place each in the bowl.

Game Instructions:

- This game is to be played like charades. Choose the first player and have him/her draw a notecard from the bowl. Ask him or her to act out the animal name written on the card.

- Ask everyone to guess what animal the player is portraying. Whoever guesses the right answer first is the next contestant.

- Repeat until everyone has a turn (with a larger group, you can split into groups or teams).

Game Goal:

Correctly guess all the animals being demonstrated.

Final Word:

WOW! It got really loud in here. Everyone was shouting and talking over one another and every person wanted to be right and win!

Superkids, our words are a gift to us from God—they can speak both life and death. No other species has the power that we do, because we were made in GOD's image. Today, let's choose our words to build up and encourage each other rather than tear one another down.

Series: The Superkid Creed II

Home Bible Study for Kids • Week 7: I Do Not Complain

ACTIVITY PAGE — CUT OUT COMPLAINING

 **Memory Verse:** Do everything without complaining and arguing. —Philippians 2:14

 Teacher Tip: Your younger kids may need help or supervision in cutting out their stars

Supplies: ☐ 1 Copy for each child, ☐ Safety scissors

The best way to cut out complaining is to be thankful! The Word says that when you leave complaining behind, you shine like a star. Color the stars below and write something you are thankful for in the middle. Cut them out and hang them on the refrigerator, bathroom mirror or next to your bed to remind you of all the GOOD things God has given you!

Cut out Complaining — Shine Like a STAR

WEEK 8: I WORK HARD TO HELP MY FAMILY

DAY 1: BIBLE LESSON—
KING OF TOUGH WORK ▶ 126

DAY 2: ACADEMY LAB—
LET'S MAKE SOME LAVA ▶ 128

DAY 3: GIVING LESSON—MR. ANT ▶ 130

DAY 4: OBJECT LESSON—
THE HASTY HUNT ▶ 132

DAY 5: GAME TIME—NOSE JOB ▶ 133

BONUS: ACTIVITY PAGE—LAZY LETTERS ▶ 135

Memory Verse: Never be lazy, but work hard and serve the Lord enthusiastically. —Romans 12:11

Home Bible Study for Kids • Week 8: I Work Hard to Help My Family

WEEK 8: SNAPSHOT — I WORK HARD TO HELP MY FAMILY

DAY	TYPE OF LESSON	LESSON TITLE	SUPPLIES
Day 1	Bible Lesson	King of Tough Work	None
Day 2	Academy Lab	Let's Make Some Lava	Clear drinking glass, Salt, Water, Food coloring (red is a good color to go with the lava theme), Vegetable oil (¼ cup)
Day 3	Giving Lesson	Mr. Ant	Picture of an ant, Picture of an ant colony, An ant farm (optional)
Day 4	Object Lesson	The Hasty Hunt	Pen, Notepad
Day 5	Game Time	Nose Job	Cotton balls (several packages), Wet wipes, Petroleum jelly, Tarp/dropcloth, 2 Large bowls or buckets, Spoon, Small table, Stopwatch
Bonus	Activity Page	Lazy Letters	1 Copy for each child

Lesson Introduction:

I've noticed that God is able to bless people who work hard and do things for others. The Bible says He blesses what we set our hands to do. We can't just be lazy, sit around and expect everything to be done for us! When we help others or work around the house, we open the door for the Lord to bless us.

Remember the lessons I've called "Home Improvement"? This is definitely one of them! Help your Superkids to develop an eagerness to help at home!

As you tell David's story, summarize, pulling out the best details to show the hardworking, courageous boy that he was…and how God blessed him for it!!

Love,

Commander Kellie

Commander Kellie

Series: The Superkid Creed II

Lesson Outline:

Hard work pays off! This is an important lesson that is all through Proverbs. Only a fool doesn't know how to work hard. King David also proved that you don't get to be king by sitting around.

I. DAVID'S HARD WORK FOR HIS FAMILY PREPARED HIM TO BE KING I Samuel 16-17

   a. When opportunity came from God, David was hard at work. 1 Samuel 16:1-13

   b. David was serving the king, but he still went home to help his father. 1 Samuel 16:14-23, 17:12-20

   c. His brothers were ungrateful and rude, making fun of him. 1 Samuel 17:22-28

II. WHEN YOU ARE A HARD WORKER, YOU OPEN THE DOOR FOR GOD TO BLESS AND PROMOTE YOU

   a. David gained the courage and experience to kill Goliath while tending sheep! 1 Samuel 17:32-37

   b. A hardworking, courageous shepherd boy became king!

   c. A lazy person always sees obstacles in the way, but God will get rid of them! Proverbs 15:19

   d. Everybody wants things, but the hard worker will have them. Proverbs 13:4

III. SUPERKIDS WHO HELP THEIR FAMILIES ARE SERVING THE LORD Romans 12:11

   a. Don't wait to be asked to help—when something needs doing, you do it!

   b. Don't let fantasies (TV, videos, games, etc.) keep you from working hard. Proverbs 12:11, 28:19

   c. Do every job to the best of your ability—no shortcuts. Proverbs 21:5

   d. The Lord will BLESS you like He BLESSED David!

Notes:

Home Bible Study for Kids • Week 8: I Work Hard to Help My Family

DAY 1: BIBLE LESSON — KING OF TOUGH WORK

Memory Verse: Never be lazy, but work hard and serve the Lord enthusiastically.
—Romans 12:11

God sees your hard work. He knows who is faithful, and who is not. For years, David helped his father with sheep and other small, no-fun tasks. But David's hard work paid off. When it was time to defeat a giant, he had already practiced for years defending his father's sheep from lions and bears. And better yet—because he was FAITHFUL, he had GOD's HELP—and that made all the difference. David killed the giant, even though he was just a young boy. Remember, you may work hard for God—but He sees your heart, and He is ALWAYS hard at work for you.

Read 1 Samuel 16:7, 17:17-25, 32-37:
The Shepherd King

But the Lord said to [the prophet] Samuel, "Don't judge by his appearance or height, for I have rejected him. The Lord doesn't see things the way you see them. People judge by outward appearance, but the Lord looks at the heart."

One day Jesse [David's father] said to David, "Take this basket of roasted grain and these ten loaves of bread, and carry them quickly to your brothers. And give these ten cuts of cheese to their captain. See how your brothers are getting along, and bring back a report on how they are doing." David's brothers were with Saul and the Israelite army at the valley of Elah, fighting against the Philistines.

So David left the sheep with another shepherd and set out early the next morning with the gifts, as [his father] Jesse had directed him. He arrived at the camp just as the Israelite army was leaving for the battlefield with shouts and battle cries. Soon the Israelite and Philistine forces stood facing each other, army against army. David left his things with the keeper of supplies and hurried out to the ranks to greet his brothers. As he was talking with them, Goliath, the Philistine champion from Gath, came out from the Philistine ranks. Then David heard him shout his usual taunt to the army of Israel. As soon as the Israelite army saw him, they began to run away in fright. "Have you seen the giant?" the men asked. "He comes out each day to defy Israel. The king has offered a huge reward to anyone who kills him. He will give that man one of his daughters for a wife, and the man's entire family will be exempted from paying taxes!"

"Don't worry about this Philistine," David told [King] Saul. "I'll go fight him!"

"Don't be ridiculous!" [King] Saul replied. "There's no way you can fight this Philistine and possibly win! You're only a boy, and he's been a man of war since his youth."

But David persisted. "I have been taking care of my father's sheep and goats," he said. "When a lion or a bear comes to steal a lamb from the flock, I go after it with a club and rescue the lamb from its mouth. If the animal

Series: The Superkid Creed II

turns on me, I catch it by the jaw and club it to death. I have done this to both lions and bears, and I'll do it to this pagan Philistine, too, for he has defied the armies of the living God! The Lord who rescued me from the claws of the lion and the bear will rescue me from this Philistine!"

Discussion Questions:

1. **Who told David to go to the army camp to deliver food?**

   Jesse, his father

2. **If David hadn't obeyed, would he have ever found out about fighting Goliath?**

   No. Discuss how obeying your parents and working hard results in blessings for you.

3. **What sort of practice in fighting did David have? (hint: He helped his father.)**

   He was fighting lions and bears while guarding his father's sheep.

4. **What blessings were David given because he defeated Goliath?**

   He received a huge reward: He married the king's daughter, and his entire family was exempt from paying taxes.

5. **King Saul said that David was ridiculous—he was just a boy going against a giant. But that's not how God sees us. The Lord told the prophet Samuel that man looks on the outside, but what does God look at (1 Samuel 16:7)? Discuss.**

   The heart

6. **Proverbs 12:11: "A hard worker has plenty of food, but a person who chases fantasies has no sense." How much time do you spend playing on the computer, video games, watching TV or playing games during the day?**

   Discuss.

7. **How much time do you usually spend helping your family during the day?**

   Discuss. It's good to be a kid, and you should spend time playing, but are you spending a lot more time playing than helping out?

8. **Is there an EXTRA task you can do all week to help out? (Making your bed doesn't count!)**

   Let your kids come up with how they want to help (examples: help with the dishes, sweep, take out the trash when it's full, wash the sinks or counters, yard work). Parents, do your best to not badger them about it, but maybe give a prize to whomever consistently accomplishes the task all week.

Home Bible Study for Kids • Week 8: I Work Hard to Help My Family

DAY 2: ACADEMY LAB — LET'S MAKE SOME LAVA

 Suggested Time: 10 minutes

 Memory Verse: Never be lazy, but work hard and serve the Lord enthusiastically. —Romans 12:11

 Supplies: ☐ Clear drinking glass, ☐ Salt, ☐ Water, ☐ Food coloring (red is a good color to go with the lava theme), ☐ Vegetable oil (¼ cup)

Lesson Instructions:

Today we are doing an exciting experiment! We're going to make lava! But I need help from you because you're hard workers. *(Choose one or more of your Superkids to help.)*

I have this really cool experiment here. Everything we need is here to complete it. *(Hold up and name all ingredients and supplies.)* How cool! Who knew this regular stuff from your house could actually make "lava"? Everything is ready to go. Now we just need to put the elements together. *(Without giving further direction, hand over the experiment to the volunteer.)*

Here you go—make some lava! *(Stare straight ahead, nudge the volunteer and smile,* **BUT DON'T GIVE ANY HELP OR SUGGESTIONS.** *After waiting a few moments, give your helpers the instructions, and help him/her complete the experiment.)*

Oh yeah… you want instructions, don't you? OK… *(Take children through the verbal instructions, step by step. Let them follow your commands.)*

- First, let's fill the glass about 3/4 full of water.
- Next, add about 5 drops of the food coloring.
- Measure out the vegetable oil, and slowly pour the oil into the glass.
- Sprinkle salt on top of the oil.
- Watch blobs of lava move up and down in your glass!
- Just continue adding salt to keep the effect going.

Great job! At first, I didn't give you any instructions how to complete this experiment. It would have been very hard to finish it without knowing what to do or the exact amounts to make this experiment work.

You are such diligent workers, so I knew you were willing to work hard and would've gotten the job done when I gave you a little more help! And when you were given the instructions, it made the task so much easier. That's exactly what happens when we ask God for His help. He makes tasks that seem hard, very easy—just like when we mixed the right amounts of ingredients to make lava. The lava is now working on its own!

Series: The Superkid Creed II

Home Bible Study for Kids • Week 8: I Work Hard to Help My Family

You have the right stuff inside you to do a task we or your teachers ask you to do, but sometimes, you need a little guidance on how to start. Next time, instead of becoming frustrated or begging someone else to do a task for you, ask the Holy Spirit for guidance and help.

As you continue to work hard and get instructions from the Holy Spirit, YOU CAN ACCOMPLISH ANYTHING!

Notes:

Home Bible Study for Kids • Week 8: I Work Hard to Help My Family

DAY 3: GIVING LESSON — MR. ANT

 **Suggested Time:** 10 minutes

 Offering Scripture: Take a lesson from the ants, you lazybones. Learn from their ways and become wise! Though they have no prince or governor or ruler to make them work, they labor hard all summer, gathering food for the winter. —Proverbs 6:6-8

Supplies: ☐ Picture of an ant, ☐ Picture of an ant colony, ☐ Optional: An ant farm

Lesson Instructions:

Hey, Superkids! How many of you have ever seen ants on the ground? Sometimes you'll see just one busily scurrying along, but sometimes you'll see what looks like thousands of them in lines taking apart a dead bug or building a nest. They are busy and efficient creatures. Today, we are going to learn more about the ant.

Did you know an ant can carry up to 20 times its body weight? Though ants are tiny insects, they have a specific work system. Some ants have the specific job of cleaning up the ant colony. They even have their own special disposal area where they put their trash. Their legs are long and very strong, giving them the ability to run very fast for their size.

Ants are hard workers. They only sleep about 1 minute at a time. Would you like to work hard like this every day of your life and sleep less than an hour a day? Probably not.

The Bible talks about a lot of things, but do you think it has anything to say about ants? *(Wait for responses.)*

Let's open our Bibles and turn to Proverbs 6:6-8. *(Read passage.)* "Take a lesson from the ants, you lazybones. Learn from their ways and become wise! Though they have no prince or governor or ruler to make them work, they labor hard all summer, gathering food for the winter."

Mr. Ant is always prepared and working hard. He always has more than enough and is always taken care of. He works hard every day to take care of the colony. He can't sit around all day, or he won't survive in the future. He has to put in hard, physical work every day in the ant system so he can have a harvest.

We have to be diligent just like the ants with the things of God. Our job is to work at keeping our hearts open to hear from Him about what He wants us to do and to give to others. When we do what He says, His system goes to work on our behalf and blesses others through us.

Let's take a minute and see what He says that we are supposed to give this week. Say this with me: "Lord, I believe I hear Your voice. Your system is at work for me. I am blessed to be a BLESSING. Please show me who to bless and how. In Jesus' Name, Amen." *(Get quiet, and give your kids a chance to hear from the Lord and then encourage them to act on what they hear Him say.)*

Notes:

Home Bible Study for Kids • Week 8: I Work Hard to Help My Family

DAY 4: OBJECT LESSON — THE HASTY HUNT

 Suggested Time: 10-20 minutes

 Memory Verse: *Never be lazy, but work hard and serve the Lord enthusiastically.* —Romans 12:11

 **Teacher Tip:** This may be your favorite object lesson, yet. Feel free to set aside more time to clean if necessary. You will find that many hands make light work. Remember: This is a TEAM effort!

 Supplies: ☐ Pen, ☐ Notepad

Lesson Instructions:

Have you ever been in a hurry to get something finished, and found that it really didn't turn out all that great? Sometimes mistakes are made and things just don't go as well as they would have had we taken our time and done our best. Proverbs 21:5 says, "Good planning and hard work lead to prosperity, but hasty shortcuts lead to poverty." These aren't good shortcuts (like a smarter way of doing something). Hasty shortcuts are taken when you rush through a job and don't finish it with excellence.

Can you think of some hasty shortcuts you have taken in the past?

- Are there clothes under your bed?
- Are dishes and storage containers shoved haphazardly into kitchen cabinets?
- What's behind those couch pillows?
- Is dirt shoved under your rug?

Hasty Shortcut Hunt:

1. Do a family assessment: Get all the family together and go room to room (even bedrooms) and look for all those hasty shortcuts! Take a notepad and pen with you, and list every shortcut that needs attention. *(Have your Superkids take turns writing the list if they are good writers.)*

2. The fun part: Now, start at the top of your list and EVERYONE together tackle those shortcuts! (It's important to now divide and conquer the list of tasks—stay together to HELP ONE ANOTHER with this.) You'll be surprised how quickly you can work when everyone works together. Remember: Clearing away those hasty shortcuts will make room for God to prosper you!

Series: The Superkid Creed II

Home Bible Study for Kids • Week 8: I Work Hard to Help My Family

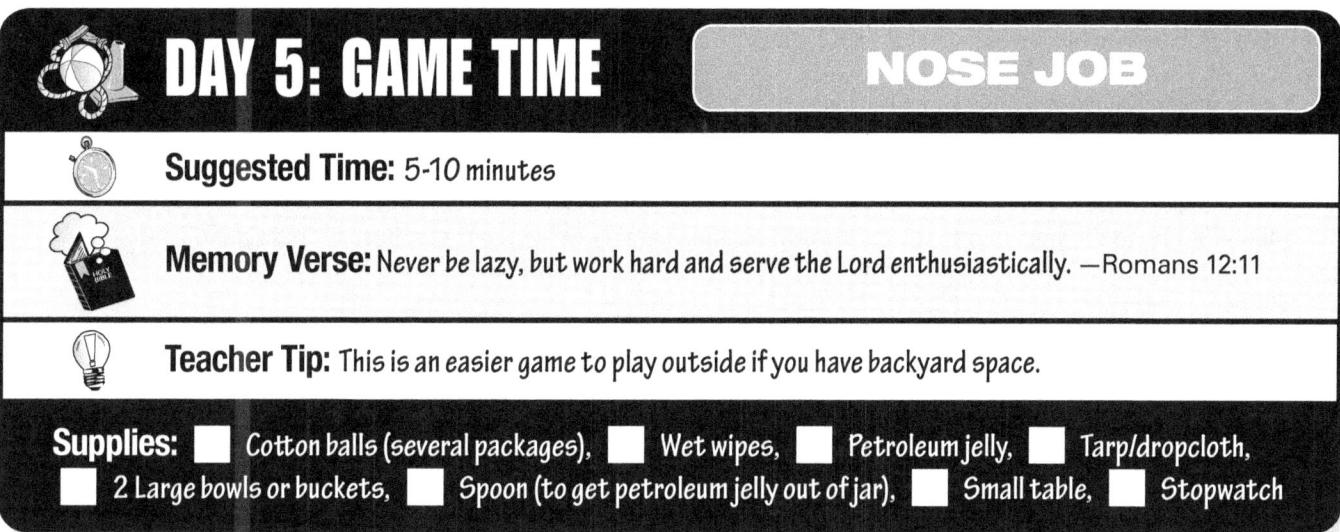

DAY 5: GAME TIME — NOSE JOB

Suggested Time: 5-10 minutes

Memory Verse: Never be lazy, but work hard and serve the Lord enthusiastically. —Romans 12:11

Teacher Tip: This is an easier game to play outside if you have backyard space.

Supplies: ☐ Cotton balls (several packages), ☐ Wet wipes, ☐ Petroleum jelly, ☐ Tarp/dropcloth, ☐ 2 Large bowls or buckets, ☐ Spoon (to get petroleum jelly out of jar), ☐ Small table, ☐ Stopwatch

Prior to Game:

- Place tarp/dropcloth on the ground.
- Place 2 buckets on top of the tarp. (If you have an odd number of contestants, you can also play 1 on 1 and time them separately or go 2 at a time.)
- Spread cotton balls over the top of a small table.
- Make sure the table and bucket are a good distance from each other.

Game Instructions:

Who's ready to get some petroleum jelly smeared on your nose?

- Pick 2 contestants to begin (unless you're playing 1 at a time). Smear petroleum jelly on both kids' noses.
- Have contestants place hands clasped together behind their backs.
- After placing their petroleum jelly-smeared noses in the cotton balls, they will walk over to the bowl/bucket and "drop off" the cotton balls that have stuck to the petroleum jelly, into the bucket.
- Repeat back and forth for 1 minute.
- Several rounds can be played—can play 3 at once or just 1, as long as you have the materials to play it.

Game Goal:

Whoever has the most cotton balls in his/her bucket at the end of 1 minute, wins.

Series: The Superkid Creed II

Home Bible Study for Kids • Week 8: I Work Hard to Help My Family

Final Word:

It sure would have been easier and less messy to use your hands to drop the cotton balls into the bucket, but you didn't have time to think about that when the clock started, did you? You all did a great job!

This week, we are learning about working hard and how we should do everything right the first time, with a good attitude, to the best of our ability—taking no shortcuts. Now, let's put that hard work to good use!

Notes: _____

Series: The Superkid Creed II

Home Bible Study for Kids • Week 8: I Work Hard to Help My Family

ACTIVITY PAGE — LAZY LETTERS

Memory Verse: Never be lazy, but work hard and serve the Lord enthusiastically. —Romans 12:11

Supplies: 1 Copy for each child

Answer Key:

SOMEONE GOT LAZY AND DIDN'T PUT THE LETTERS IN THE RIGHT PLACE.
CAN YOU DECODE THE LAZY WORDS?

[THE BOLDED WORDS ARE SCRAMBLED]

GINK VADID was a **PHEERSHD.**
King David was a shepherd.

He **THACWED** his **THRAFE'S PEESH.**
He watched his father's sheep.

When you **ORWK DRAH** for your **YAFILM,**
When you work hard for your family,

DOG will **DRAWER** you.
God will reward you.

Series: The Superkid Creed II

Home Bible Study for Kids • Week 8: I Work Hard to Help My Family

ACTIVITY PAGE — LAZY LETTERS

Memory Verse: Never be lazy, but work hard and serve the Lord enthusiastically. —Romans 12:11

LAZY LETTERS
—Romans 12:11

SOMEONE GOT LAZY AND DIDN'T PUT THE LETTERS IN THE RIGHT PLACE.
CAN YOU DECODE THE LAZY WORDS?

[THE BOLDED WORDS ARE SCRAMBLED]

GINK VADID was a **PHEERSHD**.
_____

He **THACWED** his **THRAFE'S PEESH**.
_____

When you **ORWK DRAH** for your **YAFILM**,
_____

DOG will **DRAWER** you.
_____

WEEK 9: I HONOR AND OBEY MY PARENTS AND PEOPLE IN AUTHORITY OVER ME

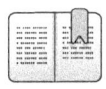 DAY 1: BIBLE LESSON—CONSEQUENCES ▸ 140

 DAY 2: STORYBOOK THEATER—
SHINE LIKE STARS, PART 2 ▸ 142

 DAY 3: GIVING LESSON—
CRYSTAL-CLEAR ▸ 148

 DAY 4: ACADEMY LAB—
SHOWING HONOR IN SCIENCE ▸ 149

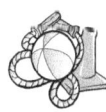 DAY 5: GAME TIME—THE SWEET LIFE ▸ 151

 BONUS: ACTIVITY PAGE—
SEARCHING FOR HONOR ▸ 153

 Memory Verse: Everyone must submit to governing authorities. For all authority comes from God, and those in positions of authority have been placed there by God. —Romans 13:1

Week 9: Snapshot

I HONOR AND OBEY MY PARENTS AND PEOPLE IN AUTHORITY OVER ME

DAY	TYPE OF LESSON	LESSON TITLE	SUPPLIES
Day 1	Bible Lesson	Consequences	None
Day 2	Storybook Theater	Shine Like Stars, Part 2	Optional Costumes, Props, Art supplies
Day 3	Giving Lesson	Crystal-Clear	2 Glasses: 1 filled with clean water and 1 filled with very dirty water
Day 4	Academy Lab	Showing Honor in Science	Table salt (optional)
Day 5	Game Time	The Sweet Life	Bag of brightly colored jelly bean candies, 2 Blindfolds, Table, 2 Chairs, Bowl
Bonus	Activity Page	Searching for Honor	1 Copy for each child, Pen or pencil

Lesson Introduction:

Obedience and honor are key ingredients to our living the life God created us to live. Yes, Jesus' sacrifice paid the price, but if we won't obey God, how can He lead us to THE BLESSING? I've said it before: Kids who won't obey their parents most likely won't obey God, either.

However, that principle works in reverse, too. If a Superkid will make it a practice to obey and honor his/her parents, he/she will be quick to honor and obey God, too.

There is such safety and security in an obedient lifestyle. Think about it this way: correction—direction—protection. It is a logical (and spiritual) sequence. And like the rest of our Creed, it's comparatively easy for your Superkids to develop at a young age. Your Superkids are on their way to a life with God that will inspire all of us to live by the Creed, too—BLESSED!

Love,

Commander Kellie

Commander Kellie

Lesson Outline:

This week is another exciting week for parents teaching their children that it's God's will for them to obey their parents in the Lord. Having them look at the Scriptures will help them to see, you're not just on a power trip this week. God seriously wants to bless children who obey their parents. Long life and things going well with you—who wouldn't want that?

I. A SUPERKID ALWAYS HONORS GOD

   a. To honor means to show high respect and esteem.

   b. If you honor someone, you obey him/her (follow his/her instructions).

   c. If you honor and obey Mom and Dad, you've honored and obeyed God. Ephesians 6:1-2

   d. The Bible promises things will go well for you, and you'll have a long life.

II. JESUS HONORED AND OBEYED HIS PARENTS

   a. Jesus honored and obeyed His mother, even when He didn't feel like it. John 2:1-11

   b. He honored and obeyed His Father, always! John 5:30

   c. We can learn from Jesus' example; He wants to teach us. Matthew 11:29

III. WHO SHOULD YOU HONOR AND OBEY?

   a. The Father, Jesus, the Holy Spirit. John 14:15-17, 23, 16:13-15

   b. Your mother and father. Deuteronomy 5:16

   c. Submit to governing authorities. Romans 13:1-7

   d. Obey everyone whom your parents appoint: teachers, babysitters, pastors, etc.

   e. The Sweet Life is the result!

Notes: _____

_____

_____

_____

_____

_____

Home Bible Study for Kids • Week 9: I Honor and Obey My Parents and People in Authority Over Me

 **DAY 1: BIBLE LESSON** — **CONSEQUENCES**

 **Memory Verse:** Everyone must submit to governing authorities. For all authority comes from God, and those in positions of authority have been placed there by God. —Romans 13:1

God takes disobedience more seriously than we realize. Disobedience comes with some serious consequences, just as obedience comes with some serious blessings.

Read 1 Samuel 15:22-29:
After King Saul Disobeyed the Lord's Command…

But [the Prophet] Samuel replied [to King Saul], "What is more pleasing to the Lord: your burnt offerings and sacrifices or your obedience to his voice? Listen! Obedience is better than sacrifice, and submission is better than offering the fat of rams. Rebellion is as sinful as witchcraft, and stubbornness as bad as worshiping idols. So because you have rejected the command of the Lord, he has rejected you as king."

Then [King] Saul admitted to [the Prophet] Samuel, "Yes, I have sinned. I have disobeyed your instructions and the Lord's command, for I was afraid of the people and did what they demanded. But now, please forgive my sin and come back with me so that I may worship the Lord."

But [the Prophet] Samuel replied, "I will not go back with you! Since you have rejected the Lord's command, he has rejected you as king of Israel."

As [the Prophet] Samuel turned to go, [King] Saul tried to hold him back and tore the hem of his robe. And [the Prophet] Samuel said to him, "The Lord has torn the kingdom of Israel from you today and has given it to someone else—one who is better than you. And he who is the Glory of Israel will not lie, nor will he change his mind, for he is not human that he should change his mind!"

Discussion Questions:

1. **The Lord said to the Prophet Samuel that rebellion (direct disobedience) is as sinful as what?**

   Witchcraft!

2. **The Lord said that stubbornness was as bad as what?**

   Worshipping idols

3. **Why did King Saul disobey the Lord's commands?**

   He was afraid of the people and did what they said (peer pressure) instead of what Samuel had told him to do.

Series: The Superkid Creed II

4. **Even though King Saul disobeyed because of peer pressure, what happened to his kingdom?**

   The Lord took the kingdom away from him for his disobedience.

5. **Many times peer pressure—other people making demands on us—will pressure us to disobey and do things we don't want to do. Is it still considered the sin of disobedience?**

   Yes.

6. **Clearly, God takes obedience very seriously. Could you imagine yourself worshipping an idol or participating in witchcraft?**

   No!

7. **God is saying disobedience is as evil as witchcraft. Think of a time that you've disobeyed your parents, teachers, God or other authorities in the last few days?** *(Draw the children into a discussion of possible problems that arise from disobedience.)*

   Thankfully, disobedience is under the blood of Jesus. So we can repent right now of any stubbornness, rebellion or disobedience we remember. But even like King Saul, we have to remember that our actions have consequences. And disobedience can alter our destiny! That's why God dislikes it so much! But we don't have to let it.

   Let's say this prayer together, "Dear Jesus, thank You for forgiving my sins always. I repent for disobedience, stubbornness and rebellion. I make a decision to obey today, in Jesus' Name! Amen."

Notes:

Home Bible Study for Kids • Week 9: I Honor and Obey My Parents and People in Authority Over M

DAY 2: STORYBOOK THEATER

SHINE LIKE STARS, PART 2

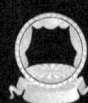
Suggested Time: 20 minutes

Key Scripture: Do everything without complaining and arguing (NLT), so that you may become blameless and pure, "children of God without fault in a warped and crooked generation." Then you will shine among them like stars in the sky (NIV). —Philippians 2:14-15

Concept: "Shine Like Stars" is an illustrated story of how stars are made. Feel free to look up more scientific information about it. According to the NIV Bible, people are able to "shine like stars" when they show themselves blameless and pure by not complaining.

Teacher Tip: Choose the best variation that works for you. No matter which you choose, having the photos of various stages of becoming a star really helps your kids to have the visual.

List of Characters:

- Narrator: Extremely energetic and dramatic reader!
- Siri: Young and imaginative. Wants to be a star and shine brightly
- Jaro: Leader, but rebellious
- Tootie: Stinky, bratty brother who has a change of heart
- Cantore: Strongest, but not the smartest
- Particle: Scared, older female

Supplies:

(Variation 1) ☐ Blank paper, ☐ Crayons or colored pencils
(Variation 2) ☐ Copies of the skit
(Variation 3) ☐ Glitter, Vacuum (to clean up the glitter), ☐ Optional: Create costumes
(Variation 4) ☐ Whiteboard, chalkboard or easel with paper, ☐ Dry-erase markers if using whiteboard, colored chalks if using chalkboard, or pencil (art pencils work best) and eraser, ☐ Black marker and rags (to blend chalks) if using paper, ☐ Art smock (to keep your artist's clothes clean)

Variation No. 1:

Read the story as part of your read-aloud time. Remember: Reading the story beforehand and giving different voices to each character will help bring life to the story. You may even give your kids a blank sheet of paper (or sketch paper) and crayons or colored pencils to draw what they are seeing in the story or versions of the pictures you've shown them.

Series: The Superkid Creed II

Variation No. 2:

Read the story as an old-time radio skit, choosing different children for each part. If you are limited on participants, assign more than one part per person, and change the voice. Make copies of the skit and have each actor highlight his/her lines. *Great for a large family, Bible study group or co-op.

Variation No. 3:

Act out the story as a fun skit. Perhaps your children can practice during the day (even creating costumes from everyday items) and then perform it in the evening before the whole family. Before beginning your skit remember to introduce your cast! *Great for a large family, Bible study group or co-op.

Variation No. 4:

Create a storybook theater where one or more family members sketch the story on a whiteboard, chalkboard or artist's easel as another member reads the story. Initially, there will be a few supplies to purchase but don't let this be a deterrent from using the illustrated story option! Once the supplies have been purchased, they'll be long-lasting and reusable.

To make your presentation easier, lightly sketch the drawing with a pencil prior to presentation. Time may not allow the picture to be completely drawn and colored at the time of the lesson. Erase pencil lines, so light lines are visible to the artist but not visible to your children. Review the story ahead of time to determine the amount of time needed to complete the illustration while telling the story. When the story begins, use black markers to "draw" the picture, following the sketched pencil lines. Next, apply color using the pastel chalk. Then, blend the color with the rags. Finally, cut the illustration from the board, roll it up, secure it with rubber bands, and share it with one of your children!

Recap of Shine Like Stars, Part 1:

(Remember to reintroduce your cast if you're putting on a show!)

Siri began as a small dust particle that couldn't speak or move, but like all dust particles in space, she desired to be a star! So, when Mariochre (Mary-oker) the comet came through her nebular cloud with her strange ways, proclaiming that she could teach particles how to be a star, Siri became Mariochre's first and most enthusiastic pupil.

Siri grew, and so did her cluster of friends among the dust particles. By the time Mariochre's light went out, Siri had amassed a large cluster of particles. Together, Siri's cluster had endured centuries of searing heat and horrible pressure from the outside. But, they stuck together at all costs.

Although many particles were tempted to grumble or complain, Siri's cluster worked through their differences and followed the teachings Mariochre had imparted to them before her light went out.

With Mariochre's advice and Siri's leadership, Cantore, Deena, Jaro, Misha, Tootie and many, many other dust particles had endured the heat and pressures in space and had fused together to become a PROTOSTAR!

They were no longer just pieces of dust particles floating around aimlessly through space; they were now important parts of a protostar. They had light energy bursting out of their core. Their protostar was now pushing out its own energy while taking in hydrogen elements to create helium for fuel. Although blistering heat was no longer an issue because of their structural change, they now faced the challenge of needing to put out more and more energy.

Story:

Siri continued to guide her protostar into stardom. "And…push! You can do it!"

"Arrrghhhh!" *(The group throws glitter out, but weakly.)* The hydrogen pressures of the outside elements were still emitting more pressure than the energy their helium fuel was creating. Siri continued to lead in the center of the little protostar, but the days were not much easier than before.

Although no longer worried about the rising temperatures, the pressure outside pushed harder as their mass grew. They were close to a mass of .1, when Jaro became concerned they would never grow large enough to be a lasting star. "Are we there yet?" Jaro asked.

Before they could help it, some of the newer particles laughed even though they knew complaining was one of the biggest "no-no's."

Cantore, one of the largest and oldest particles, sped to put down the riot. "What's your problem, Jaro?"

Jaro replied: "My problem isn't with you…. But how much longer are you going to let some girl tell you what to do?"

Siri was leading their protostar from the center, but swiftly began making her way to them near the outer rim of the struggling protostar. She knew Jaro was talking about her, but their protostar had become so large, it was going to be a while until she got all the way out there.

Cantore, who tended to act before thinking, shoved Jaro into another group of particles. "We're almost there, man, don't ruin it for the rest of us."

"Really?" Jaro countered. "Almost there? And you know this, how?"

"Siri said…"

But Jaro interrupted Cantore mockingly, "Siri said…. You're more pathetic than I thought."

Cantore tried to control his anger for Siri's sake. Through his teeth, he replied: "Siri has gotten us this far. Everything that…"

But Jaro interrupted him again, "Everything except we're still not shining at ALL. We've been through blistering heat and horrible pressure, and the helium we're releasing is still not near enough to overcome the outside pressure. I read the scales…"

Cantore became uncomfortable as more and more particles began listening in on Jaro's ranting: "We're approaching…"

But Cantore cut him off before he could say any more. "Shhhh! Let's talk about this more quietly…maybe…"

"No! They all deserve to know the truth!" Jaro insisted.

Now, every particle in the northwest quarter was paying attention. Before Jaro could shout again, Cantore placed him in a headlock that denied him air.

"Can't…"Jaro choked out, "…breathe."

"Good," Cantore retorted. Siri arrived just in time as Jaro began turning blue.

"Stop this at once!" Siri commanded. While others focused on the quarrel, Siri noticed the division that was created by Jaro's outburst. Siri stepped between them, and Cantore let go of Jaro. Jaro coughed, gasping for air.

Siri took the opportunity to investigate. "What's the problem?"

"Jaro has a problem with the way you're running things," Cantore answered.

But Jaro defended himself as soon as he had breath to do so. "I just think people should know the truth! That we're almost at .1 mass…."

The particles began whispering their disappointments. They all knew what this meant. "Everybody knows that the pressure outside is still breaking our backs…and everybody knows that Mariochre said we should be producing more energy by now…"

"Every star is different, Jaro." Siri tried to explain, "Sometimes the pressure outside is the greatest right before the victory on the inside. We have to continue to trust Mariochre's teachings. It's led us this far and…"

But Jaro interrupted her. "It led us this far? Like it's been some sort of fun adventure getting stuck with all of you, burning millions of degrees hotter than I've ever burned, putting up with your stupid rules…"

Without warning, the protostar is blasted by pressure on the outside. The division had let in the push from the outer hydrogen elements in space and RIPPPP! The surface of their budding star had been torn.

Siri cried out: "Everyone band together! Quick!"

Siri, focused on closing the gap, didn't notice Jaro making a run for it. Jaro turned to escape but ran into Tootie—who had put on a LOT of dust weight since Cantore saved him from the big scatter of particles that occurred as Mariochre's light faded.

Jaro dodged Tootie to run outside, but Tootie quickly grabbed his arm and slammed him into the massive chest of Cantore.

Cantore smiled and chuckled: "Ha, ha…going somewhere?" Jaro gulped as he was pulled in to the center.

Siri yelled again, almost forgetting the fight that caused the great divide. "Everyone pull together! Get as close as possible! We have to close the gap before more fuel escapes!"

A scared particle cried in the midst! "We're going to fail! We're going to be obliterated for sure!"

"Stop at once!" Siri couldn't stand any more complaining or arguing. "Stop this negativity right now! There is no room for division! We MUST now, more than ever, stick together!" Siri began to scan the crowd for the particle who started the argument in the first place. Her eyes landed on Cantore and Tootie dragging a near-unconscious Jaro to the place where she stood.

Siri measured Jaro as they grew closer and hushed the crowd so all could hear. "Shhhhhhhh!" The murmurs of the crowd fell silent.

"Pick him up, please," Siri said to Cantore. Cantore and Tootie picked Jaro up to stand on his feet. His right eye was swollen but he looked at Siri through his other.

"What are the two rules of our star?" Siri asked, but Jaro immediately threw his head back and laughed disrespectfully. "Ha, ha…! This is not a star!"

Siri nodded at Cantore, and Tootie and Cantore both hammered their fists into Jaro's stomach until he fell to the ground. Siri stopped them with a wave of her hand, and commanded: "Pick him back up."

Cantore and Tootie pulled Jaro to his feet. "What…are our two rules?"

Jaro swallowed hard, then answered, "No complaining, and no arguments."

"Correct—and why is this part of our creed?"

"Because complaining allows fuel to escape and arguing puts cracks in our surface."

"Yes, and cracks in our surface can cause serious damage. But you…Jaro, have done the unthinkable. With complaints and doubts you put division among us. Everybody heed my words. The reason we don't even speak of REBELLION is because just the thought of it is so hurtful to our star—it could cause us to split in half."

Even as Siri spoke, another crack ran across the surface. Other particles cried in terror, but Siri hushed them quickly. "Everyone squeeze together. Bridge the gap! Send the strongest to the outsides!"

All the particles knew the drill, even though they'd never needed to use it. Older, tougher and thicker particles began taking the outside ranks while the younger ones moved to the middle.

"Take Jaro to the other side while we secure this one," Siri commanded Cantore and Tootie. They turned to leave, but Siri whistled in her own special way and they turned back. "Feel free to shut his mouth so he doesn't cause any other riots!"

Quickly, Tootie took a large piece of lint out of his back pocket and stuffed it into Jaro's mouth. Jaro tried to talk but was muted by the lint. "That oughtta do it," Tootie said. Cantore laughed, and the three headed to the safe zone as Siri continued work on the northwest. "We can do it! Group together! Nice and close! Let gravity bring you closer!"

As particles let the gravity pull them together, the protostar began to stabilize against the pressure from the outside.

"That's it!" Siri called in encouragement. "We're going to make it! We can do this! Remember the songs we sang in the old days when we watched and followed the wisdom of Mariochre. Remember what she said: 'We need one another to stand against the pressure from the outside.' Let's prove that hydrogen pressure wrong! Stand together! Link arms!"

The particles pulled closer and closer and the gap became smaller. Siri watched joyfully as the gap closed, and their fuel began releasing heat energy again. "You're doing great! Keep pulling together. We're almost there!"

In swift obedience, the crowd pulled even closer. Among the older ranks, they started to sing and encourage one other. The song floated all the way into the inside of their star until all the particles became so close, they completely closed the gap. Even though the pressure from the hydrogen elements raged and swirled, Siri's ranks unified more than ever. The pull of gravity they created became so strong it began pulling particles and dust from other surrounding clouds into its core.

Siri watched in amazement as their protostar grew in mass and heat. Suddenly, the particles became so close that it put pressure on the fuel inside their core, and two huge streams of helium fuel burst to the outside. "POW!" *(Everyone throws massive amounts of glitter at once.)* The blast cleared away all floating dust and debris that tried to hide the new blaze that could be seen galaxies away from where Siri stood.

"We did it!" Siri exclaimed. She had never been happier in all her days. For the first time in her life, she felt bright, stable and strong. The inward heat energy from their hydrogen fusion had finally overpowered the pressure of elements that pushed from the outside! The light their star emitted warmed Siri's heart.

As it left, she knew that she had accomplished what her mentor and leader taught her to do. "Hold fast to my teaching, and one day you will shine brighter than me. You will shine like a star!" Those were Mariochre's last words. And, after years and years of obeying her mentor's orders, Siri looked out from their STAR that shone forth a bright golden yellow in the darkness.

With all the wonderful knowledge and wisdom Mariochre taught her, Siri knew her star was going to last and shine brightly for a long time.

THE END

> **Teacher Tip:** Discuss the story and how it relates to our walk with God and each other in the Body of Christ.

Notes: _____

Home Bible Study for Kids • Week 9: I Honor and Obey My Parents and People in Authority Over Me

DAY 3: GIVING LESSON — CRYSTAL-CLEAR

Suggested Time: 10 minutes

Offering Scripture: Children, obey your parents because you belong to the Lord, for this is the right thing to do. "Honor your father and mother." This is the first commandment with a promise: If you honor your father and mother, "things will go well for you, and you will have a long life on the earth."
—Ephesians 6:1-3

Supplies: ☐ 2 Glasses: 1 filled with clean water and 1 filled with VERY DIRTY water, ☐ Optional: Use crystal glasses

Lesson Instructions:

(Put both glasses in front of you, ready for your lesson.) Superkids, our heavenly Father talks to us about many things. A good leader gives crystal-clear instructions so people can follow them easily. God is the best at giving crystal-clear directions to His kids so they can have The Sweet Life.

(Show the children the two glasses.) Which glass would you like to take a drink from? The crystal-clear one, right? As you can see, these are both crystal glasses, but one of them is obviously not clear and pure, is it?

I want to read some crystal-clear instructions God gives to kids in Ephesians 6:1-3. *(Read Bible verse.)* "Children, obey your parents because you belong to the Lord, for this is the right thing to do. 'Honor your father and mother.' This is the first commandment with a promise: If you honor your father and mother, 'things will go well for you, and you will have a long life on the earth.'"

God's Word says when you honor and obey your parents, you will live a long life, and things will go well for you!

God is so easy to understand! Whatever He says is crystal-clear. Did you notice that this scripture has a promise attached to it? What a bonus!

What are some crystal-clear instructions your parents, teachers or pastors have taught you from the Bible that God says are your responsibility to do? *(Wait for responses, and encourage kids as they share. Examples: homework assignments, cleaning your room, being kind and considerate of others, etc.)*

The Bible has lots of scriptures that provide crystal-clear instructions about giving, and what God does on our behalf as a result. We've learned some of those things already, and we'll be talking more about how God blesses us when we give from a heart of love!

As you give your offerings today, make a decision to be crystal-clear with your obedience to His instructions. That will bring honor to Him, your parents and teachers!

DAY 4: ACADEMY LAB — SHOWING HONOR IN SCIENCE

 Suggested Time: 5-7 minutes

 Memory Verse: Everyone must submit to governing authorities. For all authority comes from God, and those in positions of authority have been placed there by God. —Romans 13:1

 Teacher Tip: Set the mood with different science gear on the stage—maybe include some colored water in test tubes, a toy microscope and some beakers. Add some small pieces of dry ice to the tubes and beakers to make bubbles and smoke.

Supplies: ☐ Table salt (optional)

Lesson Instructions:

Let's talk about honor in science. When some people talk about honoring someone, they think of things like making a statue of them. They think of placing a statue of a famous scientist like Albert Einstein, for example, outside the science building as a way to honor him.

Think about what the Bible says about honor in Ephesians 6:1-3: It says, "Children, obey your parents because you belong to the Lord, for this is the right thing to do. 'Honor your father and mother.' This is the first commandment with a promise: If you honor your father and mother, 'things will go well for you, and you will have a long life on the earth.'" That's quite a promise! If you honor your parents, God promises things will go well for you and you will live a long life.

Verse 1 shows us that one way to honor our parents is to obey them. That means to listen to them and do what they say with a good attitude. That's how we have a blessed, long life!

OK, now let's see how that relates to science. Let's say that a certain scientist has written an experiment using the element *sodium*.

Remember, we talked about sodium when we were in Lesson 5? We discussed how sodium and chlorine make salt. We also said that sodium is very unstable, and if you put it in water it will explode. So, let's say our scientist laid out the instructions for conducting his experiment and wrote a list of safety procedures for you to follow—maybe something about keeping water away from the sodium. That list would be a great idea, wouldn't it? We don't want our experiment to explode and someone get hurt!

Let's also say this is one of your favorite scientists. You have told all your friends how smart he is, and you've built a great statue of him in your yard to show him honor.

So, the day finally comes for you to conduct the experiment, but you've decided that the sodium looks a little dirty and you want to wash it…*in water!* What do you think is going to happen? That's right! When the sodium hits the water, it's going to…explode!

Let's make a connection here. Remember we mentioned that if we obey our parents things will go well with us, and we will live a long life? Well, if you put sodium in water will things go well with you? Will you live a long life? *(Maybe not if you do your experiments like this!)*

Even though the scientist doesn't want anyone to get hurt, people can still get hurt if they don't follow his safety instructions, can't they? Those safety instructions are there to protect us and to make sure things go well for us, but we have to honor them by following what they say. In this case, the scientist would be the person in authority over us. It's the same way with the Word of God. God doesn't want anyone to get hurt. He gave us His Word to protect us and make things go well with us. It's up to us to study His Word, listen to what He says, and obey Him.

Your parents, your teachers, your pastors, police officers and others in authority are also here to help you. We don't want you to get hurt, either. When you honor us by listening to and obeying our instructions, it protects you. That's one reason why when you obey us, things will go well for you.

So, let me ask you: If you were to build a beautiful statue of me *(your mom/dad/teacher),* thinking that's how to honor us, but don't obey us, will that make things go well with you? No, it won't. The statue may be nice, but God wants you to listen to and obey people in authority over you.

When you choose to do that, good things will happen for you, and you will have a long and happy life!

Superkids, you are awesome! I know things will go well with all of *you* because you honor and obey your mom and dad and other people in authority over you!

Notes: _____

DAY 5: GAME TIME — THE SWEET LIFE

Suggested Time: 10 minutes

Memory Verse: Everyone must submit to governing authorities. For all authority comes from God, and those in positions of authority have been placed there by God. —Romans 13:1

Supplies: ☐ Bag of brightly colored jelly bean candies, ☐ 2 Blindfolds, ☐ Table, ☐ 2 Chairs, ☐ Bowl

Prior to Game:

Decide how many players will be participating, which ones will be blindfolded and which ones will be guides. If the only participants are you and 1 child, take turns being the guide and the one blindfolded. The supplies listed are for 4 players, but with some creativity, you can make it work for your group!

Game Instructions:

- First, have ALL players wash their hands.
- Designate 2 contestants to be the blindfolded ones, and the other 2 to be the guides.
- Each blindfolded contestant will sit down at the table with the guide standing behind him/her.
- Put the blindfolds on the seated contestants and place a large bowl of colored candies between the 2 blindfolded players.
- Each contestant must sit on 1 of his/her hands.
- Assign each team a designated candy color.
- Once the game has begun, the blindfolded partner will dig through the bowl to retrieve 10 of their designated colored candies with the guide's help, and then place the candies on the table, directly in front of the blindfolded contestant, until all 10 pieces of the same color are gathered.
- Guide will then stand in front of the table with the blindfolded player in a fixed position.
- Blindfolded player will then feed the guide 1 candy at a time.
- Guide should not move.
- Guide is allowed to give verbal commands until all 10 pieces are eaten.
- Several rounds can be played, using alternating colors and contestants.

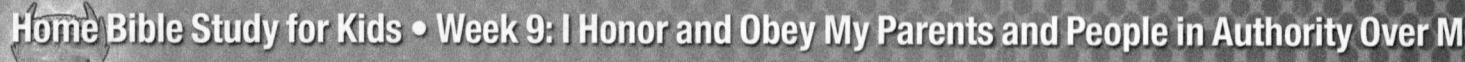

Game Goal:

The team that finishes first, wins.

Final Word:

In our game, we saw that having a guide is very helpful. God has given us guides in our lives to help direct us. Guides can be parents, pastors and teachers and others in authority in our lives. These people all want to help us reach our goals. And if we'll listen to their guidance and instruction in God's ways, we'll always be sure to have The Sweet Life!

Notes: _____

Home Bible Study for Kids • Week 9: I Honor and Obey My Parents and People in Authority Over Me

ACTIVITY PAGE: SEARCHING FOR HONOR

 **Memory Verse:** Everyone must submit to governing authorities. For all authority comes from God, and those in positions of authority have been placed there by God. —Romans 13:1

Supplies: 1 Copy for each child

Answer Key:

Words are hidden in the puzzle ➡ and ⬇.

ADORE
APPRECIATE
APPROVE
BLESS
CELEBRATE
CHERISH
COURTESY

ELEVATE
ESTEEM
LIFT
LOVE
OBEY
OBSERVE
PRIZE

RESPECT
REVERE
TREASURE
VALUE

Series: The Superkid Creed II

Home Bible Study for Kids • Week 9: I Honor and Obey My Parents and People in Authority Over M

ACTIVITY PAGE — SEARCHING FOR HONOR

Memory Verse: Everyone must submit to governing authorities. For all authority comes from God, and those in positions of authority have been placed there by God. —Romans 13:1

Find the words that mean "honor." This is how God wants you to treat your parents!

Name: _____

SEARCHING FOR HONOR

```
O B E Y E L E V A T E O W G J J E J
C I R G E H C M Y K O L O V E C R T
E I E J M H J O U J M S N E P O T R
L O A P P R E C I A T E E B M U R E
E I L Z R A A P P R O V E L Y R E A
B S V D E D J Z H W C V X E T T S S
R Y A E V O E S T E E M Q S E E P U
A B L F E R S J B Q H R S S S S E R
T F U P R E P R I Z E T Q J Y Y C E
E P E W E K C H E R I S H Z E E T E
Y L K C U H E W I D C K H U N N Y L
T O B S E R V E Y E R M D L I F T K
```

HONOR

Words are hidden in the puzzle ➡ and ⬇.

ADORE	ELEVATE	RESPECT
APPRECIATE	ESTEEM	REVERE
APPROVE	LIFT	TREASURE
BLESS	LOVE	VALUE
CELEBRATE	OBEY	
CHERISH	OBSERVE	
COURTESY	PRIZE	

WEEK 10: I WALK IN LOVE

- **DAY 1: BIBLE LESSON— LOVE: THE COMMANDMENT** ▶ 158
- **DAY 2: REAL DEAL— WILLIAM WILBERFORCE** ▶ 160
- **DAY 3: GIVING LESSON—GIFTS OF LOVE** ▶ 166
- **DAY 4: FOOD FUN—HEART KRISPIES** ▶ 167
- **DAY 5: GAME TIME—FILLED WITH LOVE** ▶ 169
- **BONUS: ACTIVITY PAGE— THE LOVE CODE** ▶ 170

Memory Verse: Live a life filled with love, following the example of Christ. He loved us and offered himself as a sacrifice for us, a pleasing aroma to God. —Ephesians 5:2

Home Bible Study for Kids • Week 10: I Walk in Love

WEEK 10: SNAPSHOT — I WALK IN LOVE

DAY	TYPE OF LESSON	LESSON TITLE	SUPPLIES
Day 1	Bible Lesson	Love: The Commandment	None
Day 2	Real Deal	William Wilberforce	Pictures of Wilberforce's home, a slave ship, etc., from internet or books, Scroll (to represent a political bill of Wilberforce's day) Optional Costume: 18th Century suit, White wig
Day 3	Giving Lesson	Gifts of Love	Wrapped gift, Small wrapped gifts or wrapped snacks for each child (optional)
Day 4	Food Fun	Heart Krispies	11x17-Inch baking sheet, Waxed paper, Hot plate, Large spoon, Measuring cup, Large cooking pot, Hot pads (potholders), Plastic bags, Yarn or ribbon, Heart-shaped cookie cutter, Cooking spray or oil, 3 Tablespoons butter, 6 Cups mini-marshmallows, Red food coloring, 9 Cups crisped rice cereal
Day 5	Game Time	Filled With Love	14 Pieces of paper, Markers
Bonus	Activity Page	The Love Code	1 Copy for each child, Pencil or pen

Lesson Introduction:

We have the awesome responsibility to *show* Jesus to the world. That sounds huge! And I've given emphasis to the word *show(ed)* on purpose. It really comes down to the fact that we can't act any old way we want to, or treat people in an unkind way. Whatever we do is going to be what others think Jesus would do. And, we can't decide for ourselves what love looks like, because Jesus showed us what love looks like, sounds like and does!

So we take His love inside us, walk and live in it. First, we receive it, and then we give it. And our point this week should bring a real understanding of *show*: the manifestation and full expression of God living and giving His love to others—through us (1 John 4:12)! Again, it says the full expression of His love flows through us! That sounds so big to take in, but we have that love inside us waiting to be seen. So, bring this thought home to your Superkids: When someone makes you mad, will they see that? Or, will you show them God's love? What about when you are given an opportunity to share or give? Will people see selfishness, or will you show love? I believe our Superkids will show love! And God's love will be seen by everyone they know!

Love,

Commander Kellie

Commander Kellie

Series: The Superkid Creed II

Lesson Outline:

When Superkids find out that Jesus is Love, it simplifies "What would Jesus do?" Knowing that God/Jesus always operates in love helps us to know how He would respond in every situation. Knowing "What would love do?" will change their lives forever.

I. GOD HAS GIVEN US A BIG RESPONSIBILITY John 15:12

   a. Jesus commands us to love each other.

   b. We should love others the same way Jesus loves us.

   c. This makes us a friend of Jesus! Verses 13-14

II. OUR FRIEND JESUS IS A GREAT EXAMPLE TO FOLLOW

   a. Jesus shows us what real love looks like. 1 John 3:16

   b. He didn't get angry at His enemies—He healed them. Luke 22:47-51

   c. He forgave His enemies. Luke 23:26-43

   d. He loves us and gave Himself as a sacrifice for us. Ephesians 5:2

III. JESUS LIVED A LIFE FILLED WITH LOVE, AND YOU CAN TOO 1 John 2:7-8

   a. People can be hard to love sometimes, but remember, God's love is in you to help you love others. Romans 5:5 AMPC

   b. Love isn't just words—our actions should show love. 1 John 3:16-19

   c. God showed His love for us, so we show love for others. 1 John 4:9-11

   d. When we love others, they see God's love, too. 1 John 4:12

Notes:

Home Bible Study for Kids • Week 10: I Walk in Love

DAY 1: BIBLE LESSON — LOVE: THE COMMANDMENT

Memory Verse: Live a life filled with love, following the example of Christ. He loved us and offered himself as a sacrifice for us, a pleasing aroma to God. —Ephesians 5:2

When Jesus speaks about the importance of love, it is clearly NOT a suggestion. It is a command. But it was a command He personally followed to the letter.

Read Mark 12:28-34:
The Greatest Commandment!

One of the teachers of religious law was standing there listening to the debate. He realized that Jesus had answered well, so he asked, "Of all the commandments, which is the most important?" Jesus replied, "The most important commandment is this: 'Listen, O Israel! The Lord our God is the one and only Lord. And you must love the Lord your God with all your heart, all your soul, all your mind, and all your strength.' The second is equally important: 'Love your neighbor as yourself.' No other commandment is greater than these."

The teacher of religious law replied, "Well said, Teacher. You have spoken the truth by saying that there is only one God and no other. And I know it is important to love him with all my heart and all my understanding and all my strength, and to love my neighbor as myself. This is more important than to offer all of the burnt offerings and sacrifices required in the law." Realizing how much the man understood, Jesus said to him, "You are not far from the Kingdom of God." And after that, no one dared to ask him any more questions.

Read John 15:12-15:
True Friendship

This is my commandment: Love each other in the same way I have loved you. There is no greater love than to lay down one's life for one's friends. You are my friends if you do what I command. I no longer call you slaves, because a master doesn't confide in his slaves. Now you are my friends, since I have told you everything the Father told me.

Discussion Questions:

1. **Jesus said part of the most important commandment is to love the Lord our God with what four things?**

    ALL our hearts, ALL our souls, ALL our minds (understanding) and ALL our strength

2. **Who else are we to love?**

    Our neighbor as ourselves

Series: The Superkid Creed II

3. Look at 1 John 3:16. What did Jesus do to show His love for us? He gave up His _____ for us.

   life

4. John 15:13-14: There is no _____ love than to _____ _____ one's life for one's friends. You are my _____ if you do what I command.

   greater, lay down, friends

5. **The Commandment from the Great Commander (Jesus):**
   John 15:12—This is my commandment: Love each other in the _____ way I have loved you.

   same

6. **Think about it:** List ONE way you can better follow Jesus' commandment to walk in love with…

   - Your mom
   - Your dad
   - Your brothers and sisters
   - Your friends
   - Your enemies

   Notes:

Home Bible Study for Kids • Week 10: I Walk in Love

DAY 2: REAL DEAL — WILLIAM WILBERFORCE

Suggested Time: 15 minutes

Memory Verse: Live a life filled with love, following the example of Christ. He loved us and offered himself as a sacrifice for us, a pleasing aroma to God. —Ephesians 5:2

Concept: Highlighting an interesting historical place, figure or event that illustrates the theme of the day. The theme of the day is: I walk in love.

Teacher Tip: Entering in costume is an attention grabber for your Cadets. Bringing in other media such as photos (onscreen or printed), videos or props is helpful to keep the Superkids engaged and gives more clarity to your presentation.

Supplies: ☐ Pictures of Wilberforce's home, a slave ship, etc., from internet or books, ☐ Scroll (to represent a political bill of Wilberforce's day)

Optional Costume: ☐ 18th Century suit, ☐ White wig

Intro:

"Let us not despair; it is a blessed cause, and success, ere long, will crown our exertions. Already we have gained one victory; we have obtained, for these poor creatures, the recognition of their human nature, which, for a while was most shamefully denied. This is the first fruits of our efforts; let us persevere and our triumph will be complete. Never, never will we desist till we have wiped away this scandal from the Christian name, released ourselves from the load of guilt, under which we at present labour, and extinguished every trace of this bloody traffic, of which our posterity, looking back to the history of these enlightened times, will scarce believe that it has been suffered to exist so long a disgrace and dishonour to this country."[6]

This was William Wilberforce's reply to the second year his bill was turned down in British Parliament in 1791. So sure of his evidence and the Christian morality of his nation, he originally had no idea that the quest to abolish (to completely put an end to) slavery would be a lifelong goal and a pursuit that would fill his career for 50 of his 74 years.

Lesson:
Big Business:

William Wilberforce was born August 24, 1759, in Hull, England, at a time when slavery was not only socially acceptable, but an established British institution and highly developed business that had the stamp of approval from many who considered themselves devout Christians.

Series: The Superkid Creed II

In the 1700s, the slave trade was in full force around the world. English ships' crews were luring free Africans onto their ships or purchasing captured Africans, and then chaining their arms, legs and often their necks, into tiny spaces filled with disease, dirt and foul odors. With such poor conditions, malnutrition and change of climate, only an average of 50 percent of the captured African people survived the long and arduous voyage.[7]

If the captured people survived, the filth was scrubbed off them and they were sold naked to the highest bidder. Then, the real horror began. These men, women and children were branded with hot irons and stripped of all rights to be considered human beings. They became slaves forever to the men and women who "purchased" them and were made to do as they were told until they died. When William Wilberforce was just a teen, about 4,000 African men and women were being captured every month!

Born into a wealthy merchant family, William Wilberforce didn't take life too seriously. He succeeded in his schooling with his charming speech and manners, but never fully applied himself. He studied at Cambridge University where he met his good friend, William Pitt (who later became prime minister).

Meeting Jesus:

After college (in 1780), both he and Pitt managed to get elected into Parliament, though both were only 21 years old (the youngest age you could enter Parliament). Although William Wilberforce's powerful way with words quickly catapulted him into higher-seated positions, he later admitted: "The first years in Parliament I did nothing—nothing to any purpose. My own distinction was my darling object."[8]

In 1786, William became deeply troubled in his soul, and around Easter of that year, experienced a true salvation and rebirth through the witness of a childhood friend. Making Jesus his Lord changed Wilberforce's life completely. He began spending time with God every morning, listening to hear His voice, and journaling all that he prayed and heard. He quit gambling and resigned from clubs to become more devout in his faith.

Wilberforce spent his days studying the Bible—"about nine or ten hours a day"[9] for 11 years. The Bible became his favorite book, and he memorized large portions of it.[10] For a time, he considered quitting politics altogether. But, he prayed and sought the counsel of another childhood friend, John Newton, former slave-runner, turned preacher (writer of the classic church hymn "Amazing Grace"). John Newton encouraged Wilberforce that God had placed him in politics. He also shared with him the horrors of the slave trade.

Encouraged by these meetings, Wilberforce realized: "My walk is a public one, my business is in the world, and I must mix in the assemblies of men or quit the post which Providence seems to have assigned me."[11] John Newton's feeling toward abolishing slavery was seconded by Wilberforce's friend William Pitt, who, at age 24, was soon to become the youngest prime minister Great Britain had ever seen. Wilberforce began meeting with abolitionists like Thomas Clarkson, a lobbyist and activist who had been publishing pamphlets against the slave trade and the cruelty he had witnessed firsthand.

Once Wilberforce saw the evidence Clarkson gave, he was persuaded that something must be done. He said, "A trade founded in iniquity, and carried on as this was, must be abolished, let the policy be what it might. Let the consequences be what they would, I from this time determined that I would never rest till I had effected its abolition."[12]

But, Wilberforce was one of the few in Parliament who thought the abolition of slavery was possible. One publicist wrote, "The impossibility of doing without slaves in the West Indies will always prevent this traffic being dropped."[13]

Home Bible Study for Kids • Week 10: I Walk in Love

The large majority of Parliament and the people agreed that Britain and her colonies could simply not operate without the slave trade. But that didn't stop Wilberforce and the Society for Effecting the Abolition of the Slave Trade, which was made up of Quakers, Thomas Clarkson, Hannah More, Granville Sharp, Henry Thornton, Zachary Macaulay, James Stephen, Edward James Eliot, Thomas Gisbourne, John Shore, Charles Grant and others.

John Wesley (great hymn writer, evangelist and founder of the Methodist church) knew perhaps more than Wilberforce how much dedication was required to bring down the slave trade. In his last letter written before his death, he wrote to Wilberforce: "Unless God has raised you up for this very thing, you will be worn out by the opposition of men and devils. But if God be for you, who can be against you? Are all of them together stronger than God? O be not weary of well doing! Go on, in the name of God and in the power of his might…."[14]

A Force Against Slavery:

Wilberforce did move forward, confident of his success and the morality of the British people. He introduced the Abolition Bill of 1789, and in May of that year, delivered one of the most eloquent speeches ever to be given in the House of Commons.[15] How could people hear about such atrocities taking place in their Christian nation and continue in this awful trade? Nonetheless, the bill was defeated by a huge margin.

But the abolitionist spirit was not. The abolitionists decided to double their efforts in the first-ever grass-roots campaign. They reached out to the people, rather than the politicians, to rally their support and sympathy. With the spread of Clarkson's pamphlets, containing narratives of slaves' firsthand experiences, coupled with Wilberforce's speeches, the movement began to gain extreme popularity with the people.

April 1791, Wilberforce put forth another Abolition of the Slave Trade Bill, and debated passionately for two days, but again, the bill quickly lost—163 to 88 votes.

Once people realized just how serious Wilberforce was about abolishing the slave trade, the death threats came rolling in. Captains of slave ships and other politicians threatened him, while even the royal family and the famous Lord Nelson (national hero of the Battle of Trafalgar) openly ridiculed him. Even his good friend and Prime Minister, William Pitt, withdrew his support. The forces against him became so fierce, one of his friends was afraid he would read that Wilberforce had been "carbonadoed [broiled] by Indian planters, barbecued by African merchants, and eaten by Guinea captains."[16]

Through all this, and despite poor health, Wilberforce fought on. He sponsored more abolition bills in 1792, 1793, 1797, 1798, 1799, 1804 and 1805. But, all his attempts, either due to current events (wars, etc.), bribery, sickness or political fear, were shot down, time after time. In 1793, one bill lost by only three votes. Then, in 1793 and 1804, the Abolition Bill passed in the House of Commons, but was defeated in the House of Lords. (Britain has two houses of Parliament.)

During the years of trials in Wilberforce's efforts to defeat slavery, he also fought for the "reformation of manners (morality)." He was dubbed "Prime Minister of Philanthropy," championing health rights for the poor, helping the orphaned, single mothers and juvenile delinquents. He gave 25 percent of his annual income to the needy. He worked for the Better Observance of Sundays, the Royal Society for the Prevention of Cruelty to Animals, the Society for Bettering the Condition of the Poor and the Church Missionary Society.

In 1797, Wilberforce found time to fall head-over-heels in love with Barbara Ann Spooner, whom he married after a quick engagement. They were married 36 years before he died, and had six children together. He was known to be a loving husband and father who actively played with his children.

With wars in France and the Americas, death threats and failing health (he had stomach issues and bad eyesight), Wilberforce pushed through, despite the defeat in 1805. In January 1807, Wilberforce again introduced a bill to the House of Commons: The Slave Trade Act. This time, the bill won with an overwhelming 283 to 16 votes! Wilberforce said, "How popular Abolition is just now! God can turn the hearts of men!"[17] The bill became law on March 25, 1807. It put an end to the slave trade in all of Great Britain and the English colonies. But those already in the bonds of slavery had yet to be freed.

William Wilberforce spent the next few years making sure the new anti-slave trade laws were enforced by creating bills like the Slave Registration Bill, which passed in 1812. Shortly after passing the bill, the Prime Minister, Spencer Percival, was assassinated. The pressure became heavier from attackers, and by 1815, William Wilberforce was so tired of working to appease his enemies in Parliament that he began campaigning to abolish the whole institution of slavery, not just the slave trade.

In 1825, Wilberforce continued his support of abolitionist efforts, but retired from Parliament due to his failing health. July 26, 1833, the Emancipation Bill was read and guaranteed huge support from the House of Commons. This law would free the slaves in Britain and its colonies. £20 million (£ is the symbol for "pounds," the British currency) were put aside to compensate owners for their slaves. "Thank God!" Wilberforce exclaimed, "that I have lived to witness the day in which England is willing to pay twenty million pounds sterling for the abolition of slavery."[18] Three days later, William Wilberforce died, a happy man. A month later, the bill was made law and slavery was abolished throughout Great Britain and her colonies. Christopher D. Hancock said that "[t]he most malignant evil of the British Empire ceased largely because of the faith and persistence of William Wilberforce."[19]

Making History:

Before William Wilberforce teamed up with others, he became an abolitionist voice in Parliament and later president of the Abolition Society when slavery was socially acceptable to the majority of the known Western world. He and the Abolitionists worked hard for over 40 years to change the way people viewed the slave trade, slaves, freedom and the African human being. After hours and days spent in debates, research, writing pamphlets and speeches, Wilberforce was the driving force to get the Abolition of Slave Trade Act passed and enforced as law. And, he opened the door to the Slavery Abolition Act of 1833.

When others accepted slaves as a social commodity, Wilberforce insisted, "In the Scripture, no national crime is condemned so frequently and few so strongly as oppression and cruelty, and the not using of our best endeavors to deliver our fellow creatures from them."[20]

Great Britain was the first country in the Western world to admit slavery was inhumane and expel it from her borders, and eventually, her commonwealth. As a leading world power, it opened the eyes of other countries around the world (including the United States) to see that all men were created equal, and therefore freedom for slaves was a cause worth fighting for.

Some of the founding fathers of the United States who were influenced by Wilberforce include John Quincy Adams, John Jay, Thomas Jefferson, Rufus King, the Marquis de Lafayette and James Monroe.

Many distinguished African-Americans' lives were also influenced by Wilberforce. Among them were Frederick Douglass, Paul Cuffe and William Wells Brown.

Other famous Americans whose lives were influenced by Wilberforce include Harriet Beecher Stowe, Jonathan Edwards, Abraham Lincoln, E.M. Bounds, Caspar Morris, Lyman Beecher, William Lloyd Garrison, Edward

Home Bible Study for Kids • Week 10: I Walk in Love

Everett Jr., William Jay, George Ticknor, William Buell Sprague, Charles Sumner, William Cabell Rives, Arthur and Lewis Tappan, Henry Ingersoll Bowditch, Henry David Thoreau, Emerson, and John Greenleaf Whittier.

America's oldest African-American college, Wilberforce University of Ohio, continues in Wilberforce's tradition, educating young people today. "Democratic and Republican leaders in the House and Senate continue to draw inspiration from Wilberforce's legacy through Prison Fellowship, the Wilberforce Forum and the Trinity Forum groups which honor and perpetuate his commitment to cultural renewal."[21] Wilberforce's work and influence continues.

Outro:

William Wilberforce died a national hero July 29, 1833. But, to slaves across Great Britain and in its colonies, he was more than just a hero—he was a savior from captivity, a true demonstrator of Jesus' love.

Oh, me good friend, Mr. Wilberforce, make we free!

God Almighty thank ye! God Almighty thank ye!

God Almighty, make we free!

—A Barbados slave song from 1816

Wilberforce proved that Jesus' command to us is NOT an impossible task: "This is my commandment: Love each other in the same way I have loved you. There is no greater love than to lay down one's life for one's friends" (John 15:12-13).

Variation No. 1:

Entering in costume is an attention grabber for your Superkids. Feel free to present the information as if you were William Wilberforce himself!

Variation No. 2:

If you are in a co-op and have other teens or adults involved, consider having another person play William Wilberforce and you can be the interviewer.

---

6 Speech before the British House of Commons, April 18, 1791.

7 Abolition speech given by William Wilberforce before the House of Commons, Tuesday, May 12, 1789, abolition.e2bn.org/file_download.php?ts=1196553600&id=207 (10/11/2012).

8 *Christian History*, "William Wilberforce: Antislavery Politician," http://www.christianitytoday.com/ch/131christians/activists/wilberforce.html (10/15/2012).

9 John Pollock, *Wilberforce* (Oxford: Lion Publishing Corporation, 1986).

10 Ibid.

11 *Christian History*, "William Wilberforce," http://www.christianitytoday.com/ch/131christians/activists/wilberforce.html (10/9/2012).

12 From abolition speech before the House of Commons, Tuesday, May 12, 1789.

13 John Hippisley (1764) quoted by F.W. Pitman in *The Development of the British West Indies, 1700-1763* (New Haven, Conn.: Yale University Press; Oxford University Press, 1917) p. 63.

14 "John Wesley: Holiness of Heart and Life, Letter to William Wilberforce," United Methodist Women, http://gbgm-umc.org/umw/wesley/wilber.stm (10/10/2012).

15 To read the text of Wilberforce's 1789 speech before the House of Commons, go to: abolition.e2bn.org/file_download.php?ts=1196553600&id=207 (10/11/2012).

16 "William Wilberforce: Antislavery Politician," *Christian History,* Issue 53, 8/8/2008, *Christianity Today,* http://www.christianitytoday.com/ch/131christians/activists/wilberforce.html?start=2 (10/15/2012).

17 *The Life of William Wilberforce: In Five Volumes, Volume 3,* by his sons, Robert I. Wilberforce, Samuel Wilberforce (London: John Murray) p. 295.

18 "The Scourge of Slavery," *Christian Action Magazine,* 2004 Vol. 4, http://www.christianaction.org.za/articles_ca/2004-4-thescourgeofslavery.htm (10/15/2012).

19 Christopher D. Hancock, "William Wilberforce and The Century of Reform,"*Christian History,* Issue 53 (1997).

20 "William Wilberforce and the Abolition of the Slave Trade: Did You Know?," Little-known or remarkable facts about William Wilberforce and the Century of Reform, by Richard V. Pierard, *Christianity Today, Christian History* Issue, Issue 53 (1997), http://www.christianitytoday.com/ch/1997/issue53/53h002.html (10/15/2012).

21 "William Wilberforce: A Man for All Seasons," by Kevin Belmonte, The Christian Broadcasting Network, Excerpted from *A Hero for Humanity,* by Kevin Belmonte, © 2002. Published by Zondervan. Used with permission, http://www.cbn.com/special/amazingGrace/Articles/Wilberforce-Bio.aspx (10/15/12012).

Notes:

Home Bible Study for Kids • Week 10: I Walk in Love

DAY 3: GIVING LESSON — GIFTS OF LOVE

Suggested Time: 5-7 minutes

Offering Scripture: Love each other in the same way I have loved you. —John 15:12

Supplies: ☐ Wrapped gift, ☐ Small wrapped gifts or wrapped snacks for each child (optional)

Prior to Lesson:

If you have a small group, wrapping one gift for each person can make it extra special. You can just wrap a snack or something small, but whatever you wrap, try to make it look exciting for your kids.

Lesson Instructions:

Receiving presents is always fun, isn't it? I really enjoy giving presents.

(Show the children the wrapped gift.) You know, I didn't have to get this gift, but I did it because I love the person I'm giving it to, and I love to bless him/her with gifts!

You know, this gift reminds me of what Jesus did for us. Let's open our Bibles to John 15:12. It says, "Love each other in the same way I have loved you."

Just like I didn't *have* to buy this gift, Jesus didn't *have* to give Himself as a sacrifice for us, either, but He loved us so much that He offered up Himself so we could receive the gift of eternal life!

And, that's what an offering is. It's something you give to God because you love Him. Let's show God how much we love Him with all of our gifts. *(If you wrapped small gifts for the kids—it would be a great time to give them!)*

Notes: _____

_____

_____

_____

_____

_____

_____

Series: The Superkid Creed II

DAY 4: FOOD FUN — HEART KRISPIES

Suggested Time: 10 minutes

Memory Verse: Live a life filled with love, following the example of Christ. He loved us and offered himself as a sacrifice for us, a pleasing aroma to God. —Ephesians 5:2

Ingredients: ☐ Cooking spray or oil, ☐ 3 Tablespoons butter, ☐ 6 Cups mini-marshmallows, ☐ Red food coloring, ☐ 9 Cups crisped rice cereal

Supplies: ☐ 11x17-Inch baking sheet, ☐ Waxed paper, ☐ Hot plate, ☐ Large spoon, ☐ Measuring cup, ☐ Large cooking pot, ☐ Hot pads (potholders), ☐ Plastic bags, ☐ Yarn or ribbon, ☐ Heart-shaped cookie cutter

Lesson Instructions:

Today, we are making heart-shaped crispy treats for our family and friends! Mmmmm! We want to do our best to make them as pretty and tasty as possible.

Can you think of some people we can make them for?

Let's read through the recipe together so we will know what to do: *(Take your kids through the recipe together as you say the steps out-loud. Then let the children help as you make the crisped rice cereal treats.)*

- Lightly coat an 11x17-inch baking sheet with cooking spray, and set aside.
- Melt butter in a large pot over low heat.
- Add the marshmallows, stirring constantly until melted.
- Remove pan from heat.
- Stir in drops of red food coloring until the color is just the right shade.
- Add the crisped rice cereal, stirring until evenly coated with marshmallow mixture.
- Spoon onto the oil-coated or cooking-sprayed baking sheet.
- With waxed paper (or lightly buttered hands), smooth out the mixture, spreading to an even thickness.
- When mixture cools, use cookie cutter to cut out heart shapes, placing each treat in a clear plastic bag.
- Tie a yarn bow on each bag, and they're ready for giving!

Home Bible Study for Kids • Week 10: I Walk in Love

Final Word:

I really enjoyed cooking with you. *(You can enjoy some of the treats with the children, but remember to save some to give away!)* And I'm so excited you are giving these treats away to _____. *(Name some of the people the children mentioned earlier.)* What about you? Are *you* excited to give them away too?

Having someone in mind when you're doing something makes it so much more special. Because you love the person you're baking for, you put love into every step from pouring in the marshmallows to making sure the color's just right, and even making sure not to eat them all yourself! It's actually very enjoyable to insert love into ALL that we do. When we do things for God, we are inserting love into every area of our lives.

Option:

Have your Superkids write a note to attach to each ribbon, telling the person who receives the gift what the giver loves most about him/her.

Notes: _____

_____

_____

_____

_____

_____

_____

_____

_____

_____

_____

_____

_____

_____

_____

_____

_____

Home Bible Study for Kids • Week 10: I Walk in Love

DAY 5: GAME TIME

FILLED WITH LOVE

Suggested Time: 10-15 minutes

Memory Verse: Live a life filled with love, following the example of Christ. He loved us and offered himself as a sacrifice for us, a pleasing aroma to God. —Ephesians 5:2

Supplies: ☐ 14 Pieces of paper, ☐ Markers

Prior to Game:

Cut the 14 pieces of paper in half. With your markers, write 1 word of the day's memory verse on each, with the reference on the last piece. Place out of order and hand the first contestant the stack. It may be best to start with the oldest, and move down to the youngest so the younger ones can watch before their turn.

Game Instructions:

(One at a time, have your kids compete to place the stack in order. Time them with your stopwatch. They may need to spread them out on the floor. Note all the times, and after the last child has had a turn, everyone can work on it together.)

Today, we're going to test our memories! Let's see who can remember our memory verse. One word from the verse is placed on each piece of paper, with the reference on its own sheet too. Let's see who can put the words in the correct order.

Game Goal:

Get to know the memory verse and enjoy working together at the end.

Final Word:

I hope you enjoyed the game! And with all that practice, I think you *really* know your memory verse now. Did you enjoy the puzzle? Was it more fun working together and competing or putting the verse together by yourself? *(Allow the children to answer.)* It's fun to win in this world, but the best times we'll ever have are when we are working in love, helping one another as Jesus would. Let's follow our memory verse and lead lives FILLED with love!

Series: The Superkid Creed II

Home Bible Study for Kids • Week 10: I Walk in Love

ACTIVITY PAGE — THE LOVE CODE

 Memory Verse: Live a life filled with love, following the example of Christ. He loved us and offered himself as a sacrifice for us, a pleasing aroma to God. —Ephesians 5:2

 Teacher Tip: Feel free to help your younger Superkids with writing on this one.

Supplies: 1 Copy for each child

Answer key:

DECODE THE MESSAGE USING THE CODE

A	B	C	D	E	F	G	H	I	J	K	L	M	N	O	P	Q	R	S	T	U	V	W	X	Y	Z
Z	Y	X	W	V	U	T	S	R	Q	P	O	N	M	L	K	J	I	H	G	F	E	D	C	B	A

OLEV RH:
LOVE IS

KZGRVMG
PATIENT

PRMW
KIND

IVQLRXRMT DSVM GIFGS DRMH
REJOICING WHEN TRUTH WINS

MVEVI TRERMT FK
NEVER GIVING UP

MVEVI OLHRMT UZRGS
NEVER LOSING FAITH

ZODZBH SLKVUFO
ALWAYS HOPEFUL

MVEVI UZRORMT
NEVER FAILING

OLEV RH MLG...
LOVE IS NOT

KILFW
PROUD

IFWV
RUDE

WVNZMWRMT
DEMANDING

RIIRGZYOV
IRRITABLE

HXLIV-PVVKRMT DILMTH
SCORE-KEEPING WRONGS

IVQLRXRMT ZYLFG RMQFHGRXV
REJOICING ABOUT INJUSTICE

Series: The Superkid Creed II

Home Bible Study for Kids • Week 10: I Walk in Love

 ## ACTIVITY PAGE — THE LOVE CODE

 Memory Verse: Live a life filled with love, following the example of Christ. He loved us and offered himself as a sacrifice for us, a pleasing aroma to God. —Ephesians 5:2

—Ephesians 5:2

THE LOVE CODE

DECODE THE MESSAGE USING THE CODE

| A B C D E F G H I J K L M N O P Q R S T U V W X Y Z |
| Z Y X W V U T S R Q P O N M L K J I H G F E D C B A |

OLEV RH:
____ __

KZGRVMG
_____

MVEVI OLHRMT UZRGS
_____ _____ _____

PRMW
____

ZODZBH SLKVUFO
_____ _____

IVQLRXRMT DSVM GIFGS DRMH
_____ ____ _____ ____

MVEVI UZRORMT
_____ _____

MVEVI TRERMT FK
_____ _____ __

OLEV RH MLG...
____ __ ___

KILFW
_____

RIIRGZYOV
_____

IFWV
____

HXLIV-PVVKRMT DILMTH
_____-_____ _____

WVNZMWRMT
_____

IVQLRXRMT ZYLFG RMQFHGRXV
_____ _____ _____

Home Bible Study for Kids • Week 10: I Walk in Love

Notes:

WEEK 11: I DO NOT GOSSIP, I AM NOT RUDE AND I AM NEVER MEAN

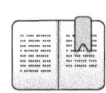 **DAY 1: BIBLE LESSON—
WHAT KIND OF FRIEND ARE YOU?** ▶ 176

 **DAY 2: YOU-SOLVE-IT MYSTERY—
CLUELESS** ▶ 178

 **DAY 3: GIVING LESSON—
FAITH MUSCLES** ▶ 180

 **DAY 4: OBJECT LESSON—
SNOWBALL EFFECT** ▶ 181

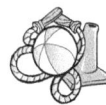 **DAY 5: GAME TIME—BUILT UP!** ▶ 183

 **BONUS: ACTIVITY PAGE—GAB-LIB** ▶ 184

 Memory Verse: Don't use foul or abusive language. Let everything you say be good and helpful, so that your words will be an encouragement to those who hear them. —Ephesians 4:29

Home Bible Study for Kids • Week 11: I Do Not Gossip, I Am Not Rude and I Am Never Mean

WEEK 11: SNAPSHOT

I DO NOT GOSSIP, I AM NOT RUDE AND I AM NEVER MEAN

DAY	TYPE OF LESSON	LESSON TITLE	SUPPLIES
Day 1	Bible Lesson	What Kind of Friend Are You?	None
Day 2	You-Solve-It Mystery	Clueless	"CLUE!" sign or flashing light, Optional Costume: A cute blouse or red shirt if narrating as Superkid Amelia
Day 3	Giving Lesson	Faith Muscles	None
Day 4	Object Lesson	Snowball Effect	Videos: Rolling a snowball to make it larger; making a snowman; an avalanche
Day 5	Game Time	Built Up!	2 Bags of large-sized marshmallows, Table, Stopwatch
Bonus	Activity Page	Gab-Lib	1 Copy for the group, Pencil or pen

Lesson Introduction:

This week you are teaching on a very needed topic. In today's culture, too many people have lost their sensitivity toward others' feelings. Perhaps it stems from our major dependence on electronic communication. We don't see someone's eyes tear up or their feelings obviously hurt as they read or hear the mean things someone may send via email, social media, texting, etc.

Many kids may have become hateful and rude, but it's not going to affect our Superkids! As we said last week, Superkids show love, not gossip, rudeness or cruelty!

Since our kids are surrounded by this behavior, we must bring attention to it, clearly stating, "This kind of behavior is NOT OK with God!" And, one thing about a rude, gossipy, mean spirit—it's contagious! God's Word clearly tells us to stay away from people like that. Why is that important? Because we want people to see that God is love, NOT: God is mean!

Love,

Commander Kellie

Commander Kellie

Series: The Superkid Creed II

Lesson Outline:

Sometimes people will judge you because of the way your children act. In the same way, people judge our God by the way we, His children, act. So often God gets a bad reputation because His kids are rude, mean or gossiping. This week, help your kids to see how hurtful they can be to God, others and themselves when they don't put those things behind them and treat people with respect the way God does.

I. YOUR WORDS AFFECT PEOPLE—BUILD THEM UP OR TEAR THEM DOWN

   a. If you are mean or rude, it can affect friendships. Proverbs 11:9-11

   b. If you can't say something nice, don't say anything at all! Verse 12

   c. Neither God, family nor friends will trust you if you are rude or mean, and gossip. Verse 13

   d. "Your kindness will reward you, but your cruelty will destroy you." Verse 17

II. GOSSIP AND HATRED WILL BRING TROUBLE ON YOU! Numbers 12:1-14

   a. Miriam and Aaron gossiped about Moses.

   b. The Lord always hears what we say (and so does your enemy Satan!).

   c. The Lord's presence (and protection) departed, and Miriam became sick with leprosy.

   d. Moses was kind and pleaded with God to heal her—and He did!

III. IF YOU WANT TO ENJOY LIFE, SPEAK AND DO GOOD THINGS 1 Peter 3:8-12

   a. Be encouraging and kind. Ephesians 4:29-32

   b. Tame your tongue, or it can mess up your whole life! James 3:2-12

   c. The wisdom from God will help you say good things and not be mean to people. James 3:13-17

   d. As you practice good conversation, you'll begin to know the right things to say to people. Colossians 4:5-6

Notes: _____

Home Bible Study for Kids • Week 11: I Do Not Gossip, I Am Not Rude and I Am Never Mean

DAY 1: BIBLE LESSON

WHAT KIND OF FRIEND ARE YOU?

Memory Verse: Don't use foul or abusive language. Let everything you say be good and helpful, so that your words will be an encouragement to those who hear them. —Ephesians 4:29

Words are powerful! Listening to God's wisdom on the power of words will certainly make you think twice before letting your mouth be a tool for gossip, lies and rudeness. When you build others up, you're also building up your spirit man! But tearing others down tears down your spirit, too.

Read Proverbs 11:5-17:
We Live by Our Words

The godly are directed by honesty; the wicked fall beneath their load of sin. The godliness of good people rescues them; the ambition of treacherous people traps them.

When the wicked die, their hopes die with them, for they rely on their own feeble strength. The godly are rescued from trouble, and it falls on the wicked instead. With their words, the godless destroy their friends, but knowledge will rescue the righteous.

The whole city celebrates when the godly succeed; they shout for joy when the wicked die. Upright citizens are good for a city and make it prosper, but the talk of the wicked tears it apart.

It is foolish to belittle one's neighbor; a sensible person keeps quiet. A gossip goes around telling secrets, but those who are trustworthy can keep a confidence.

Without wise leadership, a nation falls; there is safety in having many advisers. There's danger in putting up security for a stranger's debt; it's safer not to guarantee another person's debt.

A gracious woman gains respect, but ruthless men gain only wealth. Your kindness will reward you, but your cruelty will destroy you.

Discussion Questions:

1. **Proverbs 11:9**—With their _____, the godless _____ their friends, but knowledge will rescue the _____.

    words, destroy, righteous

2. **Proverbs 11:12**—It is foolish to _____ one's neighbor; a sensible person keeps _____.

    belittle, quiet

Series: The Superkid Creed II

Home Bible Study for Kids • Week 11: I Do Not Gossip, I Am Not Rude and I Am Never Mean

3. **Proverbs 11:13**—A _____ goes around telling _____, but those who are _____ can keep a confidence.

   gossip, secrets, trustworthy

4. **Proverbs 11:17**—Your kindness will _____ you, but your _____ will _____ you.

   reward, cruelty, destroy

5. **When was the last time you spoke unkind things about someone behind his/her back? Discuss.**

6. **Have you recently hurt someone's feelings by saying something you didn't mean? Discuss.**

7. **When was the last time you spoke <u>good</u> things about someone behind his/her back? Discuss.**

   Remember, it takes just as much energy to say good things behind someone's back as it does to say bad things about him/her. But when you speak good things, you're building UP your spirit and the other person's—NOT tearing down.

   Notes: _____

Series: The Superkid Creed II

Home Bible Study for Kids • Week 11: I Do Not Gossip, I Am Not Rude and I Am Never Mean

DAY 2: YOU-SOLVE-IT MYSTERY — CLUELESS

Suggested Time: 10 minutes

Memory Verse: Don't use foul or abusive language. Let everything you say be good and helpful, so that your words will be an encouragement to those who hear them. —Ephesians 4:29

Teacher Tip: If you have four girls, you can let them each play a character as you narrate, or do the whole thing yourself, assuming a different voice for each character.

Supplies: ☐ "CLUE!" sign or flashing light
Optional Costume: ☐ A cute blouse or red shirt if narrating as Superkid Amelia

Background:

Are you ready for a mystery? You can solve it yourself! Listen closely for clues and see if you can figure out the answer by the time we get to the end of the story. (**Bolded words** are slightly stressed because they help solve the mystery. For younger kids, you could hold up a "CLUE!" sign, or flash a light when a clue is revealed.)

Story: Clueless

(Superkid Amelia begins to tell the story):

Cadet Melissa loved to joke around with people. She knew God had made her funny, and she loved to make people laugh.

One day during the Cadets' morning run, Melissa's friend Jenny tripped on a tree branch in the middle of the road. Melissa could tell that Jenny was hurt, so after she prayed for her, she laughed, trying to lighten the mood and said, **"Well, you're just a regular klutz, aren't you?"**

Jenny stood up, smiled and said, "Thanks, Melissa, for praying for me. You run ahead, I'm going to walk and talk to Jesus."

"You sure, Jen? I can walk with you," said Melissa.

Jenny smiled as she replied, "No, I'm absolutely sure! You go on without me."

Melissa waved to her as she jogged back to Headquarters. That day at lunch, as Melissa and her friends Jayden and June were loading their lunch trays, Jayden slipped in a small puddle of water that was on the floor as they made their way back to their seats. Jayden's tray full of food flipped UP into the air and then straight back DOWN onto her new, yellow squad shirt. (Spaghetti on a yellow shirt is kind of hard to cover up!)

Jayden let out a dejected moan as she looked at the mess she had unintentionally made, and tears began to fill her eyes. Melissa could see that she was about to cry. She HATED to see her friends cry.

Series: The Superkid Creed II

Melissa quickly changed the subject. **"Do you remember that time June dropped that test tube in Academy Lab and it started a fire? Your mess is bad, but hers was SO much worse!"** June's face turned bright red as both **June and Jayden looked at each other.**

June reached down to help Jayden up, saying, "Come on Jay, we'll get you all cleaned up and get you another lunch."

"Here, let me help," Melissa said, attempting to assist June in lifting their friend off the floor.

"Thanks Mel, but I think I can do it on my own," said Jayden as she hopped to her feet. "Thanks though," she said, walking away with June.

That weekend was the Cadet retreat for the Yellow Squad. Melissa was so excited, not only because all of her friends were going to be there, but also because she LOVED making s'mores by the campfire.

Melissa's excitement dwindled, however, when they got to the campsite. None of her friends wanted to sit with her, talk to her or room with her! She found herself alone and clueless about the reason why.

That night, during Cadet Evaluations, Commander Kellie helped her see why her friends weren't spending time with her.

So, Superkids, have you solved the mystery? Do you know why Melissa's friends didn't want to be around her? Does anyone know what some of the clues were? *(Allow time for kids to take turns guessing. If no one gets the answer, suggest the clues to them again. Finally, reveal the answer by reading the Solution.)*

Solution:

Commander Kellie gently told Melissa: "Sometimes, you're clueless that your words are hurtful and rude." *She always has the right words to say!* thought Melissa.

Commander Kellie had just mentioned she was going to begin teaching about how the pirates in Proverbs can invade your actions and words.

She said, "Sweetie, you haven't been speaking with love. In your attempt to lighten the mood, you sometimes use your words to tear down rather than to build up. Your friends don't want to spend time with you because when they do, you hurt them rather than love them. That's what pirates do: They sneak in and try to sabotage everything. That's why you're trained in Superkid Academy to put His Word in your heart, so HIS WORDS come out of your mouth. I'll be teaching you all about that in the weeks to come. For now, why don't you repent to the Lord and to your friends for not walking in love toward them?"

Melissa nodded. She knew Commander Kellie was speaking the truth. The first thing she did after her meeting with Commander Kellie was to rush over to her friends, share what she had learned and promise to never be clueless again with her words. They all hugged and assured her she was loved and forgiven!

Notes: _____

Home Bible Study for Kids • Week 11: I Do Not Gossip, I Am Not Rude and I Am Never Mean

DAY 3: GIVING LESSON — FAITH MUSCLES

Suggested Time: 10 minutes

Offering Scripture: For the Scriptures say, "If you want to enjoy life and see many happy days, keep your tongue from speaking evil and your lips from telling lies. Turn away from evil and do good. Search for peace, and work to maintain it. The eyes of the Lord watch over those who do right, and his ears are open to their prayers. But the Lord turns his face against those who do evil." —1 Peter 3:10-12

Lesson Instructions:

Who's got muscles here? *(Begin flexing your arms, and get your kids to flex theirs as well.)* Wow! Look at all those muscles! You're all so strong!

Does anyone here ever work out? Let's see—who would like to volunteer? *(You could arm-wrestle with a volunteer to make it fun.)*

You know, our arms may be powerful, but did you know that our words are even *more* powerful? *(Read 1 Peter 3:10-12 aloud.)*

God's Word says *our* words are powerful, and when our speech is good and pleasing to God, He can bless us. When we are believing God for something, our words must line up with His words. His words are kind, loving, truthful and full of faith.

When we speak what He speaks, we are putting ourselves in the perfect place for THE BLESSING.

Let's begin using our faith muscle—OUR MOUTHS. Let's say this together: "I am BLESSED. Everything I set my hands to will prosper. I live in The Sweet Life. THE BLESSING is fully at work in me!"

Superkids, this week continue to speak what God speaks and watch THE BLESSING pour into your life!

Notes: _____

_____

_____

_____

_____

_____

_____

_____

Series: The Superkid Creed II

Home Bible Study for Kids • Week 11: I Do Not Gossip, I Am Not Rude and I Am Never Mean

DAY 4: OBJECT LESSON — SNOWBALL EFFECT

Suggested Time: 5-7 minutes

Memory Verse: Don't use foul or abusive language. Let everything you say be good and helpful, so that your words will be an encouragement to those who hear them. —Ephesians 4:29

Teacher Tip: If you have access to snow outside, this is a great time to build a snowman and show your kids what a "snowball effect" really is.

Supplies: ☐ Videos: rolling a snowball to make it larger; making a snowman; an avalanche

Lesson Instructions:

Do you like snow? It's cold, but it's beautiful, and it's fun to play in. Snow is very interesting. Did you know that there are no two snowflakes alike? Even though there are millions and millions of them, each one is unique. Snowflakes are little ice crystals that float down from the sky and turn everything white and pretty. Some people gather up fresh snow and make snow ice cream out of it while others pack snow together in their hands and make a snowball.

If you roll a snowball in wet, sticky snow, it will collect more snow and grow in size. That's the way snowmen are made. You roll three snowballs around in the snow until they get big enough to make your snowman. *(Show video of making a snowman, and rolling a snowball that gets bigger and bigger.)*

If you roll a snowball down a snow-covered hill, the snowball will grow bigger and bigger until it can do some real damage. What starts out soft and fluffy can become so big and heavy, it can knock you down or start a dangerous avalanche. It's amazing that something that looks so harmless and starts out so small could cause so much damage! *(Show video of an avalanche.)*

This is much like our topic this week: "I do not gossip. I am not rude and I am never mean." You see, words are kind of like snow; you can make something good out of them, or you can make something mean by gossiping.

Gossip often starts out small like a snowflake. Then the small statement said about someone starts to grow, becoming a huge mess and causing a lot of damage. The damage is not only to the person you're gossiping about, but also to you. Nobody wants to hang around a gossiper. You see, if someone is whispering gossip about someone TO you, then you can be sure they will be whispering gossip to someone else ABOUT you.

Proverbs 11:17 says, "Your kindness will reward you, but your cruelty will destroy you."

Have you ever noticed that a lot of gossip is whispered? When people gossip, they want to hide what they're saying so they whisper it. They are talking behind someone's back. That's a sure sign that what they have to say is not good. If what you have to say is good, you won't mind shouting it from the rooftops, but if it's bad, you'll want to hide it. That's one way to tell if you should speak or keep quiet.

If you have a snowball in your hand and you decide not to throw it, then it will melt away and not cause anyone harm. It's the same with gossip. When you have a thought that's not too nice, it will melt away if you don't speak it. When those thoughts come, take them captive and replace them with God's thoughts. When you speak God's Word, great things happen.

Say this after me: "I take evil thoughts captive and replace them with God's Word. I only speak good things." Praise God! We are going to have a great day!

Notes:

Home Bible Study for Kids • Week 11: I Do Not Gossip, I Am Not Rude and I Am Never Mean

DAY 5: GAME TIME

BUILT UP!

Suggested Time: 10 minutes

Memory Verse: Don't use foul or abusive language. Let everything you say be good and helpful, so that your words will be an encouragement to those who hear them. —Ephesians 4:29

Supplies: ☐ 2 Bags of large-sized marshmallows, ☐ Table, ☐ Stopwatch

Game Instructions:

Choose your contestants. Each contestant will be given 5 large marshmallows.

Contestants must place their hands behind their backs and, using only their mouths, stack 5 marshmallows that must remain stacked for at least 3 seconds. Use your stopwatch to time contestants.

Game Goal:

The Cadet who stacks his/her marshmallows the fastest and whose stack remains standing for all 3 seconds, wins!

Final Word:

Today we had to carefully use our mouths to stack marshmallows. If we didn't really watch where we were placing each marshmallow, the whole stack tumbled over.

It's the same way with our words. We must carefully watch the words that come out of our mouths. Just like you used your mouths to build up the marshmallow towers, choose today to use your mouth to speak words that help people stay built up!

Notes: _____

_____

_____

_____

_____

_____

_____

_____

Series: The Superkid Creed II

Home Bible Study for Kids • Week 11: I Do Not Gossip, I Am Not Rude and I Am Never Mean

ACTIVITY PAGE — GAB-LIB

Memory Verse: Don't use foul or abusive language. Let everything you say be good and helpful, so that your words will be an encouragement to those who hear them. —Ephesians 4:29

Teacher Tip: This activity page's fun to do as a group. If you choose to use it as a group activity, you'll only need one copy. Choose children who are good writers to write on the gab-lib and allow the kids to take turns choosing words and phrases.

Supplies: ☐ 1 Copy for the group

When you begin to gossip or speak words, it's amazing how out of control your mouth can get! Fill in the gab-lib below. Read aloud, then compare the differences with the original passage.

Remember:

Noun: person, place or thing (strawberry, dog, Jimmy, home)

Adjective: describing words (like awesome, pretty)

Verb: action (often ending in -ing)

Adverb: describing word (often ending in –ly)

Original Story/Answer Key:

While the Israelites were stuck in the wilderness, Miriam and Aaron talked about Moses behind his back because he had married a Cushite woman. But God heard them talking. God said, "Come out, you three to the Tent of Meeting." They walked out, and God told them how close He and Moses were, that they spoke closely together as friends. His anger blazed, and when He left, Miriam had leprosy! Aaron begged Moses for forgiveness, and Moses prayed to God that He would heal Miriam. God told him to leave her outside the camp for seven days, and then she would be healed.

Series: The Superkid Creed II

Home Bible Study for Kids • Week 11: I Do Not Gossip, I Am Not Rude and I Am Never Mean

ACTIVITY PAGE — GAB-LIB

Memory Verse: Don't use foul or abusive language. Let everything you say be good and helpful, so that your words will be an encouragement to those who hear them. —Ephesians 4:29

When you begin to gossip or speak words, it's amazing how out of control your mouth can get! Fill in the gab-lib below. Read aloud, then compare the differences with the original passage.

Remember: *Noun:* person, place or thing (strawberry, dog, Jimmy, home), *Adjective:* describing words (like awesome, pretty), *Verb:* action (often ending in -ing), *Adverb:* describing word (often ending in –ly)

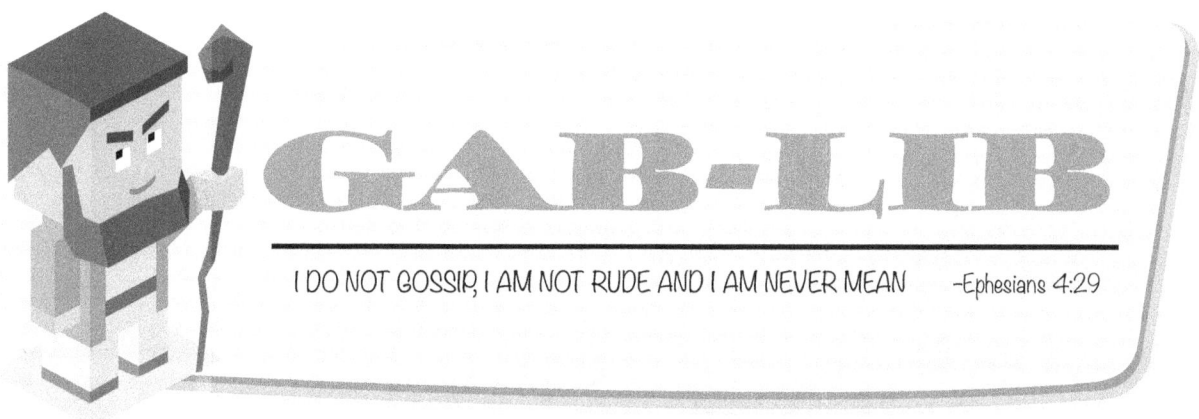

I DO NOT GOSSIP, I AM NOT RUDE AND I AM NEVER MEAN —Ephesians 4:29

While the _____ were _____ in the _____ , _____ and _____
    (group of people)   (action ends in -ing)   (place)   (person/Name #1)   (person/Name #2)

talked about _____ behind his/her _____ because _____ had _____ a Cushite woman.
    (person/Name #3)   (part of body)   (Name #3) (action ends in -ed)

But _____ heard them _____. _____ said, "Come out, you 3 to the _____."
  (person/Name #4)   (action end in -ing) (Name #4)   (place)

They walked out, and _____ told them how _____ _____ and _____ were, that they
                     (Name #4)   (describing word) (Name #4) (Name #3)

spoke _____ together as _____ . _____ anger _____ , and when he/she left, _____
(describing word ending in -ly) (plural thing –ends in s) (Name #4) (action ending in –ed)   (Name #1)

had _____ ! _____ begged _____ for _____ , and _____ _____ to _____
    (disease)   (Name #2)   (Name #3)   (thing)   (Name #4) (action ends in –ed) (Name #4)

that he/she would _____ _____. _____ told him/her to leave _____ outside the _____
               (action)   (Name #1) (Name #4)   (Name #1)   (place)

for _____ days, and then _____ would be _____.
   (number)   (Name #1) (action ending in –ed)

Home Bible Study for Kids • Week 11: I Do Not Gossip, I Am Not Rude and I Am Never Mean

Notes:

Series: The Superkid Creed II

WEEK 12: THE PIRATES IN PROVERBS, PART 1

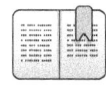 DAY 1: BIBLE LESSON—NEVER FORGET ▸ 190

 DAY 2: READ-ALOUD—
SOLOMON IN ALL HIS GLORY, PART 1 ▸ 192

 DAY 3: GIVING LESSON—
X MARKS THE SPOT ▸ 199

 DAY 4: FOOD FUN—SUMMER IN A CUP ▸ 200

 DAY 5: GAME TIME—
MAP YOUR TREASURE ▸ 202

 BONUS: ACTIVITY PAGE—
TREASURE HUNT ▸ 204

 Memory Verse: My child, listen to what I say, and treasure my commands. —Proverbs 2:1

Home Bible Study for Kids • Week 12: The Pirates in Proverbs, Part 1

WEEK 12: SNAPSHOT — THE PIRATES IN PROVERBS, PART 1

DAY	TYPE OF LESSON	LESSON TITLE	SUPPLIES
Day 1	Bible Lesson	Never Forget	1 Per child: pen/pencil, paper
Day 2	Read-Aloud	Solomon in All His Glory, Part 1	None
Day 3	Giving Lesson	X Marks the Spot	Printed treasure map, Gold candy coins (optional)
Day 4	Food Fun	Summer in a Cup	2 Quarts cranberry juice, 2 Quarts cherry soda, 2 Quarts fruit punch, 1 Pint strawberry sherbet, Large punch bowl, Ladle, Cups for everyone, Ice cream scoop, Can opener, Straws
Day 5	Game Time	Map Your Treasure	Printed treasure maps (1 per person or team), Pencils or crayons
Bonus	Activity Page	Treasure Hunt	1 Copy for each child, Crayons or colored pencils

Lesson Introduction:

Hopefully, your kids met our pirates in Volume 3, weeks 1-4, and remember the lessons they learned about how pirates are out to steal God's best from you! The kids understood pirates so quickly that we wanted to bring them back to do our review weeks! If you need to, pull those lessons out and go over them again for yourself so you can remember things you may want to remind your Superkids about pirates and treasure!

So, get those pirate threads out again! Have fun with the seafaring talk, and you might even dress like a captain as you bring them the Word for the next two weeks. Superkids will enjoy this week and next. It's also a great reminder to your kids if you decorate, make it fun, and be creative! Aye, and just follow the leading of the Holy Spirit, Matey!

Love,

Commander Kellie

Commander Kellie

Series: The Superkid Creed II

Lesson Outline:

For those who've discussed the "Pirates of Proverbs" before, you know that a pirate is a thief, and God's Word is your treasure map. Pirates are always trying to steal God's words that have been planted into our hearts. This review will help your Superkids hold fast to what they've been taught.

I. REMEMBER WHY WE HAVE A CREED

   a. Our Creed is God's Word that we store in our hearts. Proverbs 3:1-2

   b. The Creed helps us to commit ourselves to God's ways and instructions. Isaiah 55:7 NKJV

   c. Our Creed will help us remember and choose ways and instructions when we are under pressure to do wrong. Proverbs 3:5-6

II. GOD'S WORD AND THE CREED ARE LIKE A TREASURE MAP
2 Timothy 3:14-17

   a. They tell you which way to go.

   b. They warn you of traps.

   c. They will correct you, direct you and protect you.

   d. They will prepare you for every good thing God has planned for you—treasure!

III. PROVERBS IS FULL OF WISDOM AND WARNS YOU OF PIRATES
Proverbs 1:1-4, 2:1-4

   a. A pirate will steal from you.

   b. A pirate will get you off track.

   c. A pirate will bring you trouble.

   d. When you allow a pirate in, it will steal God's plan for you!

   e. Say, "No Pirates Here!"

Notes: _____

Home Bible Study for Kids • Week 12: The Pirates in Proverbs, Part 1

DAY 1: BIBLE LESSON — NEVER FORGET

Memory Verse: My child, listen to what I say, and treasure my commands. —Proverbs 2:1

Supplies: 1 Per child: pen/pencil, paper

Even after the Lord freed them from slavery in Egypt, the children of Israel doubted His love and goodness and created a false idol to worship in His place. This passage is a great reminder of how far we can move away from God when we don't listen to Him and value His presence in our lives. God desires that we follow Him faithfully and remember The Sweet Life He has given us through His Son, Jesus.

Read Exodus 32:1-26, 29:

(Read these verses aloud and remind the children of the Memory Verse. Discuss how the children of Israel didn't do what God said and didn't value His words to them. They ended up grieving the heart of God—the One who had delivered them from slavery in Egypt and fed them with manna in the wilderness. Discuss Proverbs 3:1-6 and the blessings of listening to and treasuring God's commands.)

Our Proverbs:
(Proverbs 3:1-6)

My child, never forget the things I have taught you.

Store my commands in your heart.

If you do this, you will live many years,

and your life will be satisfying.

Never let loyalty and kindness leave you!

Tie them around your neck as a reminder.

Write them deep within your heart.

Then you will find favor with both God and people,

and you will earn a good reputation.

Trust in the Lord with all your heart;

do not depend on your own understanding.

Seek his will in all you do,

and he will show you which path to take.

(Lead the children in the confession of the Superkid Creed.)

Series: The Superkid Creed II

YOUR SUPERKID CREED:
The Superkid Creed

I am a Superkid—Servant and child of the Most High God.
Jesus is my Savior and my Lord. I am filled with His Holy Spirit. I obey His written Word.
I hear every word that He speaks to me, and I obey quickly without arguing.
I live and walk by faith, not by what I see. I walk in the power of my strong spirit.
I am full of wisdom and understanding. I lay hands on the sick and they recover.
I win people to Jesus. I do not lie—I am always quick to tell the truth.
I do not steal—I am a tither and a giver, not a taker.
My Father makes me wealthy. I do not complain. I work hard to help my family.
I honor and obey my parents and people in authority over me.
I walk in love—I do not gossip, I am not rude and I am never mean.
I put others first and I am not selfish.
I treat other people with respect.
I am always grateful for everything good in my life.
I am fiercely loyal.
I am full of courage and I refuse fear of any kind.
I am merciful and kind.
I am generous and fair-minded.
I do not get offended, and I am quick to forgive.
I always do what is right and I do it right.
I do all things with excellence.
I am diligent and I am not a quitter.
I only allow my eyes and ears and mouth to let in good things.
I keep my heart pure.
I live my life in honor and humility.
I allow nothing to come before God.

Discussion Questions:

1. **Why do we have a Superkid Creed?**

    So we won't forget what we've been taught.

2. **What kind of life will you have if you keep the Superkid Creed?**

    We'll have a long, rich and satisfying life.

3. **What should you never let leave you?**

    Loyalty and kindness

4. **When we seek God's will in all we do, what will He do?**

    He will show us the path to take.

5. **Have each child write down as much as he/she can remember of the Superkid Creed.**

    Help children to memorize the Superkid Creed.

Home Bible Study for Kids • Week 12: The Pirates in Proverbs, Part 1

DAY 2: READ-ALOUD — SOLOMON IN ALL HIS GLORY, PART 1

Suggested Time: 15 minutes

Memory Verse: *My child, listen to what I say, and treasure my commands.* —Proverbs 2:1

Background:

This is a fun twist on Solomon's story in 1 Kings 3 when he asked God for wisdom. After reading today's story, discuss how it affects your kids. What value does wisdom have today, especially in a world driven by money, cool cars and vanity?

Story:

Although Jamie seemed like an ordinary boy with an ordinary desk and bed in his ordinary bedroom, Jamie was actually quite EXTRA-ordinary. But even extraordinary 11-year-olds can sometimes deal with the stresses and anxieties of life. He sat at his desk that was covered in homework, papers and books with an equal amount of homework on his floor.

He sat, just staring at his walls, wide-eyed and in shock. His sister, Natalie, entered, but he was so engrossed, he didn't even see her.

"Hey, Jamie!" Natalie said. But nothing. Not even a blink. "Jamie!" she tried again. Jamie continued to stare at the void in front of him.

Natalie cleared her throat: "Jameson Porter Grayson the third!" She screamed and rushed at his face waving her hands like a crazy person.

"Ahhhhhhh!" Jamie snapped into action. "You scared me!" he said, trying to recover his senses.

Natalie laughed, "Your face…was…haha…hilarious!"

"Please, don't do that to me ever again!" Jamie continued to try and shake it off. But Natalie's laughing didn't help calm his nerves. He shot her an icy look.

"I kept calling you, but you were on another planet," she said, trying to squelch her giggles.

"What?" He really didn't hear her until she was in his face.

"When I came in, I said your name like 10 times, and you just stared into space like your life was over or something," Natalie continued.

"My life *is* over," said Jamie, remembering his previous troubles. His head fell.

"You're 11."

"Eleven and a half."

Series: The Superkid Creed II

Home Bible Study for Kids • Week 12: The Pirates in Proverbs, Part 1

Though not much older, Natalie was not fooled. "Your life is *not* over," she said.

Jamie looked at her so hopelessly; she took pity on him. "What's up?" she asked.

Jamie just shook his head.

"You can tell me. I won't tell anyone," Natalie said.

He opened his mouth to start, but didn't know where to begin. He let out a dramatic sigh.

Natalie became genuinely curious, "What? What is it?"

With another sign, Jamie confessed, "I got an F on my science quiz."

"It's just a quiz. It's not even a test!"

Jamie was incredulous, "An F!"

Natalie couldn't understand his freak-out. "It probably won't affect your grade at all."

"F, as in *failure!*"

"What's the big deal? You'll get a better grade next time," she said.

But Jamie had lost faith. "No...I just...I can't...like...it's impossible. I've been staring at my science book for hours, and I don't get it! And I NEED to get it because I want to be an important doctor someday. And I read that doctors have to take a lot of science in school, and all these different sciences like chemistry and anatomy and physiology and organic chemistry."

"What is that? Like organic fruit?" Natalie asked, clearly not wanting to become a doctor herself.

But Jamie was still so extremely stressed, "I don't *know!*" he said. "I just read that I'm going to have to take it in college, but Nats, if I can't even understand this science, how am I ever going to get into a good college like...like Harvard, or something, so I can get my medical degree? Good schools won't want me if I've gotten F's in all my science classes since the 5th grade. They'll laugh at me. And then I won't be able to get into a good medical school, which I have to go to for four MORE years. And then I won't have any money, and no girl will want to marry me, so I'll have to get stuck with someone like Carrie Cowlicker."

"Carrie Cowlicker—with the pig face?" Nat asked.

"Yeah," Jamie said with a gulp, "she asked me out."

"Yikes! Hope you said no," Natalie said with a frown.

"Of course I did. Mom and Dad would flip!"

But Natalie poked fun at him. "You don't like her...just a little bit?"

"Ewwww, stop it! Girls aren't supposed to ask boys out anyway," Jamie said.

Natalie nodded. Jamie continued his rant: "But if I don't start passing science, that's who I'm going to end up with. Forget being the president of the United States or an astronaut or something cool like that. I'll be stuck with a horrible life. No friends..."

"Hey," Natalie interrupted, "you'll have me."

Jamie nodded. "One friend...and Carrie Cow-face-licker will probably ask me to marry her, and I'll have to say yes because no one else would ever like me because I'm stupid and…"

"Hold it!" Natalie couldn't take any more of this talk. "You are not stupid!"

Jamie's head fell onto his desk. "Yes I am. How am I going to be a doctor when…"

Natalie interrupted again, "That is a really, really long way from now."

Jamie lifted his head up. "Would you let me operate on you when I'm a doctor?"

Natalie laughed. "No way!"

"See," Jamie's head fell again, "I'm a failure."

"OK, stop it. You're not a failure. You *are* a little pathetic, though." Nat didn't know how much more of this she could take.

"Sorry. You asked. I just want to know what to do. I wish I knew how…to know," Jamie said with urgency.

"Know what?"

"What to do with my life! Like they talk about at church and stuff. Or at school. I mean, I think I want to be a doctor."

"Why?" Nat asked.

"They're smart, and they make a lot of money."

"Great reasons," Nat said sarcastically.

Jamie defended himself, "I mean, they help people, too."

"Of course," Nat retorted.

"And I want to have a sweet ride—a cool car and a nice house."

"Wow. You're like…getting wayyyy ahead of yourself. What are you…35 now?"

"I just like to think about the future."

"Umm, I'm pretty sure thinking about the future almost put you in a state of shock," Natalie pointed out.

"It's a lot to think about! I want a lot of things, but I'm never really sure because different days, I really do want to be an astronaut."

Nat couldn't help but dash his dream, "That requires a lot of science, too."

"Ahhhh!" Jamie slammed his head on his desk. "I can't win!"

"OK. That's it!"

"What?"

"Where's your Bible?" Natalie was also a Superkid.

"I dunno," Jamie said sheepishly.

"No wonder you don't know what God wants you to do."

Home Bible Study for Kids • Week 12: The Pirates in Proverbs, Part 1

"I think it's under my bed." Jamie looked under his bed. After a little digging, he found his Bible. "Here it is!"

He handed it to her, and she wiped the dust off with a little cough. "OK. Do you know King Solomon's story?" she asked.

"Yeah, he was the richest guy to ever live! He was the king of Israel. He had the biggest house, the nicest clothes…."

Natalie rolled her eyes, "Yes, but do you know how he got all that stuff?"

"Uhhh…der," Jamie said matter-of-factly, "he was the king."

"Yeah, but how did he become the richest king ever?" she asked.

Jamie guessed, "He had a lot of wealthy wives?"

"He did, but that's another story," Nat said.

Jamie countered, "See! He didn't have to marry Carrie."

But Nat laughed, "Actually, he had a lot of wives. Chances are some of them were really ugly."

"Yeah, but that probably just means they had more money."

Natalie opened the Bible. "Forget the money and the wives. In 1 Kings 3, Solomon had just become king, and he was really nervous because…"

Jamie sighed, "See…I wish I was a king. That would be easy."

"What? Are you crazy?" Nat said.

"No. Because you'd be a prince for all your life—and you'd know that, no matter what, whether you did good in class or not, you'd still be king someday."

Natalie was done with the excuses. "You are not allowed to talk anymore. Let me read. So, Solomon had just become king. And even though he was trained for it, he was still really nervous because all of Israel depended on him. He had just married Pharaoh's daughter…."

"See…he wasn't stuck with the cow-licker…" Jamie started.

"Stop talking." Nat interrupted his train of thought. "So Solomon loved the Lord and followed the decrees of his father. He was worshiping God at an altar in Gibeon." She began reading from 1 Kings 3:5, "That night, the Lord appeared to Solomon in a dream,"

"At the place of worship?" Jamie asked, confused.

"No, he was asleep. Probably in his bed somewhere." Natalie opened her mouth to read again, but…

Jamie asked, "And he was staying at Gideon's house?"

"No…. Pay attention! He was at Gibeon. It was a holy place where he went to worship God. And he had a dream."

"Got it…!" Jamie tried to make a mental note not to interrupt again, but to really listen.

Natalie looked back down at the Bible and opened her mouth to read, but Jamie had another question: "So

Home Bible Study for Kids • Week 12: The Pirates in Proverbs, Part 1

Solomon was dreaming in his bed at the Temple?"

"No!" Nat burst out. "He was at home by this time."

Jamie made an even bigger mental note to really, really not interrupt again.

Natalie composed herself. "So, he worshipped at the Temple, then went home and went to sleep—in his bed, at home." Jamie nodded.

She continued reading her Bible, "That night the Lord appeared to Solomon in a dream, and God said, 'What do you want? Ask, and I will give it to you!'"

"OOOoooh. Like Aladdin and the genie in the lamp!" Jamie said, but then clamped his hands over his mouth.

Natalie started to explode again, but she thought about it. "Yeah, actually, kind of like that—except this really happened. There's no such thing as a genie in a lamp."

"Wouldn't it be awesome if there were, though?"

Nat was getting frustrated again. "Urggghhh. You don't need a genie or a lamp!"

"But I'd get three wishes!"

"Do you want to know King Solomon's secret to success or not?"

"Yes."

"Then remember, there is no genie in a lamp and no three wishes. But God is real, and He asked King Solomon what he wanted."

"OK. Chill out." Jamie said the words you should *never* say to an angry sister!

Natalie threw him a look and he piped down. She looked down at her Bible again, and got an idea. "Out of curiosity..." she asked, "if you did get three wishes from a genie what would they be?"

"You just said that genies weren't real."

"All right then, if God said, 'Jamie, what do you want? Ask, and I will give it to you.'"

Jamie thought about it. "That's a big question. I'd have to think about it."

"King Solomon answered it in his sleep, so don't think too hard," Nat retorted.

Jamie shrugged. "OK. I want to be a doctor. I want an awesome car that goes really, really fast...and a huge house with a pool...and lots of money. And I want to be famous." He paused. "I mean, I want to be able to give money to poor people, too, and..."

Natalie looked back down at her Bible. "Good to know. So this is what Solomon said to the Lord: 'You showed faithful love to your servant my father, David, because he was honest and true and faithful to you. And you have continued your faithful love to him today by giving him a son to sit on his throne.'"

Jamie was confused. "What kind of answer is that?" he asked.

Natalie replied, "A good answer. He was giving praise to God. That's probably why God had asked him what he wanted in the first place, because Solomon had spent time worshipping Him that day."

Jamie was ready for the punchline. "When does he say what he wants?"

Natalie read the rest of Solomon's reply, "Now, O Lord my God, you have made me king instead of my father, David, but I am like a little child who doesn't know his way around." Nat looked up and added: "See…he admits to God he was nervous about not knowing how to handle the huge responsibility of being king. He doesn't know what to…"

"But what does he pick?" Jamie earnestly wanted to know.

Natalie continued reading. "And here I am in the midst of your own chosen people, a nation so great and numerous they cannot be counted." Nat gave a pointed look to Jamie.

Jamie responded, "Yeah, I guess his job doesn't sound so easy."

Nat smiled and continued reading, "Give me an understanding heart so that I can govern your people well and know the difference between right and wrong. For who by himself is able to govern this great people of yours?"

"That's it?" Jamie was shocked. "He asked to know right and wrong?"

Natalie nodded.

Jamie didn't understand. "But he could have asked for anything!"

"Yeah," Nat replied, "and he asked for wisdom."

"But he could have asked for a lot of other things, too. God didn't even tell him that he only had three wishes."

Natalie was glad he had begun to understand. "But, that just shows you how much Solomon valued the wisdom from God to know right from wrong."

Jamie shook his head. "That's just weird," he said.

But Nat smiled, "God didn't think so." She looked back down to read, "The Lord was pleased that Solomon had asked for wisdom. So, God replied, 'Because you have asked for wisdom in governing my people with justice and have not asked for a long life or wealth or the death of your enemies…'" She threw Jamie a look. He felt bad for his response earlier. She continued, "God said, 'I will give you what you asked for! I will give you a wise and understanding heart such as no one else has had or ever will have! And I will also give you what you did not ask for—riches and fame!'"

"God really said that?" Jamie was astounded.

"Look!" Nat showed him the Bible, pointing to what she just read.

Jamie mumbled while reading it for himself, "And I will also give you what you did not ask for—riches and fame!"

He was shocked! He kept reading. "'No other king in all the world will be compared to you for the rest of your life. And if you follow me and obey my decrees and my commands as your father, David, did, I will give you a long life.' Then Solomon woke up and realized it had been a dream."

Jamie questioned Natalie, "But, it says here that he realized it had just been a dream."

She nodded, "But it was a prophetic dream. God speaks to us in dreams, too. Like He did to Joseph. And what God said in Solomon's dream came true."

Jamie soaked it all in for just a moment. But he had another question: "How much money did Solomon have?"

"Ummm...let me see." Natalie looked it up. "Whoa! No one's really sure how much he had, but some say over...." Jamie looked at the information on the screen.

"200 trillion dollars!" Jamie exclaimed.

"That's a lot of money," Nat added.

Jamie repeated it: "200 TRILLION dollars!"

"And he was known around the world and was the wisest ruler," Nat added. But Jamie was stuck on the number.

"That's 14 zeros!"

Natalie laughed as she watched Jamie go to another planet again.

To Be Continued…

Discussion Questions:

1. **How much value do *you* place on wisdom? Would it be the first thing you'd ask for if you could have *anything*?**

   Discuss.

2. **Do you have any friends who value wisdom?**

   Discuss the importance of having wise friends and not hanging around with people obsessed with worldly things.

Notes: _____

_____

_____

_____

_____

_____

_____

_____

_____

_____

_____

_____

Home Bible Study for Kids • Week 12: The Pirates in Proverbs, Part 1

DAY 3: GIVING LESSON — X MARKS THE SPOT

Suggested Time: 10 minutes

Offering Scripture: [I thank my God] for your fellowship (your sympathetic cooperation and contributions and partnership) in advancing the good news.... —Philippians 1:5, AMPC

Supplies: ☐ Printed treasure map, ☐ Gold candy coins (optional)

Prior to Lesson:

Print a treasure map. It can be used again for the upcoming lesson on Day 5.

Lesson Instructions:

Have you ever been on a scavenger hunt?

What was the one thing that helped you find your prize? That's right, a map!

God's Word is like a map, and it is full of treasures. It guides us as we navigate through life and helps us find what we've been looking for—kind of like an "X" on a treasure map. When we follow God's Word and give our tithes and offerings, we will always have the desires of our hearts.

What are some things that *you* would consider treasure? *(Allow kids to give you several examples.)*

Treasures are not always gold, riches and fine things. Some of the greatest treasures God gives us are not things we can touch. The Holy Spirit, wisdom and love are all treasures we have been given that cannot be bought with money. Jesus paid the price for us to inherit all His treasures, and He shows us how to take God's Word and go on the ultimate treasure hunt. He will show you where X marks the spot so you can unlock any treasure you need in your life.

What are some things *God* considers treasure? *(Allow kids to answer. Discuss.)*

Let's thank God that He not only blesses us with physical treasures, but spiritual ones also!

(If you decide to use the gold candy coins for this lesson, give some to each child.) When we follow God and value His treasures, He will *always* bless us with earthly treasures as well. If we'll seek Him above everything else, and live righteously, He will give us *everything* we need—including money! As we enjoy our yummy chocolate coins, let's remember that doing things God's way will lead us to The Sweet Life He has planned for us!

Series: The Superkid Creed II

Home Bible Study for Kids • Week 12: The Pirates in Proverbs, Part 1

DAY 4: FOOD FUN — SUMMER IN A CUP

Suggested Time: 10-15 minutes

Memory Verse: *My child, listen to what I say, and treasure my commands.* —Proverbs 2:1

Ingredients: ☐ 2 Quarts cranberry juice, ☐ 2 Quarts cherry soda, ☐ 2 Quarts fruit punch, ☐ 1 Pint strawberry sherbet

Supplies: ☐ Large punch bowl, ☐ Ladle, ☐ Cups for everyone, ☐ Ice cream scoop, ☐ Can opener, ☐ Straws

Lesson Instructions:

Do you know what's always great for a party? A really awesome punch! Today, we're going to make what I like to call "summer in a cup"! Catchy sounding, isn't it? I love summer, and I think about it when it's really cold outside. With this recipe, you can have your own summer any time of the year, or even after a long day of school!

This recipe is so easy to remember and very easy to make. The best part is it makes enough to share with others!

First, you're going to need the following ingredients: *(Show the ingredients to the children.)*

- 2 Quarts cranberry juice
- 2 Quarts cherry soda
- 2 Quarts fruit punch
- 1 Pint strawberry sherbet

Now that we have all the ingredients, we'll measure them out, except the strawberry sherbet, and pour them into the punch bowl. *(Combine the ingredients, except the strawberry sherbet, in the punch bowl.)*

Next, we'll stir all the liquids together and make sure they are mixed well. *(Let the children help you stir the ingredients.)*

Now we're going to put 1-2 scoops of sherbet into each of the glasses, and then pour the punch over the sherbet. Mmm…it looks and smells so good!

Are you ready for "summer in a cup"? Get your spoon and straw, and ENJOY! *(Allow your kids to enjoy the punch with you!)*

On a scale of 1-10, 1 being the most awful thing you've ever tried in your life, and 10 being simply delicious, where would you rate "summer in a cup"? *(Allow the children to answer.)*

Series: The Superkid Creed II

Final Word:

Our "summer in a cup" is so good, and yet, it's so easy to make, isn't it? The ingredients are perfect when we mix them together, and it turns out so yummy and even fancy looking!

It makes me think about how easy our Creed—God's Word—is, and when we follow HIS recipe, we end up enjoying The Sweet Life, too!

Thank you so much for your help! Now we have plenty to share!

Notes: _____

Home Bible Study for Kids • Week 12: The Pirates in Proverbs, Part 1

DAY 5: GAME TIME — MAP YOUR TREASURE

 **Suggested Time:** 10 minutes

 Memory Verse: My child, listen to what I say, and treasure my commands. —Proverbs 2:1

 **Teacher Tip:** This is sort of a reverse scavenger hunt. Have fun and make sure to list "treasures" that work for you.

Supplies: ☐ Printed treasure maps (1 per person or team), ☐ Pencils or crayons

Prior to Game:

Find and print a standard treasure map online. This game can be played in teams (2 maps needed) or separately (1 treasure map per person).

Once you've printed the map(s), write different places in your home or meeting space on them (kitchen, bedroom, den, backyard, etc.), creating a map of your search area.

On the back, write a "treasure list" of things the children will have to find. Put them in a different order on each map. (To make the game more exciting, place a few of the list items in places they wouldn't normally be. (For example, place a hammer in the kitchen or bathroom.)

Game Instructions:

Your treasure seekers must hunt for the "treasures" on the back of the map. Once a treasure is found, players must write or draw what they found on the map in the area in which it was found. *(Example: Bobby and Suzi found the hammer in the kitchen, so they would draw a hammer on the map in the "kitchen" area.)*

List Examples:
1. Cheese
2. Spoon
3. Desk
4. Lamp
5. Pillow
6. Hammer
7. Magnet
8. Candle
9. Tennis shoes
10. Umbrella

Series: The Superkid Creed II

Game Goal:

The first person/team to find and write or draw all the items on their map in the correct areas, wins.

Final Word:

Great job, everyone! You worked hard to find the things on your treasure map! While you were searching for the treasures on your list, I'm sure you probably learned where a lot more items are located—even things that weren't on your list!

When we have difficulties in our everyday lives, we need to go to our real Treasure Map—God's Word. His Word will always lead us to the *best* treasures, AND the more we hunt through this map (the Bible), the more we will find even *more* treasures we weren't even searching for!

Notes: _____

Home Bible Study for Kids • Week 12: The Pirates in Proverbs, Part 1

ACTIVITY PAGE — TREASURE HUNT

Memory Verse: My child, listen to what I say, and treasure my commands. —Proverbs 2:1

Supplies: 1 Copy for each child

Find your way to the treasure—the Superkid Creed. Color your "treasure" and display in a familiar place where you will see it every day.

Answer Key:

Series: The Superkid Creed II

Home Bible Study for Kids • Week 12: The Pirates in Proverbs, Part 1

 **ACTIVITY PAGE** — TREASURE HUNT

 Memory Verse: My child, listen to what I say, and treasure my commands. —Proverbs 2:1

Find your way to the treasure—the Superkid Creed. Color your "treasure" and display in a familiar place where you will see it every day.

TREASURE HUNT

START

FINISH

SUPERKID CREED

Home Bible Study for Kids • Week 12: The Pirates in Proverbs, Part 1

Let's confess the Superkid Creed that we've learned so far!

SUPERKID CREED

I am a Superkid—Servant and child of the Most High God. Jesus is my Savior and my Lord.

I am filled with His Holy Spirit. I obey His written Word.

I hear every word that He speaks to me, and I obey quickly without arguing.

I live and walk by faith, not by what I see. I walk in the power of my strong spirit.

I am full of wisdom and understanding. I lay hands on the sick and they recover.

I win people to Jesus. I do not lie—I am always quick to tell the truth.

I do not steal—I am a tither and a giver, not a taker.

My Father makes me wealthy. I do not complain. I work hard to help my family.

I honor and obey my parents and people in authority over me.

I walk in love—I do not gossip, I am not rude and I am never mean.

Stay tuned as we learn the rest of the Superkid Creed in the next editions of the Superkid Home Bible Studies!

WEEK 13: THE PIRATES IN PROVERBS, PART 2

 **DAY 1: BIBLE LESSON— WISDOM CRIES OUT** ▸ 211

 **DAY 2: READ-ALOUD— SOLOMON IN ALL HIS GLORY, PART 2** ▸ 213

 **DAY 3: GIVING LESSON— SWEET TREASURES** ▸ 216

 **DAY 4: ACADEMY LAB—CLOUDY VISION** ▸ 218

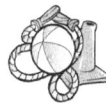 **DAY 5: GAME TIME—LOCK OUT** ▸ 220

 **BONUS: ACTIVITY PAGE— THIEVING PIRATES** ▸ 222

 Memory Verse: My advice is wholesome. There is nothing devious or crooked in it. —Proverbs 8:8

Home Bible Study for Kids • Week 13: The Pirates in Proverbs, Part 2

WEEK 13: SNAPSHOT — THE PIRATES IN PROVERBS, PART 2

DAY	TYPE OF LESSON	LESSON TITLE	SUPPLIES
Day 1	Bible Lesson	Wisdom Cries Out	None
Day 2	Read-Aloud	Solomon in All His Glory, Part 2	None
Day 3	Giving Lesson	Sweet Treasures	Measuring cups (several different sizes), Large glass bowl, Cookie dough (without chocolate chips), Mixing spoon, Chocolate chips
Day 4	Academy Lab	Cloudy Vision	An adult-sized white lace-up shoe with lace removed, Eye patch, Stopwatch, Small notebook, Pen
Day 5	Game Time	Lock Out	Box of notecards, Marker, Small table (big enough to display cards on), Stopwatch
Bonus	Activity Page	Thieving Pirates	1 Copy for each child

Lesson Introduction:

As we review this volume, the evil pirates should become well-known to your Superkids. As you talk about lying, stealing and greed (the pirates who want to steal God's treasure away), having helpers play those pirates, is a great way to give your kids the visual. You can even assume different voices yourself for each "character" and refer to them during your teaching—even interacting with them can help make your point. (Ex: "We say no to the lying pirates. We speak the truth.")

The pirates I've listed here and the truth in Proverbs that exposes them are from all the lessons we've learned in the past 13 weeks. It's fun to watch the kids become aware and resist the pirates in their own lives. Use this review to show them how easy it is to do this. I believe these final two weeks will solidify in their hearts the Creed they have learned and establish it in their thinking. It's a great time to make sure your kids really have it memorized from the beginning to this point (I'm sure some have already learned the entire creed!). I believe you are seeing real power and change in the lives of your Superkids!

Love,

Commander Kellie

Commander Kellie

Lesson Outline:

These pirates—lying, stealing, greed, cheating, complaining, laziness, disobedience, hate and anger, gossip, meanness, and rudeness—are all what Superkids say no to. We don't encourage our Superkids to be extraordinary because it's an easy way of life in the moment. For example, sometimes they will have to do what is unpopular with their friends and not gossip or choose to NOT say the really funny but hurtful words to cut someone down. Making uncommon choices based on our Superkid Creed (from the Word of God) will cause our Superkids *to live EXTRA-ordinary lives* because they'll be living out God's plan for them and following His Proverbs (wisdom) every step of the way.

I. PROVERBS HAS A PURPOSE Proverbs 1:1-6

a. So you can see things as God does (insight)

b. They make you smarter than your age!

c. To give you common sense and discernment—to have understanding and insight

II. GOD'S INSTRUCTIONS ARE THE KEY TO UNLOCKING HIS TREASURE Proverbs 4:13

a. Wisdom, common sense and discernment are like jewels. Proverbs 3:21-22

b. God has important things to tell us. Proverbs 8:6-7

c. Pirate ways are nothing like God's ways and cannot compare to His treasures. (Proverbs 8:8-11)

III. LET THE WORD (CREED) CORRECT YOUR ACTIONS AND KEEP PIRATES OUT OF YOUR LIFE

a. Satan comes to steal, kill and destroy—all pirates come from him. John 10:10

b. Give yourself to God, resist the devil and he (and all his pirates) will flee! James 4:7

c. Get close to your Captain (God). He has a wonderful plan for your life! (James 4:8a)

Resist these pirates that Proverbs warns us about:

Lying—Proverbs 17:20

Stealing—Proverbs 12:12

Greed—Proverbs 21:26

Cheating—Proverbs 11:3

Complaining—Proverbs 22:10 MSG

Laziness—Proverbs 13:4

Disobedience—Proverbs 15:32 MSG

Hate, anger, temper—Proverbs 10:12

Gossip—Proverbs 26:22, 11:13

Mocking (meanness, rudeness)—Proverbs 11:9

Notes:

DAY 1: BIBLE LESSON — WISDOM CRIES OUT

 Memory Verse: My advice is wholesome. There is nothing devious or crooked in it. —Proverbs 8:8

These two weeks are not just about widsom in general, but a fun way to review the wisdom you've shared with your kids the past 11-12 weeks. We want to preserve these truths and "write on the tablet of their hearts." Proverbs is so full of God's wisdom. It's amazing how many pirates want to steal it from us! Sometimes those pirates can speak through TV, neighbors, kids at school or online, and even through adults. We want our Superkids to recognize lying, cheating and mocking pirates for who they are. Proverbs 1 helps them to do just that.

Read Proverbs 1:1-23:
Wisdom and Discipline

These are the proverbs of Solomon, David's son, king of Israel. Their purpose is to teach people wisdom and discipline, to help them understand the insights of the wise. Their purpose is to teach people to live disciplined and successful lives, to help them do what is right, just, and fair. These proverbs will give insight to the simple, knowledge and discernment to the young. Let the wise listen to these proverbs and become even wiser. Let those with understanding receive guidance by exploring the meaning in these proverbs and parables, the words of the wise and their riddles.

Fear of the Lord is the foundation of true knowledge, but fools despise wisdom and discipline. My child, listen when your father corrects you. Don't neglect your mother's instruction. What you learn from them will crown you with grace and be a chain of honor around your neck.

My child, if sinners entice you, turn your back on them! They may say, "Come and join us. Let's hide and kill someone! Just for fun, let's ambush the innocent! Let's swallow them alive, like the grave; let's swallow them whole, like those who go down to the pit of death. Think of the great things we'll get! We'll fill our houses with all the stuff we take. Come, throw in your lot with us; we'll all share the loot."

My child, don't go along with them! Stay far away from their paths. They rush to commit evil deeds. They hurry to commit murder. If a bird sees a trap being set, it knows to stay away. But these people set an ambush for themselves; they are trying to get themselves killed. Such is the fate of all who are greedy for money; it robs them of life.

Wisdom shouts in the streets. She cries out in the public square. She calls to the crowds along the main street, to those gathered in front of the city gate: "How long, you simpletons, will you insist on being simple-minded? How long will you mockers relish your mocking? How long will you fools hate knowledge? Come and listen to my counsel. I'll share my heart with you and make you wise.

Home Bible Study for Kids • Week 13: The Pirates in Proverbs, Part 2

Discussion Questions:

1. **What is the purpose of the book of Proverbs?**

   Proverbs teaches people wisdom and discipline, and helps them understand the insights of the wise. It helps teach people to live disciplined and successful lives.

2. **Proverbs will give knowledge and discernment to everyone, but to whom are they directed?**

   The young—kids!

3. **What do fools despise?**

   Wisdom and discipline

4. **My child, _____ when your father corrects you. (Hint: use ears)**

   listen

5. **Don't neglect your _____'s instruction.**

   mother

6. **What are some things unwise/foolish people might want to do according to Proverbs 1?**

   They want to set traps for the innocent, take their stuff, mock them and even commit murder.

7. **What is another way people set traps for the innocent?**

   Bullying and hazing others are ALWAYS cruel and against God's wisdom. Discuss.

8. **Why does Solomon talk about a bird knowing how to avoid a trap?**

   Solomon talks about having God's wisdom that will help us to avoid evil traps—just as an innocent bird does.

9. **What/who is crying out in the street for people to listen?**

   Wisdom

10. **Who is the Person of wisdom inside us who is constantly speaking, if only we would stop and listen for His wisdom, instruction and counsel?**

    The Holy Spirit is God's wisdom who lives inside us. He was sent to us by God as our Guide. When we choose to follow His voice, we are choosing wisdom.

Notes: _____

_____

_____

_____

_____

Series: The Superkid Creed II

DAY 2: READ-ALOUD — SOLOMON IN ALL HIS GLORY, PART 2

Suggested Time: 10-15 minutes

Memory Verse: *My advice is wholesome. There is nothing devious or crooked in it.* —Proverbs 8:8

Background:

This is a fun twist on Solomon's story when he asked for wisdom. After reading, discuss how this story affects your kids. What value does wisdom have today, especially in a world driven by money, cool cars and vanity?

Story:

Natalie waved a hand in front of her younger brother Jamie's eyes. Once again he was in a state of shock! *200 trillion dollars! How could someone have that much?* Jamie thought.

Suddenly, Jamie came to. "So, let me get this straight: King Solomon was worshiping God at an altar."

"Yep," his older sister said.

"Then he went back home and went to sleep. Then, he had a dream. And God said, 'What do you want, Solomon? Ask for anything, and I'll give it to you.'"

Natalie nodded, "Basically, yeah."

Jamie continued, "And Solomon said, 'Thank You, Lord, for Your faithfulness to me and to my dad and stuff.' Then he asks for wisdom to know right from wrong and how to rule God's people with justice."

"See," Natalie said, patting her brother on the back, "you ARE smart."

Jamie continued, "Then, God told the king that He was going to give him what he asked for. And God said He would give him long life and riches, too?"

Nat answered, "Yes—$200 trillion in riches—and make him the wisest king who ever lived. God even said He would make Solomon so famous that no one in the world would be able to compare with him."

Jamie looked back down at his Bible soberly. "Should I feel bad?" he asked Nat. "I mean, for wanting to be rich and have all that stuff. I don't have to have money, I guess."

"It's not wrong to want to have money or a nice house. It's not even wrong to ask God for long life or any of that stuff," she answered. "You just have to make sure your heart is in the right place."

Jamie had heard that before. "But what does that really mean?" he asked.

"Remember what Jesus said in Matthew 6:33?"

Jamie shook his head no, and then remembered the Bible in his lap. He eagerly found Matthew 6:33: "Seek the Kingdom of God above all else, and live righteously, and he will give you everything you need."

Nat nodded. "See, Solomon knew not to seek those things first—he wanted God's wisdom more than all that other stuff." One look at Jamie's face told Natalie she needed to keep explaining. "So before Jesus said that about the Kingdom, He said, 'You cannot serve God and be enslaved to money. That is why I tell you not to worry about everyday life—whether you have enough food and drink, or enough clothes to wear. Isn't life more than food, and your body more than clothing? Look at the birds. They don't plant or harvest or store food in barns, for your heavenly Father feeds them. And aren't you far more valuable to him than they are? Can all your worries add a single moment to your life?' Well, can they, Jamie?"

"Can what?" he asked.

"Can worrying about stuff help you?" she insisted.

"No." Jamie knew it wouldn't.

Natalie continued to read in Matthew 6, "And why worry about your clothing? Look at the lilies of the field and how they grow. They don't work or make their clothing, yet Solomon in all his glory..."

"$200 trillion glory," Jamie said with a laugh.

Nat continued "...was not dressed as beautifully as they are. And if God cares so wonderfully for wildflowers that are here today and thrown into the fire tomorrow, he will certainly care for you. Why do you have so little faith?" Natalie looked at him, but Jamie didn't have an answer. "King Solomon was rich because he asked for wisdom," she added.

"That's not what I asked for," Jamie said soberly.

"I know. But it's not too late to ask for it."

Jamie wasn't so sure. "This may sound bad, but if I were to do that, I feel like it would just be me trying to trick God into giving me all that other stuff."

Natalie smiled. "I think that's why Jesus said seek first the kingdom of God."

Jamie sighed in despair. "But how do you do that?" he asked.

"OK, well earlier you said you just wanted to know God's plan for your life, remember?"

"Yeah!" Jamie said.

"Well, that's it. That's what Jesus was saying to seek after. But wanting to know is not enough. Seeking wisdom is more of an active thing. Like today, we already have a ton of wisdom that King Solomon gave to us."

"Proverbs!" Jamie said.

"Yeah. Proverbs is FULL of wisdom. If you really treasure wisdom like King Solomon did, spend time reading what he wrote in Proverbs." Natalie took the Bible and opened it to a random Proverb and read, "'Choose my instruction rather than silver, and knowledge rather than pure gold. For wisdom is far more valuable than rubies. Nothing you desire can compare with it.' Proverbs 8:10-11."

"Heyyyy, good one!" he exclaimed. "My turn." He took the Bible, opened it, and it landed on Proverbs 21:19, "It's better to live alone in the desert than with a quarrelsome, complaining wife."

Natalie laughed. "Ewww, like Carrie Cowlicker!" Natalie sobered up. "I've got one!" She took the Bible back and read Proverbs 11:12: "It is foolish to belittle one's neighbor; a sensible person keeps quiet."

"Oops…" Jamie said.

"Yeah, we should probably start using wisdom by being nicer to Carrie."

"Yeah." Jamie took the Bible back and continued reading Proverbs. "This is really good stuff!"

"Told ya," Nat said, messing up Jamie's hair as she was leaving.

But Jamie stopped her. "Ya think there's anything in here about older sisters who are bossy?"

"More like older sisters who are always right!" she laughed.

Jamie ran and gave Natalie a hug. "Thanks for helping me out!" Jamie was truly thankful. Armed with the book of Proverbs, his IQ went from ordinary to EXTRA-ordinary. And 30 years later, everyone agreed Dr. Jameson Porter Grayson the third was the wisest doctor around!

End Scene

Discussion Questions:

1. **Jamie wanted to be a doctor. Is there something you feel that the Lord is leading you to do?**

   Discuss. The children's desires could be toward a profession in the future, but God also talks to us about what He wants us to do today. It could be as simple as just guiding them toward entering the science fair or asking a school friend to come to church.

2. **What does wisdom have to do with the Superkid Creed?**

   Answers will vary. Proverbs says that wisdom is crying out for someone to listen. Everything in our Superkid Creed points us to the wisdom of God!

Notes: _____

Home Bible Study for Kids • Week 13: The Pirates in Proverbs, Part 2

DAY 3: GIVING LESSON — SWEET TREASURES

Suggested Time: 10 minutes

Offering Scripture: Remember this—a farmer who plants only a few seeds will get a small crop. But the one who plants generously will get a generous crop. —2 Corinthians 9:6

Supplies: ☐ Measuring cups (several different sizes), ☐ Large glass bowl, ☐ Cookie dough (without chocolate chips), ☐ Mixing spoon, ☐ Chocolate chips

Prior to Lesson:

You can make your own cookie dough or buy pre-made cookie dough. Just make sure it is chocolate-chip free for this lesson.

Lesson Instructions:

Will you be my helper? *(Choose one of the children to assist you as you begin mixing the ingredients. If you are using pre-made dough, have your assistant stir it in the bowl.)* I've got this basic batter for some awesome chocolate chip cookies, but it's lacking a main ingredient. *(Allow the children to look at the batter and talk about it.)*

Can anyone tell me what's missing? *(Pause for answer.)* You're right! It's missing the chocolate chips!

(Pick up the smallest measuring cup.) Do you think this is the right amount of chocolate chips? *(Pause for the children's answer.)* No! I don't know about you, but I like *lots* of chocolate chips.

(Pick up the biggest measuring cup.) Well, what about this one? Is THIS the right measuring cup? *(Pause for an answer.)* I think so, too! Let's do it! *(Pour the chocolate chips into the large measuring cup, and add into the mixture.)*

(Have your helper continue mixing the batter.) While the batter is being mixed, let's look at 2 Corinthians 9:6: "Remember this—a farmer who plants only a few seeds will get a small crop. But the one who plants generously will get a generous crop."

The Word says when we sow a big seed, we'll reap a big harvest just like these chocolate chip cookies. If we had put in only a few chocolate chips, we would have been able to only make a few cookies. But since we poured in a *huge* amount of chocolate chips, we will be able to have a HUGE harvest of chocolate chip cookies! *(Have your helper stop stirring the mixture.)*

It's the same thing when we sow our seeds, or offerings, to God. Second Corinthians 9:6 says that "the one who plants generously will get a generous crop." Superkids are as generous with their offerings as they are with the chocolate chips! So when we <u>mix</u> that with our faith in God's promises, we can expect a generous crop! Our God is so good to us, He makes our lives so much sweeter than any cookies could ever be!

(Bake the cookies and present "the harvest"!)

Series: The Superkid Creed II

Notes:

Home Bible Study for Kids • Week 13: The Pirates in Proverbs, Part 2

DAY 4: ACADEMY LAB — CLOUDY VISION

Suggested Time: 10 minutes

Memory Verse: My advice is wholesome. There is nothing devious or crooked in it. —Proverbs 8:8

Teacher Tip: Treat this lesson a bit more seriously, like a scientist conducting an experiment.

Supplies: ☐ An adult-sized white lace-up shoe with lace removed, ☐ Eye patch, ☐ Stopwatch, ☐ Small notebook to write down your observations, ☐ Pen, ☐ Optional: White lab coat for the "scientist"

Prior to Lesson:

Remove the lace from the adult-sized, white lace-up shoe. A white tennis shoe would work best for this lesson. The large size will ensure that the kids won't be lacing a familiar-sized shoe.

Lesson Instructions:

Today, we're doing a science experiment that analyzes our vision. In a science experiment, a *subject* is the person or thing you are studying. So who wants to volunteer to be my subject for the experiment? *(Choose one of the children to be a helper. Using an eye patch, cover one eye of the volunteer.)* I am going to cover one eye with this eye patch and observe you as you begin to lace up your shoe.

(When the eye patch is secure so your helper can't see around it, start the stopwatch and have him or her thread the shoelace through the lacing holes in the shoe. When every hole has been threaded, stop the stopwatch and record the time it took to complete the task in your observation notebook.)

And now we'll have our subject lace up the shoe again, but this time we'll put the patch over the other eye. *(Pull the lace from the shoe. Put the eye patch on your volunteer's other eye, and repeat the process.)*

Interesting. One more time please, but with both eyes *uncovered*. *(Pull the lace from the shoe. Restart the stopwatch and have the volunteer repeat the process with both eyes uncovered.)*

(Share the results with the children.) How fast did my subject thread the shoelace through the holes when using his/her right eye? What about the left eye? Which eye was easier to work with? Why do you think that eye was faster? *(Allow time for the children to guess.)*

(Ask the subject:) So now that you have laced up the shoe three different ways, which way do you think was the easiest, having one of your eyes covered while lacing up the shoe or being able to use both? Why do you think it was easier when you were allowed to use both?

Series: The Superkid Creed II

Final Word:

Our eyes are *very* important. The left and right eyes see a little differently. When we use both eyes together, we can see the most clearly. When using only one eye our vision can be a bit distorted. This reminds me of the pirates we have been talking about. When we allow pirates in, they distort our spiritual eyes and ears. Just like the eye patch takes away some of our ability to see clearly, pirates take away some of our ability to see and hear God clearly.

When we remove those pirates from our lives, we are able to see all God has for us, and hear His voice loudly and clearly so we can do what He asks us to do without obstacles. Let's remember to keep our eyes on Jesus and to not allow the pirates of this world to cloud our spiritual eyes and ears!

Notes:

Home Bible Study for Kids • Week 13: The Pirates in Proverbs, Part 2

DAY 5: GAME TIME — LOCK OUT

Suggested Time: 10 minutes

Memory Verse: My advice is wholesome. There is nothing devious or crooked in it. —Proverbs 8:8

Supplies: ☐ Box of notecards, ☐ Marker, ☐ Small table (big enough to display cards on), ☐ Stopwatch

Prior to Game:

Divide the notecards into 2 piles of 10. *(Option: Print a picture to correspond with each word to aid memory.)*

Choose 1 pile of 10 cards and label each with 1 of the following:

- Lying (Proverbs 17:20)
- Stealing (Proverbs 12:12)
- Greed (Proverbs 21:26)
- Cheating (Proverbs 11:3)
- Laziness (Proverbs 13:4)
- Disobedience (Proverbs 15:32 MSG)
- Hate (Proverbs 10:12)
- Gossip (Proverbs 11:13)
- Complaining (Proverbs 22:10 MSG)
- Mocking (Proverbs 11:9)

Label the other 10 cards with the following Scripture verses: *(Option: Use the same picture, but smaller, and place in the corner of each card under the verse.)*

- "The crooked heart will not prosper; the lying tongue tumbles into trouble." Proverbs 17:20
- "Thieves are jealous of each other's loot, but the godly are well rooted and bear their own fruit." Proverbs 12:12
- "Some people are always greedy for more, but the godly love to give!" Proverbs 21:26
- "Honesty guides good people; dishonesty destroys treacherous people." Proverbs 11:3
- "Lazy people want much but get little, but those who work hard will prosper." Proverbs 13:4

Series: The Superkid Creed II

- "An undisciplined, self-willed life is puny; an obedient, God-willed life is spacious." Proverbs 15:32 MSG
- "Hatred stirs up quarrels, but love makes up for all offenses." Proverbs 10:12
- "A gossip goes around telling secrets, but those who are trustworthy can keep a confidence." Proverbs 11:13
- "Kick out the troublemakers and things will quiet down; you need a break from bickering and griping!" Proverbs 22:10 MSG
- "With their words, the godless destroy their friends, but knowledge will rescue the righteous." Proverbs 11:9

Place cards in random order on the table.

Game Instructions:

Choose 1 cadet at a time to participate in this game. The player will match the "pirate" words with the scriptures.

When a player has correctly matched all the words with the scriptures, stop the clock. You can play as many rounds of this game as you like to allow everyone to have a turn. Rearrange the cards on the table after each round.

Game Goal:

Whoever correctly matches all the pirate words with the correct scriptures the fastest, wins.

Final Word:

God's Word is a treasure. We use it to lock out all the pirates in our lives.

Notes: _____

Home Bible Study for Kids • Week 13: The Pirates in Proverbs, Part 2

ACTIVITY PAGE — THIEVING PIRATES

Memory Verse: My advice is wholesome. There is nothing devious or crooked in it. —Proverbs 8:8

Answer Key:

Home Bible Study for Kids • Week 13: The Pirates in Proverbs, Part 2

ACTIVITY PAGE — THIEVING PIRATES

Memory Verse: My advice is wholesome. There is nothing devious or crooked in it. —Proverbs 8:8

THIEVING PIRATES

By now you know what pirates want to steal—your treasure! Find and circle the 6 thieving pirates in the ship below:

Home Bible Study for Kids • Week 13: The Pirates in Proverbs, Part 2

Notes:

www.ingramcontent.com/pod-product-compliance
Lightning Source LLC
Chambersburg PA
CBHW082118230426
43671CB00015B/2735